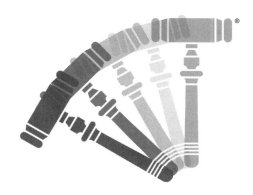

Casenote™ Legal Briefs

CRIMINAL PROCEDURE

Keyed to Courses Using

Dressler and Thomas's
Criminal Procedure: Principles, Policies and Perspectives

Fourth Edition

Wolters Kluwer
Law & Business

AUSTIN   BOSTON   CHICAGO   NEW YORK   THE NETHERLANDS

This publication is designed to provide accurate and authoritative information in regard to the subject matter covered. It is sold with the understanding that the publisher is not engaged in rendering legal, accounting, or other professional services. If legal advice or other expert assistance is required, the services of a competent professional person should be sought.

— From a Declaration of Principles adopted jointly by a Committee of the American Bar Association and a Committee of Publishers and Associates

To contact Customer Care, e-mail customer.service@aspenpublishers.com, call 1-800-234-1660, fax 1-800-901-9075, or mail correspondence to:

Aspen Publishers
Attn: Order Department
P.O. Box 990
Frederick, MD 21705

Printed in the United States of America.

1 2 3 4 5 6 7 8 9 0

ISBN 978-0-7355-9770-9

About Wolters Kluwer Law & Business

Wolters Kluwer Law & Business is a leading provider of research information and workflow solutions in key specialty areas. The strengths of the individual brands of Aspen Publishers, CCH, Kluwer Law International and Loislaw are aligned within Wolters Kluwer Law & Business to provide comprehensive, in-depth solutions and expert-authored content for the legal, professional and education markets.

CCH was founded in 1913 and has served more than four generations of business professionals and their clients. The CCH products in the Wolters Kluwer Law & Business group are highly regarded electronic and print resources for legal, securities, antitrust and trade regulation, government contracting, banking, pension, payroll, employment and labor, and health-care reimbursement and compliance professionals.

Aspen Publishers is a leading information provider for attorneys, business professionals and law students. Written by preeminent authorities, Aspen products offer analytical and practical information in a range of specialty practice areas from securities law and intellectual property to mergers and acquisitions and pension/benefits. Aspen's trusted legal education resources provide professors and students with high-quality, up-to-date and effective resources for successful instruction and study in all areas of the law.

Kluwer Law International supplies the global business community with comprehensive English-language international legal information. Legal practitioners, corporate counsel and business executives around the world rely on the Kluwer Law International journals, loose-leafs, books and electronic products for authoritative information in many areas of international legal practice.

Loislaw is a premier provider of digitized legal content to small law firm practitioners of various specializations. Loislaw provides attorneys with the ability to quickly and efficiently find the necessary legal information they need, when and where they need it, by facilitating access to primary law as well as state-specific law, records, forms and treatises.

Wolters Kluwer Law & Business, a unit of Wolters Kluwer, is headquartered in New York and Riverwoods, Illinois. Wolters Kluwer is a leading multinational publisher and information services company.

Format for the Casenote Legal Brief

Nature of Case: This section identifies the form of action (e.g., breach of contract, negligence, battery), the type of proceeding (e.g., demurrer, appeal from trial court's jury instructions), or the relief sought (e.g., damages, injunction, criminal sanctions).

Fact Summary: This is included to refresh your memory and can be used as a quick reminder of the facts.

Rule of Law: Summarizes the general principle of law that the case illustrates. It may be used for instant recall of the court's holding and for classroom discussion or home review.

Facts: This section contains all relevant facts of the case, including the contentions of the parties and the lower court holdings. It is written in a logical order to give the student a clear understanding of the case. The plaintiff and defendant are identified by their proper names throughout and are always labeled with a (P) or (D).

Palsgraf v. Long Island R.R. Co.

Injured bystander (P) v. Railroad company (D)

N.Y. Ct. App., 248 N.Y. 339, 162 N.E. 99 (1928).

NATURE OF CASE: Appeal from judgment affirming verdict for plaintiff seeking damages for personal injury.

FACT SUMMARY: Helen Palsgraf (P) was injured on R.R.'s (D) train platform when R.R.'s (D) guard helped a passenger aboard a moving train, causing his package to fall on the tracks. The package contained fireworks which exploded, creating a shock that tipped a scale onto Palsgraf (P).

🏛 RULE OF LAW
The risk reasonably to be perceived defines the duty to be obeyed.

FACTS: Helen Palsgraf (P) purchased a ticket to Rockaway Beach from R.R. (D) and was waiting on the train platform. As she waited, two men ran to catch a train that was pulling out from the platform. The first man jumped aboard, but the second man, who appeared as if he might fall, was helped aboard by the guard on the train who had kept the door open so they could jump aboard. A guard on the platform also helped by pushing him onto the train. The man was carrying a package wrapped in newspaper. In the process, the man dropped his package, which fell on the tracks. The package contained fireworks and exploded. The shock of the explosion was apparently of great enough strength to tip over some scales at the other end of the platform, which fell on Palsgraf (P) and injured her. A jury awarded her damages, and R.R. (D) appealed.

ISSUE: Does the risk reasonably to be perceived define the duty to be obeyed?

HOLDING AND DECISION: (Cardozo, C.J.) Yes. The risk reasonably to be perceived defines the duty to be obeyed. If there is no foreseeable hazard to the injured party as the result of a seemingly innocent act, the act does not become a tort because it happened to be a wrong as to another. If the wrong was not willful, the plaintiff must show that the act as to her had such great and apparent possibilities of danger as to entitle her to protection. Negligence in the abstract is not enough upon which to base liability. Negligence is a relative concept, evolving out of the common law doctrine of trespass on the case. To establish liability, the defendant must owe a legal duty of reasonable care to the injured party. A cause of action in tort will lie where harm,

though unintended, could have been averted or avoided by observance of such a duty. The scope of the duty is limited by the range of danger that a reasonable person could foresee. In this case, there was nothing to suggest from the appearance of the parcel or otherwise that the parcel contained fireworks. The guard could not reasonably have had any warning of a threat to Palsgraf (P), and R.R. (D) therefore cannot be held liable. Judgment is reversed in favor of R.R. (D).

DISSENT: (Andrews, J.) The concept that there is no negligence unless R.R. (D) owes a legal duty to take care as to Palsgraf (P) herself is too narrow. Everyone owes to the world at large the duty of refraining from those acts that may unreasonably threaten the safety of others. If the guard's action was negligent as to those nearby, it was also negligent as to those outside what might be termed the "danger zone." For Palsgraf (P) to recover, R.R.'s (D) negligence must have been the proximate cause of her injury, a question of fact for the jury.

▶ ANALYSIS

The majority defined the limit of the defendant's liability in terms of the danger that a reasonable person in defendant's situation would have perceived. The dissent argued that the limitation should not be placed on liability, but rather on damages. Judge Andrews suggested that only injuries that would not have happened but for R.R.'s (D) negligence should be compensable. Both the majority and dissent recognized the policy-driven need to limit liability for negligent acts, seeking, in the words of Judge Andrews, to define a framework "that will be practical and in keeping with the general understanding of mankind." The Restatement (Second) of Torts has accepted Judge Cardozo's view.

Quicknotes

FORESEEABILITY A reasonable expectation that change is the probable result of certain acts or omissions.

NEGLIGENCE Conduct falling below the standard of care that a reasonable person would demonstrate under similar conditions.

PROXIMATE CAUSE The natural sequence of events without which an injury would not have been sustained.

Party ID: Quick identification of the relationship between the parties.

Concurrence/Dissent: All concurrences and dissents are briefed whenever they are included by the casebook editor.

Analysis: This last paragraph gives you a broad understanding of where the case "fits in" with other cases in the section of the book and with the entire course. It is a hornbook-style discussion indicating whether the case is a majority or minority opinion and comparing the principal case with other cases in the casebook. It may also provide analysis from restatements, uniform codes, and law review articles. The analysis will prove to be invaluable to classroom discussion.

Issue: The issue is a concise question that brings out the essence of the opinion as it relates to the section of the casebook in which the case appears. Both substantive and procedural issues are included if relevant to the decision.

Holding and Decision: This section offers a clear and in-depth discussion of the rule of the case and the court's rationale. It is written in easy-to-understand language and answers the issue presented by applying the law to the facts of the case. When relevant, it includes a thorough discussion of the exceptions to the case as listed by the court, any major cites to the other cases on point, and the names of the judges who wrote the decisions.

Quicknotes: Conveniently defines legal terms found in the case and summarizes the nature of any statutes, codes, or rules referred to in the text.

Note to Students

Aspen Publishers is proud to offer *Casenote Legal Briefs*—continuing thirty years of publishing America's best-selling legal briefs.

Casenote Legal Briefs are designed to help you save time when briefing assigned cases. Organized under convenient headings, they show you how to abstract the basic facts and holdings from the text of the actual opinions handed down by the courts. Used as part of a rigorous study regimen, they can help you spend more time analyzing and critiquing points of law than on copying bits and pieces of judicial opinions into your notebook or outline.

Casenote Legal Briefs should never be used as a substitute for assigned casebook readings. They work best when read as a follow-up to reviewing the underlying opinions themselves. Students who try to avoid reading and digesting the judicial opinions in their casebooks or online sources will end up shortchanging themselves in the long run. The ability to absorb, critique, and restate the dynamic and complex elements of case law decisions is crucial to your success in law school and beyond. It cannot be developed vicariously.

Casenote Legal Briefs represents but one of the many offerings in Aspen's Study Aid Timeline, which includes:

- *Casenote Legal Briefs*
- *Emanuel Law Outlines*
- *Examples & Explanations* Series
- *Introduction to Law* Series
- Emanuel *Law in a Flash* Flash Cards
- Emanuel *CrunchTime* Series

Each of these series is designed to provide you with easy-to-understand explanations of complex points of law. Each volume offers guidance on the principles of legal analysis and, consulted regularly, will hone your ability to spot relevant issues. We have titles that will help you prepare for class, prepare for your exams, and enhance your general comprehension of the law along the way.

To find out more about Aspen Study Aid publications, visit us online at *www.AspenLaw.com* or email us at *legaledu@wolterskluwer.com*. We'll be happy to assist you.

Get this Casenote Legal Brief as an AspenLaw Studydesk eBook today!

By returning this form to Aspen Publishers, you will receive a complimentary eBook download of this Casenote Legal Brief in the AspenLaw Studydesk digital format.* Learn more about AspenLaw Studydesk today at *www.AspenLaw.com*.

Name	Phone ( )
Address	**Apt. No.**
City	**State**	**ZIP Code**

Law School	Year (check one) ☐ 1st ☐ 2nd ☐ 3rd

Cut out the UPC found on the lower left corner of the back cover of this book. Staple the UPC inside this box. Only the original UPC from the book cover will be accepted. (No photocopies or store stickers are allowed.)

Attach UPC inside this box.

Email (Print legibly or you may not get access!)

Title of this book (course subject)

ISBN of this book (10- or 13-digit number on the UPC)

Used with which casebook (provide author's name)

Mail the completed form to: Aspen Publishers, Inc.
Legal Education Division
130 Turner Street, Bldg 3, 4th Floor
Waltham, MA 02453-8901

* Upon receipt of this completed form, you will be emailed a code for the digital download of this book in AspenLaw Studydesk format. The AspenLaw Studydesk application is available as a 60-day free trial at *www.AspenLaw.com*.

For a full list of print titles by Aspen Publishers, visit *www.AspenLaw.com*.
For a full list of digital eBook titles by Aspen Publishers, visit *www.AspenLaw.com*.

Make a photocopy of this form and your UPC for your records.

For detailed information on the use of the information you provide on this form, please see the PRIVACY POLICY at *www.AspenLaw.com*.

How to Brief a Case

A. Decide on a Format and Stick to It

Structure is essential to a good brief. It enables you to arrange systematically the related parts that are scattered throughout most cases, thus making manageable and understandable what might otherwise seem to be an endless and unfathomable sea of information. There are, of course, an unlimited number of formats that can be utilized. However, it is best to find one that suits your needs and stick to it. Consistency breeds both efficiency and the security that when called upon you will know where to look in your brief for the information you are asked to give.

Any format, as long as it presents the essential elements of a case in an organized fashion, can be used. Experience, however, has led *Casenotes* to develop and utilize the following format because of its logical flow and universal applicability.

NATURE OF CASE: This is a brief statement of the legal character and procedural status of the case (e.g., "Appeal of a burglary conviction").

There are many different alternatives open to a litigant dissatisfied with a court ruling. The key to determining which one has been used is to discover *who is asking this court for what.*

This first entry in the brief should be kept as *short as possible.* Use the court's terminology if you understand it. But since jurisdictions vary as to the titles of pleadings, the best entry is the one that addresses who wants what in this proceeding, not the one that sounds most like the court's language.

RULE OF LAW: A statement of the general principle of law that the case illustrates (e.g., "An acceptance that varies any term of the offer is considered a rejection and counteroffer").

Determining the rule of law of a case is a procedure similar to determining the issue of the case. Avoid being fooled by red herrings; there may be a few rules of law mentioned in the case excerpt, but usually only one is *the* rule with which the casebook editor is concerned. The techniques used to locate the issue, described below, may also be utilized to find the rule of law. Generally, your best guide is simply the chapter heading. It is a clue to the point the casebook editor seeks to make and should be kept in mind when reading every case in the respective section.

FACTS: A synopsis of only the essential facts of the case, i.e., those bearing upon or leading up to the issue.

The facts entry should be a short statement of the events and transactions that led one party to initiate legal proceedings against another in the first place. While some cases conveniently state the salient facts at the beginning of the decision, in other instances they will have to be culled from hiding places throughout the text, even from concurring and dissenting opinions. Some of the "facts" will often be in dispute and should be so noted. Conflicting evidence may be briefly pointed up. "Hard" facts must be included. Both must be *relevant* in order to be listed in the facts entry. It is impossible to tell what is relevant until the entire case is read, as the ultimate determination of the rights and liabilities of the parties may turn on something buried deep in the opinion.

Generally, the facts entry should not be longer than three to five *short* sentences.

It is often helpful to identify the role played by a party in a given context. For example, in a construction contract case the identification of a party as the "contractor" or "builder" alleviates the need to tell that that party was the one who was supposed to have built the house.

It is always helpful, and a good general practice, to identify the "plaintiff" and the "defendant." This may seem elementary and uncomplicated, but, especially in view of the creative editing practiced by some casebook editors, it is sometimes a difficult or even impossible task. Bear in mind that the *party presently* seeking something from this court may not be the plaintiff, and that sometimes only the cross-claim of a defendant is treated in the excerpt. Confusing or misaligning the parties can ruin your analysis and understanding of the case.

ISSUE: A statement of the general legal question answered by or illustrated in the case. For clarity, the issue is best put in the form of a question capable of a "yes" or "no" answer. In reality, the issue is simply the Rule of Law put in the form of a question (e.g., "May an offer be accepted by performance?").

The major problem presented in discerning what is *the* issue in the case is that an opinion usually purports to raise and answer several questions. However, except for rare cases, only one such question is really the issue in the case. Collateral issues not necessary to the resolution of the matter in controversy are handled by the court by language known as *"obiter dictum"* or merely *"dictum."* While dicta may be included later in the brief, they have no place under the issue heading.

To find the issue, ask *who wants what* and then go on to ask *why did that party succeed or fail in getting it.* Once this is determined, the "why" should be turned into a question.

The complexity of the issues in the cases will vary, but in all cases a single-sentence question should sum up the issue. *In a few cases,* there will be two, or even more rarely, three issues of equal importance to the resolution of the case. Each should be expressed in a single-sentence question.

Since many issues are resolved by a court in coming to a final disposition of a case, the casebook editor will reproduce the portion of the opinion containing the issue or issues most relevant to the area of law under scrutiny. A noted law professor gave this advice: "Close the book; look at the title on the cover." Chances are, if it is Property, you need not concern yourself with whether, for example, the federal government's treatment of the plaintiff's land really raises a federal question sufficient to support jurisdiction on this ground in federal court.

The same rule applies to chapter headings designating sub-areas within the subjects. They tip you off as to what the text is designed to teach. The cases are arranged in a casebook to show a progression or development of the law, so that the preceding cases may also help.

It is also most important to remember to *read the notes and questions* at the end of a case to determine what the editors wanted you to have gleaned from it.

HOLDING AND DECISION: This section should succinctly explain the rationale of the court in arriving at its decision. In capsulizing the "reasoning" of the court, it should always include an application of the general rule or rules of law to the specific facts of the case. Hidden justifications come to light in this entry: the reasons for the state of the law, the public policies, the biases and prejudices, those considerations that influence the justices' thinking and, ultimately, the outcome of the case. At the end, there should be a short indication of the disposition or procedural resolution of the case (e.g., "Decision of the trial court for Mr. Smith (P) reversed").

The foregoing format is designed to help you "digest" the reams of case material with which you will be faced in your law school career. Once mastered by practice, it will place at your fingertips the information the authors of your casebooks have sought to impart to you in case-by-case illustration and analysis.

B. Be as Economical as Possible in Briefing Cases

Once armed with a format that encourages succinctness, it is as important to be economical with regard to the time spent on the actual reading of the case as it is to be economical in the writing of the brief itself. This does not mean "skimming" a case. Rather, it means reading the case with an "eye" trained to recognize into which "section" of your brief a particular passage or line fits and having a system for quickly and precisely marking the case so that the passages fitting any one particular part of

the brief can be easily identified and brought together in a concise and accurate manner when the brief is actually written.

It is of no use to simply repeat everything in the opinion of the court; record only enough information to trigger your recollection of what the court said. Nevertheless, an accurate statement of the "law of the case," i.e., the legal principle applied to the facts, is absolutely essential to class preparation and to learning the law under the case method.

To that end, it is important to develop a "shorthand" that you can use to make marginal notations. These notations will tell you at a glance in which section of the brief you will be placing that particular passage or portion of the opinion.

Some students prefer to underline all the salient portions of the opinion (with a pencil or colored underliner marker), making marginal notations as they go along. Others prefer the color-coded method of underlining, utilizing different colors of markers to underline the salient portions of the case, each separate color being used to represent a different section of the brief. For example, blue underlining could be used for passages relating to the rule of law, yellow for those relating to the issue, and green for those relating to the holding and decision, etc. While it has its advocates, the color-coded method can be confusing and time-consuming (all that time spent on changing colored markers). Furthermore, it can interfere with the continuity and concentration many students deem essential to the reading of a case for maximum comprehension. In the end, however, it is a matter of personal preference and style. Just remember, whatever method you use, underlining must be used sparingly or its value is lost.

If you take the marginal notation route, an efficient and easy method is to go along underlining the key portions of the case and placing in the margin alongside them the following "markers" to indicate where a particular passage or line "belongs" in the brief you will write:

N   (NATURE OF CASE)
RL   (RULE OF LAW)
I   (ISSUE)
HL   (HOLDING AND DECISION, relates to the RULE OF LAW behind the decision)
HR   (HOLDING AND DECISION, gives the RATIONALE or reasoning behind the decision)
HA   (HOLDING AND DECISION, APPLIES the general principle(s) of law to the facts of the case to arrive at the decision)

Remember that a particular passage may well contain information necessary to more than one part of your brief, in which case you simply note that in the margin. If you are using the color-coded underlining method instead of marginal notation, simply make asterisks or checks in the margin next to the passage in question in the colors that indicate the additional sections of the brief where it might be utilized.

The economy of utilizing "shorthand" in marking cases for briefing can be maintained in the actual brief writing process itself by utilizing "law student shorthand" within the brief. There are many commonly used words and phrases for which abbreviations can be substituted in your briefs (and in your class notes also). You can develop abbreviations that are personal to you and which will save you a lot of time. A reference list of briefing abbreviations can be found on page xii of this book.

C. Use Both the Briefing Process and the Brief as a Learning Tool

Now that you have a format and the tools for briefing cases efficiently, the most important thing is to make the time spent in briefing profitable to you and to make the most advantageous use of the briefs you create. Of course, the briefs are invaluable for classroom reference when you are called upon to explain or analyze a particular case. However, they are also useful in reviewing for exams. A quick glance at the fact summary should bring the case to mind, and a rereading of the rule of law should enable you to go over the underlying legal concept in your mind, how it was applied in that particular case, and how it might apply in other factual settings.

As to the value to be derived from engaging in the briefing process itself, there is an immediate benefit that arises from being forced to sift through the essential facts and reasoning from the court's opinion and to succinctly express them in your own words in your brief. The process ensures that you understand the case and the point that it illustrates, and that means you will be ready to absorb further analysis and information brought forth in class. It also ensures you will have something to say when called upon in class. The briefing process helps develop a mental agility for getting to the *gist* of a case and for identifying, expounding on, and applying the legal concepts and issues found there. The briefing process is the mental process on which you must rely in taking law school examinations; it is also the mental process upon which a lawyer relies in serving his clients and in making his living.

Abbreviations for Briefs

acceptance	acp	offer	O
affirmed	aff	offeree	OE
answer	ans	offeror	OR
assumption of risk	a/r	ordinance	ord
attorney	atty	pain and suffering	p/s
beyond a reasonable doubt	b/r/d	parol evidence	p/e
bona fide purchaser	BFP	plaintiff	P
breach of contract	br/k	prima facie	p/f
cause of action	c/a	probable cause	p/c
common law	c/l	proximate cause	px/c
Constitution	Con	real property	r/p
constitutional	con	reasonable doubt	r/d
contract	K	reasonable man	r/m
contributory negligence	c/n	rebuttable presumption	rb/p
cross	x	remanded	rem
cross-complaint	x/c	res ipsa loquitur	RIL
cross-examination	x/ex	respondeat superior	r/s
cruel and unusual punishment	c/u/p	Restatement	RS
defendant	D	reversed	rev
dismissed	dis	Rule Against Perpetuities	RAP
double jeopardy	d/j	search and seizure	s/s
due process	d/p	search warrant	s/w
equal protection	e/p	self-defense	s/d
equity	eq	specific performance	s/p
evidence	ev	statute	S
exclude	exc	statute of frauds	S/F
exclusionary rule	exc/r	statute of limitations	S/L
felony	f/n	summary judgment	s/j
freedom of speech	f/s	tenancy at will	t/w
good faith	g/f	tenancy in common	t/c
habeas corpus	h/c	tenant	t
hearsay	hr	third party	TP
husband	H	third party beneficiary	TPB
injunction	inj	transferred intent	TI
in loco parentis	ILP	unconscionable	uncon
inter vivos	I/v	unconstitutional	unconst
joint tenancy	j/t	undue influence	u/e
judgment	judgt	Uniform Commercial Code	UCC
jurisdiction	jur	unilateral	uni
last clear chance	LCC	vendee	VE
long-arm statute	LAS	vendor	VR
majority view	maj	versus	v
meeting of minds	MOM	void for vagueness	VFV
minority view	min	weight of authority	w/a
Miranda rule	Mir/r	weight of the evidence	w/e
Miranda warnings	Mir/w	wife	W
negligence	neg	with	w/
notice	ntc	within	w/i
nuisance	nus	without	w/o
obligation	ob	without prejudice	w/o/p
obscene	obs	wrongful death	wr/d

Table of Cases

The Criminal Process: Failure, Choices, and Legitimacy

Quick Reference Rules of Law

Powell v. Alabama

Capital crime defendant (D) v. State (P)

287 U.S. 45 (1932).

NATURE OF CASE: Appeal from convictions for rape.

FACT SUMMARY: Several blacks were convicted of raping two white girls.

🏛 RULE OF LAW
In a capital case, where the defendant is unable to employ counsel and is incapable of adequately defending himself, the Due Process Clause requires that effective counsel be appointed for him.

FACTS: Several blacks (D) were charged with the rape of two white girls. The Defendants were all young, ignorant, and illiterate. They came from other states and had no family or friends in the immediate area. Six days after an indictment and arraignment at which they were not represented by counsel, the boys (D) were tried. Until the morning of the trial, no lawyer had been named to represent them.

ISSUE: In a capital case, where the defendant is unable to employ counsel and is incapable of adequately defending himself, does the Due Process Clause of the Fourteenth Amendment require that effective counsel be appointed for him?

HOLDING AND DECISION: (Sutherland, J.) Yes. In a capital case, where the defendant is unable to employ counsel and cannot adequately defend himself, due process requires that the trial court appoint effective counsel. The record of this case clearly illustrates that from the time of their arraignment until the trial, the defendants did not have the aid of counsel in any real state. This is often the most critical stage of a criminal trial during which consultation and investigation must be carried out. The right to a hearing is among the "immutable principles of justice which inhere in the very idea of free government." The right to a hearing has always included the right to counsel, for the right to be heard is often useless unless it includes the right to be heard by counsel; even the intelligent layman is often unable to adequately defend himself. Thus, the failure of the trial court to give the boys (D) reasonable time and opportunity to employ counsel was a denial of due process. In addition, assuming their inability to secure counsel even if they had been given the opportunity, the failure of the trial court to make an effective appointment of counsel was also a denial of due process. Reversed.

DISSENT: (Butler, J.) If there had been any lack of opportunity for preparation, trial counsel would have applied to the court for a postponement; however, here no such application was made. There was no suggestion, at the trial or in the new trial motion, that the defendants were denied such an opportunity or were not, in fact, fully prepared. The amended new trial motion contains the first suggestion that the defendants were denied counsel or opportunity to prepare for trial. Such silence requires a finding that the claim is groundless, since if it had any merit there would have been support for it.

▶ ANALYSIS

Powell v. Alabama is the first case to recognize the constitutional right of an indigent defendant to the assistance of court-appointed counsel. Although the *Powell* decision was limited to capital cases, its underlying due process rationale suggested the need for the appointment of counsel generally.

■═■

Quicknotes

ARRAIGNMENT The formal charging of an individual with a criminal offense.

CAPITAL CASE An action involving an offense that is punishable by death.

DUE PROCESS CLAUSE Clauses found in the Fifth and Fourteenth Amendments to the United States Constitution providing that no person shall be deprived of "life, liberty, or property, without due process of law."

INDICTMENT A formal written accusation made by the prosecution to the grand jury under oath, charging an individual with a criminal offense.

■═■

Brown v. Mississippi

Convicted murderer (D) v. State (P)

297 U.S. 278 (1936).

NATURE OF CASE: Appeal from murder conviction.

FACT SUMMARY: Brown (D) and others were convicted of murder after they were beaten into confessing to the crime, over their objection that the confessions were coerced.

RULE OF LAW
A confession obtained by inflicting physical pain during interrogation is not admissible against the accused.

FACTS: To elicit murder confessions, the Mississippi police tortured Brown (D) and other African-American men. One defendant was "hanged by a rope to the limb of a tree" three times by a sheriff and subsequently "tied to a tree and whipped," suffering intense pain and agony; later, the same defendant was severely whipped and told the whipping would continue "until he confessed." He confessed. Two other defendants were taken to jail, they were made to strip by the sheriff, and then "they were laid over chairs and their backs were cut to pieces with a leather strap with buckles on it." They too were told the whipping would continue until they confessed; they confessed. At trial, the sheriff admitted the whippings, as did other witnesses. Brown (D) and the other defendants were convicted. They appealed, challenging their conviction on due process grounds in a case of first impression.

ISSUE: Is a confession that was obtained by inflicting physical pain during the interrogation admissible against the accused?

HOLDING AND DECISION: (Hughes, C.J.) No. The method employed by the interrogating officers to obtain the confessions was a denial of due process. The rack and torture chamber may not be substituted for the witness stand. While states are free to regulate the procedure of their courts in accordance with their own conceptions of policy, such freedom is limited by the requirement of due process of law. In addition, the state's argument that the accused's counsel failed to move for the exclusion of the coerced statements after their introduction has no merit. The duty of the trial court rises above simple procedural rules, particularly when a man is on trial for his life. The trial court was fully aware there was no additional evidence upon which a conviction could stand. Reversed.

ANALYSIS

Brown v. Mississippi was the first of a long line of confession cases. In the following 20 years, the determining factors for "involuntariness" evolved from "special circumstances" involving physical brutality, upon which the defendant had the burden of proof, to "some" coercive force regardless of the methodology, and finally to a shifting of the burden to the prosecutor who must show, by a preponderance of the evidence, that no coercion occurred.

Quicknotes

COERCED CONFESSION A statement made by a person charged with the commission of a criminal offense acknowledging his guilt in respect to the charged offense, made when the confessor's free will was overcome as a result of threats, promises, or undue influence, and which is inadmissible at trial.

DUE PROCESS The constitutional mandate requiring the courts to protect and enforce individuals' rights and liberties consistent with prevailing principles of fairness and justice and prohibiting the federal and state governments from such activities that deprive its citizens of life, liberty, or property interest.

Duncan v. Louisiana

Batterer (D) v. State (P)

391 U.S. 145 (1968).

NATURE OF CASE: Appeal from conviction for simple battery.

FACT SUMMARY: Duncan (D) was convicted without the right to a jury trial of simple battery, a crime punishable by two years imprisonment and a $300 fine.

🏛 RULE OF LAW
Fourteenth Amendment due process guarantees a right of jury trial in all state criminal cases "which, were they to be tried in federal court, would come within the Sixth Amendment's guarantee."

FACTS: Duncan (D), a black youth, was convicted in Louisiana of simple battery and sentenced to 60 days imprisonment and to pay a fine of $150. Before his trial, Duncan (D) requested a jury trial but his request was denied. Under Louisiana law, a jury trial is guaranteed only in cases where capital punishment or imprisonment at hard labor may be imposed. Simple battery, however, is a misdemeanor punishable only with up to two years imprisonment and a $300 fine. After his conviction, Duncan (D) appealed on the basis that denial of a jury trial violated his Sixth and Fourteenth Amendment rights. After the supreme court of Louisiana upheld his conviction, Duncan (D) appealed to the U.S. Supreme Court.

ISSUE: Does the Constitution impose a duty upon the state to give a jury trial in any criminal case that, were it to be tried in a federal court, would come within the Sixth Amendment's guarantee?

HOLDING AND DECISION: (White, J.) Yes. Fourteenth Amendment due process guarantees a right of jury trial in all state criminal cases that, were they to be tried in a federal court, would come within the Sixth Amendment's guarantee. Furthermore, any serious crime tried in a federal court comes within the Sixth Amendment's guarantee of a jury trial. Trial by jury in such serious criminal cases is so fundamental to the American scheme of justice (i.e., as a defense against arbitrary law enforcement) that it cannot be denied by state courts either. Of course, the possible penalty for a particular crime is of major importance in determining if it is serious. Here, however, the Court does not need to settle the exact location of the line between petty offenses and serious crimes. It is sufficient for our purposes to hold that a crime punishable by two years in prison (as here) is, based on past and contemporary standards in this country, a serious crime and not a petty offense. As such, Duncan (D) should have received a jury trial. Reversed.

CONCURRENCE: (Black, J.) Although the selective incorporation process was here properly applied, the Fourteenth Amendment is intended to make the entire Bill of Rights applicable to the states. The words "No state shall make or enforce any law which shall abridge the privileges or immunities of citizens of the United States" clearly express this intention. There is no more precious "privilege" than to claim the protections of the Bill of Rights. Furthermore, the Fourteenth Amendment guarantees due process and the due process of law standard for a trial is one tried in accordance with the Bill of Rights and laws passed pursuant to constitutional power, guaranteeing to all alike a trial under the general law of the land.

CONCURRENCE: (Fortas, J.) While the Due Process Clause requires the states to accord the right to jury trial in prosecutions for offenses that are not petty, the practices of the forum states are also relevant. The Supreme Court must not automatically import all of the ancillary rules that have been, or may hereafter be, developed incidental to the right to jury trial in the federal courts. The Supreme Court may well conclude that various features of federal jury practice are by no means fundamental, are not therefore essential to due process of law hence, and are not obligatory on the states. The Due Process Clause requires that state court proceedings assure basic fairness, not that they rigidly and arbitrarily follow the exact pattern of federal proceedings.

DISSENT: (Harlan, J.) Due process of law requires nothing more than that a criminal trial be fundamentally fair. Trial by jury is not the only fair means of resolving issues of fact. Even if a jury trial were a fundamental right in some criminal cases, there is no fundamental rule saying that a simple battery is within the category of "jury crimes" rather than "petty crimes."

▶ ANALYSIS

This case illustrates the doctrine of "selective incorporation" of the Bill of Rights into the Fourteenth Amendment Due Process Clause. Under this doctrine, the Bill of Rights is incorporated by the Due Process Clause only to the extent that the Court decides that the protections and rights therein are "so essential to fundamental principles of due process of law, as to be preserved against both federal and state action (*Bloom v. Illinois*, 391 U.S. 194 (1968)). A minority of the justices of the Supreme Court (especially Black and Douglas), though, have argued for

Continued on next page.

total incorporation." Note that the Court has only specifically found two of the guarantees of the Bill of Rights to be nonfundamental. The first is the Fifth Amendment right to indictment by grand jury (some states permit criminal prosecutions to proceed upon the filing of an information only). The second is the Eighth Amendment's guarantees regarding bail and fines.

■═■

Quicknotes

BILL OF RIGHTS Refers to the first ten amendments to the federal constitution, setting forth individual rights and liberties.

FOURTEENTH AMENDMENT DUE PROCESS CLAUSE Provides that protections mandated by the constitution and observed by the federal government are equally applicable, and therefore must be observed by the States.

MISDEMEANOR Any offense that does not constitute a felony, which is generally less severe and for which a lesser punishment is imposed.

RIGHT TO JURY TRIAL The right guaranteed by the Sixth Amendment to the federal constitution that in all criminal prosecutions the accused has a right to a trial by an impartial jury of the state and district in which the crime was allegedly committed.

SIXTH AMENDMENT Provides the right to a speedy trial by impartial jury, the right to be informed of the accusation, to confront witnesses and to have the assistance of counsel in all criminal prosecutions.

■═■

CHAPTER 2

An Overview of the Fourth Amendment

Quick Reference Rules of Law

Weeks v. United States

Defendant charged with unlawful use of mails (D) v. Federal government (P)

232 U.S. 383 (1914).

NATURE OF CASE: Appeal from conviction for unlawfully using the mails to transport lottery tickets.

FACT SUMMARY: Police officers and federal marshal (P) seized lottery tickets and other incriminating evidence in warrantless search of Weeks's (D) house.

🏛 RULE OF LAW
Evidence obtained in an unlawful search and seizure by agents of the federal government may not be used against the defendant in a federal prosecution.

FACTS: Police arrested Weeks (D) at work without a warrant; other officers, also without a warrant, went to defendant's house. A neighbor told them where the key was kept, and they searched Weeks's (D) room and took possession of lottery tickets and various papers, which they turned over to the United States Marshal (P). The Marshal (P), also without a warrant, then went to defendant's house and obtained additional evidence.

ISSUE: May evidence seized unlawfully by agents of the federal government be used in a federal prosecution?

HOLDING AND DECISION: (Day, J.) No. Evidence obtained during an illegal search and seizure by agents of the federal government may not be used against a defendant in a federal prosecution. The Fourth Amendment protects all citizens from unreasonable searches and seizures by federal officials. If evidence seized in violation of the Fourth Amendment may be used against a citizen accused of an offense, its protections are of no value. Reversed.

▶ ANALYSIS

The decision in *Weeks* applies only to the conduct of federal officials; it did not reach the conduct of the state police officers who unlawfully searched Weeks's (D) house. The holding also did not bar state officials from giving illegally seized evidence to federal prosecutors, referred to as the "silver platter" doctrine.

■═■

Quicknotes

WRITS OF ASSISTANCE An equitable remedy imposed in order to enforce a previous court judgment ordering the transfer of title to real property.

■═■

Wolf v. Colorado

Owner of illegally seized evidence (D) v. State (P)

338 U.S. 25 (1949).

NATURE OF CASE: Appeal from conviction of conspiracy to commit abortion.

FACT SUMMARY: Dr. Wolf (D) was convicted of conspiracy to commit abortion, such conviction resting in part upon evidence seized from his office.

🏛 RULE OF LAW
In a prosecution in a state court for a state crime, the Fourteenth Amendment does not forbid the admission of evidence obtained by an unreasonable search and seizure.

FACTS: Appointment books were seized from Dr. Wolf's (D) office. Partly on the basis of this evidence, Dr. Wolf (D) was convicted in a state court of conspiracy to commit abortion. Under Colorado law, evidence seized in an unreasonable search and seizure is admissible against the accused. Had the case been brought in federal court, the evidence would have been inadmissible under the exclusionary rule as being in violation of Dr. Wolf's (D) Fourth Amendment rights.

ISSUE: Does a conviction by a state court for a state offense deny a defendant his due process rights under the Fourteenth Amendment solely because evidence was obtained by a search and seizure that was illegal under the Fourth Amendment, and thus would have been excluded if the case had been brought in a federal court?

HOLDING AND DECISION: (Frankfurter, J.) No. In a prosecution in a state court for a state crime, the Fourteenth Amendment does not forbid the admission of evidence obtained by an unreasonable search and seizure. While the Fourth Amendment's prohibition against unreasonable searches and seizures is incorporated under the due process clause of the Fourteenth Amendment and thus is binding upon the states, the federal exclusionary rule is not binding on the states. The exclusion of illegally obtained evidence is not fundamental to the concept of ordered liberty. It is merely one means of securing compliance with the Fourth Amendment and thus deterring unreasonable searches and seizures. The states are free to fashion other remedies to deter violations of defendants' due process rights, as long as they do indeed provide some means of redress. It is not a departure from the basic standards of individual rights to remand such individuals to the remedies of private action and to such protection as the internal discipline of the police. While it is true that exclusion of such evidence is an effective means of deterring unreasonable searches, the Supreme Court will not condemn a state's reliance upon methods which, if consistently enforced, would be equally effective. The public opinion within the state can be more effectively exerted against the local police than can local opinion be exerted against federal officers. Affirmed.

▶ ANALYSIS

In *Weeks v. U.S.*, 232 U.S. 383 (1914), the Supreme Court first held that, under the Fourth Amendment, evidence obtained by federal officials by means of an unreasonable search and seizure is inadmissible as evidence in a federal court. Evidence procured by state officials in violation of the Fourth Amendment is also inadmissible in federal court (*Elkins v. U.S.*, 364 U.S. 206 (1960)). In *Wolf*, the Court established two basic propositions: first, the Fourth Amendment's prohibition against unreasonable search and seizure is binding on the states through the Due Process Clause of the Fourteenth Amendment; and second, the rule of *Weeks*, excluding all evidence seized in an unreasonable search, is not commanded by the Fourth Amendment but is a judicially created rule of evidence for federal courts and is, therefore, not binding on the states. Under *Wolf*, then, although unreasonable search and seizure by state officials is unconstitutional, it is permissible for the state courts to use such illegally obtained evidence in state trials, if the state has some procedure other than the exclusionary rule to discourage unreasonable searches. Although this case held that the exclusionary rule is not implicit in the Fourteenth Amendment's concept of ordered liberty and fundamental justice, *Mapp v. Ohio*, 367 U.S. 643 (1961), using the same standard, overturned *Wolf* and found that the exclusionary rule was a part of the Fourteenth Amendment, binding on the states.

■■■

Quicknotes

EXCLUSIONARY RULE A rule precluding the introduction at trial of evidence unlawfully obtained in violation of the federal constitutional safeguards against unreasonable searches and seizures.

FOURTEENTH AMENDMENT Declares that no state shall make or enforce any law that shall abridge the privileges and immunities of citizens of the United States.

FOURTH AMENDMENT Provides that persons be secure as to their person and private belongings against unreasonable searches and seizures.

MOTION TO SUPPRESS Motion to exclude the introduction of evidence in a criminal prosecution that was unlawfully obtained.

■■■

Mapp v. Ohio

Lewd book-owner (D) v. State (P)

367 U.S. 643 (1961).

NATURE OF CASE: Appeal from conviction for possession of obscene material.

FACT SUMMARY: Mapp (D) was arrested and later convicted of possession of obscene material when police without a search warrant forcibly entered her home pursuant to information that a bombing suspect was hiding in the dwelling.

RULE OF LAW
In a prosecution in a federal or state court, the Fourth Amendment (by application of the Fourteenth Amendment) forbids the admission of evidence obtained by an unreasonable search and seizure.

FACTS: When three Cleveland police officers knocked on the door of her house, Mapp (D), upon the telephoned advice of her attorney, refused to admit them without a search warrant. The police had information that a person wanted for questioning regarding a bombing was hiding in the Mapp (D) home. Being refused admission, the policemen forcibly entered, waving a piece of paper they claimed was a warrant and proceeded to search extensively the second floor and the basement. During the search, certain books, pictures, and photographs deemed to be obscene and unlawful in Ohio (P) were found. Mapp (D) was convicted of their possession and appealed, arguing that the search was unlawful because no search warrant had been issued and, thus, the seized material should not have been admitted at trial. The Ohio (P) Supreme Court agreed that the search was unlawful but upheld the conviction on the basis that the materials had not been taken from Mapp's (D) "person by the use of brutal or offensive physical force against" her. The U.S. Supreme Court granted certiorari.

ISSUE: In a prosecution in a state or federal court, should the Fourth Amendment (by application of the Fourteenth Amendment) forbid the admission of evidence obtained by an unreasonable search and seizure?

HOLDING AND DECISION: (Clark, J.) Yes. In a prosecution in federal or state court, the Fourth Amendment (by application of the Fourteenth Amendment) forbids the admission of evidence obtained by an unlawful search and seizure. For more than 50 years prior to this case, the exclusionary rule has been applied in federal courts. Any forcible and compulsory extortion of one's own testimony or private papers to convict one or to forfeit goods violates the Fourth and Fifth Amendments. If unlawfully seized material could be admitted as evidence, the Fourth Amendment right to be secure against unlawful searches and seizures would be of no value. *Weeks v. United States*, 232 U.S. 383 (1914). Although this Court failed to require application of the exclusionary rule in state courts in *Wolf v. Colorado*, 338 U.S. 25 (1949), the failure to do so there was based on factual considerations not relevant to the constitutional consideration and could not be controlling here. To allow *Wolf* to continue in force would be to grant the right but in reality to withhold its privilege and enjoyment. The purpose of the rule is to deter violation of the right by the only effective way—by removing the incentive to disregard it. If a criminal must go free, it is the law that sets the criminal free. "If the government becomes a lawbreaker, it breeds contempt for law." Reversed and remanded.

CONCURRENCE: (Black, J.) Although the Fourth Amendment itself does not expressly require the exclusionary rule, it, together with the Fifth Amendment's ban against self-incrimination, not only justifies the rule, it requires it.

DISSENT: (Harlan, J.) The real issue of this case is whether the Ohio law banning mere possession of obscene material is consistent with the rights of free thought and expression assured by the Fourth Amendment. As for the exclusionary rule itself, the question is whether the individual states should be able to determine the rule's desirability. The Fourteenth Amendment does not allow this court to mold state remedies according to its own notions of how things should be done. What was recognized in *Wolf* was not that the Fourth Amendment *as such* is enforceable against the states as a facet of due process, but the principle of privacy that is at the core of the Fourteenth Amendment.

ANALYSIS

While holding that the exclusionary rule should be applied to the states, the Court noted there was a slow although "significant" trend among the states to adopt it on their own. As stated, the exclusionary rule was applied in federal courts for over 50 years prior to the *Mapp* decision and without significant controversy. The Court sought to put an end to the practice of federal prosecutors taking unlawfully seized evidence to state prosecutors "in the courthouse across the street" to initiate prosecutions they themselves could not bring constitutionally in federal court.

Continued on next page.

Quicknotes

CERTIORARI A discretionary writ issued by a superior court to an inferior court in order to review the lower court's decisions; the Supreme Court's writ ordering such review.

EXCLUSIONARY RULE A rule precluding the introduction at trial of evidence unlawfully obtained in violation of the federal constitutional safeguards against unreasonable searches and seizures.

FOURTEENTH AMENDMENT Declares that no state shall make or enforce any law that shall abridge the privileges and immunities of citizens of the United States.

FOURTH AMENDMENT Provides that persons be secure as to their person and private belongings against unreasonable searches and seizures.

Passing the Threshold of the Fourth Amendment

Quick Reference Rules of Law

Katz v. United States

Gambler (D) v. Federal government (P)

389 U.S. 347 (1967).

NATURE OF CASE: Appeal from criminal conviction for transmitting betting information over the phone.

FACT SUMMARY: Katz (D) was arrested for transmitting wagering information by telephone to another state; at his trial the government introduced recordings of his conversation made by attaching a listening and recording device to the outside of a phone booth.

🏛 RULE OF LAW
The Fourth Amendment protects a person from search and seizure if, under the circumstances, he has a justifiable expectation of privacy, regardless of whether an actual physical trespass occurred.

FACTS: Katz (D) was arrested and convicted for transmitting betting information by telephone to another state in violation of a federal statute. At his trial, the prosecution introduced recordings of phone conversations Katz (D) had made. These recordings were made by attaching a recording and listening device to the outside of a phone booth that Katz (D) used to make his calls. There was no search warrant. The government used this device only after it had made an investigation that indicated that the phone booth was being used to transmit such information, and they only recorded conversations that Katz (D) personally had.

ISSUE: Is the attachment of a listening device to the outside of a public telephone booth a search and seizure within the meaning of the Fourth Amendment?

HOLDING AND DECISION: (Stewart, J.) Yes. The Fourth Amendment protects a person from search and seizure if, under the circumstances, he has a justifiable expectation of privacy, regardless of whether an actual physical trespass occurred. The Fourth Amendment protects a person's justifiable expectations of privacy, and protects people and not places. Whatever a person knowingly exposes to the public, even in his own home, is therefore not protected by the Fourth Amendment, but what a person keeps private, even in a public place, may be protected. Earlier cases stated that a surveillance without a trespass or seizure of a material object is outside of the Fourth Amendment, and now these cases must be overturned. Even though the phone booth was a public place, and there was no physical trespass (the device was on the outside of the booth), there was a search because the government violated the privacy upon which Katz (D) justifiably relied. There also is a seizure even though no tangible property was taken because the recording of a statement overheard, even if there is no trespass, is a seizure. The remaining question, then, is whether the government complied with the constitutional standards of the Fourth Amendment. Although the government reasonably believed that the phone booth was being illegally used, and their search and seizure was carefully limited both in scope and duration, the action cannot be upheld because there was no search warrant issued. A search warrant is a safeguard in several ways: a neutral magistrate on the basis of information presented to him determined whether a warrant should issue; the search warrant carefully limits the scope of the search; and the government must report back on the evidence it finds. Without such safeguards, even if the search was in fact reasonable, it cannot be upheld.

CONCURRENCE: (Harlan, J.) In order to be protected by the Fourth Amendment, a person must have an actual, subjective expectation of privacy, and also that expectation of privacy must be reasonable.

DISSENT: (Black, J.) When the Fourth Amendment was adopted, eavesdropping was a common practice, and if the framers of the Constitution wished to limit that procedure they would have used appropriate language. This case, then, goes against the plain meaning of the Fourth Amendment that was solely aimed at limiting the practice of breaking into buildings and seizing tangible property. Therefore, wiretapping, which is a form of eavesdropping, is not subject to the Fourth Amendment.

▶ ANALYSIS

Katz rejects the old rule that held that there was no search unless there was a physical trespass and substitutes a new rule based on the defendant's expectation of privacy. One facet of this privacy concept is the place involved—for example, if, unlike *Katz*, the defendant had engaged in conversation in a public place that was audible to others, there would be no search within the meaning of the Fourth Amendment. Also, the privacy concept turns on action of the defendant. If he had engaged in a loud conversation even in his own home which was audible to a person standing outside of his door, there would be no search since the conversation was exposed by the defendant to the public.

■▬■

Continued on next page.

Quicknotes

FOURTH AMENDMENT Provides that persons be secure as to their person and private belongings against unreasonable searches and seizures.

SEARCH AND SEIZURE An inspection conducted in order to obtain evidence to be utilized for the prosecution of a crime and the subsequent taking of such evidence.

TRESPASS Unlawful interference with, or damage to, the real or personal property of another.

WIRETAP A means of acquiring the content of a communication through an electronic or other device.

United States v. White

Federal government (P) v. Narcotics convict (D)

401 U.S. 745 (1971).

NATURE OF CASE: Appeal from criminal conviction for violation of narcotics laws.

FACT SUMMARY: A government informer carrying a concealed radio transmitter engaged in conversation with White (D), and those conversations were simultaneously transmitted to federal narcotic agents. Those agents testified at White's (D) trial as to the conversations they had heard.

🏛 RULE OF LAW
The Fourth Amendment does not protect a person from having his conversations with an associate recorded by that associate or transmitted to a recording or listening device located elsewhere.

FACTS: A government informer had engaged White (D) in numerous conversations in a restaurant, White's (D) home, the informer's car, and the informer's house. During these conversations, the informer carried a concealed radio transmitter that transmitted the conversations to federal agents who had a listening and recording device. Additionally, while the conversations were carried on in the informer's house, an agent, with the informer's consent, hid in the kitchen and overheard the conversations, but this agent did not testify at White's (D) trial. The federal agents did not obtain a warrant or a court order before engaging in this activity. At White's (D) trial, the informer did not testify, but the federal agents testified as to the conversations they had overheard by the use of the radio transmitter. White (D) was convicted, but the U.S. court of appeals overturned the conviction, holding that *Katz* prohibited testimony about the conversations.

ISSUE: Does the Fourth Amendment protect a person from having his conversations transmitted and recorded by that associate or transmitted to a recording or listening device located elsewhere?

HOLDING AND DECISION: (White, J.) No. The Fourth Amendment does not protect a person from having his conversations with an associate recorded by that associate or transmitted to a recording or listening device located elsewhere. Although *Katz v. United States*, 389 U.S. 347, stated that the Fourth Amendment protects a person's justifiable expectation of privacy, it didn't hold that a person has a justifiable and constitutionally protected expectation that a person with whom he is talking will not reveal that conversation to the police. And under *Hoffs v. United States*, 385 U.S. 293, no matter how strongly a person trusts an associate, this expectation that the associate will be faithful is not protected by the Fourth

Amendment if it turns out that person is a government agent; when a person voluntarily engages in a conversation with another, he risks the chance that the other person will relate the conversation to the police. In a case with very similar facts as this case, *Lee v. United States*, 343 U.S. 747, this Court held that electronic eavesdropping on a conversation with the cooperation of one of the parties is not a violation of the Fourth Amendment. Since the law doesn't protect a person when an associate testifies as to a conversation in which they engaged, there should not be a different result if that same associate, rather than testifying, transmits the conversation to another by use of electronic equipment. Since the associate could testify as to the conversation, the recording serves the same function but with increased reliability and accuracy. Additionally, with a recording, the informant/associate is less likely to later change his story. A different result is not required because the informant did not testify at the trial; the question of whether an act violates the Fourth Amendment is determined at the time of the act and is not changed by later events. Reversed.

DISSENT: (Douglas, J.) The concepts of privacy enshrined in the Fourth Amendment vanish completely when we slavishly allow an all-powerful government, proclaiming law and order, efficiency, and other benign purposes, to penetrate all the walls and doors that men need to shield them from the pressures of a turbulent life around them and to give them the health and strength to carry on. The Court must reaffirm the need for judicial supervision of the use of judicial surveillance which, uncontrolled, promises to lead into a police state.

DISSENT: (Harlan, J.) The impact of third-party bugging undermines that confidence and sense of security in dealing with one another that is characteristic of individual relationships between citizens in a free society.

▶ ANALYSIS

Katz held that the Fourth Amendment protects a defendant's justifiable expectations of privacy; whatever a person knowingly exposes to the public is not protected, but whatever a person justifiably considers as private, and keeps from public view or hearing, is protected. *White*, however, holds that when a person engages in a conversation, he does not have a constitutionally protectable expectation that the other party to the conversation will not reveal the conversation to the authorities, either by

Continued on next page.

testifying or by contemporaneously transmitting the conversation to third-party eavesdroppers. This appears to be a sharp limitation on *Katz*'s rather broad "expectation of privacy" approach. But, under *Katz*, unless the defendant knowingly exposes a conversation to the public (by speaking too loudly in a public place), the conversation cannot be subjected to electronic surveillance without a warrant or the cooperation of the other party to the conversation.

■══■

Quicknotes

EXPECTATION OF PRIVACY Requirement that in order to invoke the Fourth Amendment's protection against unreasonable searches and seizures, the individual must have a reasonable expectation of privacy in respect to the location searched or thing seized.

FOURTH AMENDMENT Provides that persons be secure as to their person and private belongings against unreasonable searches and seizures.

WIRETAP A means of acquiring the content of a communication through an electronic or other device.

■══■

Smith v. Maryland

Convicted robber (D) v. State (P)

442 U.S. 735 (1979).

NATURE OF CASE: On writ of certiorari from robbery conviction.

FACT SUMMARY: Using evidence obtained from a pen register, police obtained a warrant to search Smith's (D) home, leading to his eventual conviction for robbery.

🏛 RULE OF LAW
The warrantless installation of a pen register to record numbers dialed from an individual's home telephone does not violate the individual's legitimate expectations of privacy.

FACTS: McDonough was robbed; she described the robber and an automobile she observed near the crime to police. She later saw the car driving past her house, and received obscene and threatening phone calls from a man identifying himself as the robber. At the request of the police, but without a warrant or court order, the phone company installed a device called a pen register at its offices to monitor and record numbers dialed from Smith's (D) home. The register revealed that Smith (D) had called McDonough, and on the basis of this and other evidence, police obtained a warrant to search his home. The trial court denied Smith's (D) motion to suppress the evidence derived from the pen register, and he was convicted of robbery. The U.S. Supreme Court granted review.

ISSUE: Does the use of a pen register to record numbers dialed from an individual's home violate his legitimate expectations of privacy?

HOLDING AND DECISION: (Blackmun, J.) No. The use of a pen register to record numbers dialed from an individual's home does not violate legitimate expectations of privacy. Users of the telephone must realize that they are conveying information about the numbers they dial to the phone company. They typically realize that the phone company has facilities for recording such numbers for a variety of purposes, including billing, detecting fraud, and identifying obscene callers. The fact that Smith (D) dialed the numbers from his home phone is immaterial; the phone company obtains the information regarding numbers dialed in the same way, regardless of where the phone is located. This Court has held that an individual does not harbor a legitimate expectation of privacy in information he voluntarily turns over to third parties. Affirmed.

DISSENT: (Stewart, J.) The majority distinguishes between the numbers dialed and the content of conversations, in which we have held an individual enjoys an expectation of privacy from surveillance. It is incorrect to say that the numbers dialed are without content, as they can easily reveal the most intimate details of a person's life.

DISSENT: (Marshall, J.) The notion that those who reveal information to third parties assume the risk of disclosure implies choice. It is idle to speak of choice in the context of use of a home telephone, an instrument that has become a necessity in our society, and one for which there is no practical alternative.

▶ ANALYSIS

In response to *Smith*, Congress passed legislation prohibiting the installation of pen registers, except for maintenance and testing, without a court order. Likewise, Congress prohibited seizure of financial institution records without a subpoena or warrant, in response to *United States v. Miller*, 425 U.S. 435 (1976), a case cited by Justice Blackmun in *Smith*.

■═■

Quicknotes

CERTIORARI A discretionary writ issued by a superior court to an inferior court in order to review the lower court's decisions; the Supreme Court's writ ordering such review.

SUBPOENA A mandate issued by court to compel a witness to appear at trial.

WARRANT An order issued by a court directing an officer to undertake a certain act (e.g., arrest or search).

■═■

Kyllo v. United States

Resident (D) v. Federal government (P)

533 U.S. 27 (2001).

NATURE OF CASE: Appeal from indictment of manufacturing marijuana.

FACT SUMMARY: Federal agents suspected Kyllo (D) of growing marijuana in his residence and used a thermal scanner to prove he was doing so.

RULE OF LAW
Where the government uses a device that is not in general public use to explore details of the home that would previously have been unknowable without physical intrusion, the surveillance is a "search" and is presumptively unreasonable without a warrant.

FACTS: Federal agents suspected Kyllo (D) was growing marijuana in his home and used a thermal imager to scan the residence. The agents concluded that Kyllo (D) was using halide lights to grow marijuana in his house and a magistrate issued a search warrant on the basis of the thermal scan, tips from informants, and Kyllo's (D) heating bills. Kyllo (D) was indicted and unsuccessfully moved to suppress the evidence. The court of appeals remanded the case for an evidentiary hearing regarding the intrusiveness of the thermal imaging. The district court upheld the warrant and affirmed denial of the motion. The court of appeals affirmed.

ISSUE: Where the government uses a device that is not in general public use to explore details of the home that would previously have been unknowable without physical intrusion, is the surveillance a "search" and presumptively unreasonable without a warrant?

HOLDING AND DECISION: (Scalia, J.) Yes. Where the government uses a device that is not in general public use to explore details of the home that would previously have been unknowable without physical intrusion, the surveillance is a "search" and is presumptively unreasonable without a warrant. Obtaining by sense-enhancing technology any information regarding the interior of a home that could not otherwise have been obtained without physical intrusion into a constitutionally protected area constitutes a search, at least where, as here, the technology in question is not in general public use. This assures preservation of that degree of privacy against government that existed when the Fourth Amendment was adopted. On the basis of this criterion, the information obtained by the thermal imaging was the product of a search. The Fourth Amendment draws a firm line at the entrance to the house. Remanded to the district court to determine whether probable cause existed independent of the evidence from the thermal visioning. Reversed.

DISSENT: (Stevens, J.) There is a distinction between "through-the-wall surveillance" that gives the observer direct access to information in a private area and the thought processes used to draw inferences from information in the public domain. The Court has crafted a rule that purports to deal with direct observation of the inside of the home. This case, however, involves indirect deductions from observations of the exterior of the home. It would be far wiser to give legislators an unimpeded opportunity to grapple with prematurely devised constitutional restraints.

ANALYSIS

The Court upholds the test of "reasonableness" set forth in *Katz v. United States*, 389 U.S. 347 (1967), that whether the individual has an expectation of privacy depends on whether society is prepared to recognize such expectation as reasonable. The Court rejects the erosion of Fourth Amendment protection by technological advances, concluding that any such technological "intrusion into a constitutionally protected area" constitutes a search, especially if the product of the use of a devices not available to the general public.

Quicknotes

FOURTH AMENDMENT Provides that persons be secure as to their person and private belongings against unreasonable searches and seizures.

PROBABLE CAUSE A reasonable basis for believing that a crime has been committed.

SEARCH An inspection conducted in order to obtain evidence to be utilized for the prosecution of a crime.

WARRANT An order issued by a court directing an officer to undertake a certain act (e.g., arrest or search).

United States v. Karo

Federal government (P) v. Accused cocaine trafficker (D)

468 U.S. 705 (1984).

NATURE OF CASE: Appeal from court of appeals judgment overturning conviction.

FACT SUMMARY: Drug Enforcement Administration (DEA) agents arranged to have a beeper placed in cans of ether that were allegedly to be used to extract cocaine from clothing.

RULE OF LAW
The delivery of an electronic tracking device in a container of chemicals to a buyer without knowledge of the device does not violate the Fourth Amendment.

FACTS: Through a government informant, the Drug Enforcement Administration (DEA) learned that Karo (D) and his confederates were planning to extract cocaine from clothing impregnated with the drug and imported into the United States. A DEA agent arranged with the informant, who was supplying Karo (D) with the ether, to substitute a can containing a beeper for one of the cans of ether. The agent had a court order for the installation and monitoring of the device. A court of appeals overturned Karo's (D) conviction, holding that his Fourth Amendment rights were violated when the can containing the beeper was given to him. The U.S. Supreme Court granted the federal government's (P) petition for certiorari.

ISSUE: Does the delivery of an electronic tracking device in a container of chemicals to a buyer without knowledge of the device violate the Fourth Amendment?

HOLDING AND DECISION: (White, J.) No. The delivery of an electronic tracking device in a container of chemicals to a buyer without knowledge of the device does not violate the Fourth Amendment. The Fourth Amendment protects against unreasonable searches and seizures. Although the monitoring of the device may have constituted a search, the mere transfer of the can to Karo (D) did not. Likewise, Karo's (D) possessory interests were not meaningfully interfered with by the transfer, so no seizure occurred. At most, there was a technical trespass. The judgment of the court of appeals is reversed.

CONCURRENCE AND DISSENT: (Stevens, J.) The attachment of the beeper was a seizure. Karo (D) had the right to exclude the world from his property; by attaching the bug, the government (P) infringed upon that exclusionary right.

ANALYSIS

The Court examined the actual monitoring of the beeper as well. It held that the use of the beeper to track Karo (D) in his private residence, an area not open to visual surveillance in which he had a legitimate expectation of privacy, violated his Fourth Amendment rights.

■=■

Quicknotes

POSSESSORY INTEREST The right to possess particular real property to the exclusion of others.

■=■

The Substance of the Fourth Amendment

Quick Reference Rules of Law

Spinelli v. United States

Gambler (D) v. Federal government (P)

393 U.S. 410 (1969).

NATURE OF CASE: Appeal from conviction of violation of gambling statutes.

FACT SUMMARY: Spinelli (D) was convicted upon evidence seized with a search warrant that was issued based upon an affidavit containing a statement from an anonymous informer and information from agents of the Federal Bureau of Investigation (FBI) agents.

🏛 RULE OF LAW
If an affidavit to obtain a search warrant is based upon an informer's tip (i.e., hearsay), the affidavit must state why the informer is "reliable" and the "underlying circumstances" from which the informer drew his conclusions, so as to enable an independent magistrate to conclude that the informer's information provides probable cause for the search.

FACTS: Spinelli (D) was convicted of violation of gambling statutes based upon evidence seized by the FBI under a search warrant. The FBI obtained this warrant based upon an affidavit containing the following information: (1) the FBI had been informed by a reliable informer that Spinelli (D) was using two specific telephones to conduct gambling operations; (2) that Spinelli (D) had been seen entering the apartment in which these two telephones were located; and (3) that Spinelli (D) had a reputation as a gambler. Upon conviction, and affirmance of that conviction by the court of appeals, Spinelli (D) brought a petition of certiorari to the U.S. Supreme Court challenging the constitutionality of the issuance of the search warrant.

ISSUE: Is an affidavit based primarily upon an informer's tip that does not state why the informer is reliable or the "underlying circumstances" as to how the informer obtained his information sufficient to establish probable cause for the issuance of a search warrant?

HOLDING AND DECISION: (Harlan, J.) No. If an affidavit to obtain a search warrant is based upon an informer's tip (i.e., hearsay), the affidavit must state why the informer is "reliable" and the "underlying circumstances" from which the informer drew his conclusions, so as to enable an independent magistrate to conclude that the informer's information provides probable cause for the search. Of course, in the absence of a statement detailing how the informer's tip was gathered, a search warrant may still issue if (1) the tip describes the accused's criminal activity in such detail (*Draper v. United States*, 358 U.S. 307 (1959)) that a magistrate may conclude that it was gained in a reliable manner, or (2) there is sufficient independent corroboration of criminal activity in the affidavit

so that a magistrate may conclude that there is probable cause that a crime is being committed. Here, first, the tip is insufficient for the issuance of a warrant. The affidavit neither states why the informer was considered reliable nor how he obtained his information. Second, there is no sufficient corroboration of the tip. The fact that Spinelli (D) entered an apartment with two telephones contains no suggestion of criminal activity by itself, and the fact that Spinelli (D) is known as a gambler is only "suspicion" entitled to no weight. Judgment below reversed.

CONCURRENCE: (White, J.) There are limited special circumstances in which an "honest" informant's report, if sufficiently detailed, will in effect verify itself and in which the magistrate when confronted with such detail could reasonably infer that the informant had gained his or her information in a reliable way. Detailed information may sometimes imply that the informant himself has observed the facts. Suppose an informant with whom an officer has had satisfactory experience states that there is gambling equipment in the living room of a specified apartment and describes in detail not only the equipment itself but also the appointments and furnishings in the apartment. Detail like this, if true at all, must rest on personal observation either of the informant or of someone else. If the latter, we know nothing of the third person's honesty or sources; he may be making a wholly false report. However, it is arguable that on these facts it was the informant himself who has perceived the facts since the information reported is not usually the subject of casual day-to-day conversation. Because the informant is honest, and it is probable that he has viewed the facts, there is probable cause for the issuance of a warrant. The *Draper* approach would reasonably justify the issuance of a warrant in this case, particularly since the police had some awareness of Spinelli's (D) past activities. The majority, however, while seemingly embracing *Draper*, confines that case to its own facts. Pending full-scale reconsideration of that case on the one hand, or of the *Nathanson-Aguilar* cases on the other, I join the opinion of the Court and the judgment of reversal, especially since a vote to affirm would produce an equally divided Court. *Nathanson v. United States*, 290 U.S. 41 (1933), *Aguilar v. Texas*, 378 U.S. 108 (1964).

▶ ANALYSIS

This case illustrates the two-pronged *Aguilar* test applicable to affidavits for search warrants based upon hearsay. *Harris v. U.S.* (1971) further specified a situation in which a

Continued on next page.

search warrant may be issued on the basis of hearsay. In *Harris* a warrant was upheld based upon hearsay because the affidavit contained sufficient information to allow the magistrate to determine that there was probable cause for a search warrant. The affidavit contained: (1) the informer's "personal and recent observations" of the accused's criminal activity; (2) the informer's statement which was against his own "penal interest"; and (3) the fact that the officer himself had certain knowledge of the accused's background consistent with the illegal activity alleged. Note, finally, that police do not have to reveal the identity of their informer on a hearing on the issue of probable cause, although they must do so when it is material at trial to establish guilt or innocence.

■■■

Quicknotes

AFFIDAVIT A declaration of facts written and affirmed before a witness.

CERTIORARI A discretionary writ issued by a superior court to an inferior court in order to review the lower court's decisions; the Supreme Court's writ ordering such review.

HEARSAY An out-of-court statement made by a person other than the witness testifying at trial that is offered in order to prove the truth of the matter asserted.

PROBABLE CAUSE A reasonable basis for believing that a crime has been committed.

■■■

Illinois v. Gates

State (P) v. Drug smugglers (D)

462 U.S. 213 (1983).

NATURE OF CASE: Appeal from grant of motion to suppress evidence.

FACT SUMMARY: Following the receipt of an anonymous letter detailing the drug-related criminal activities of Gates (D), the Bloomingdale Police Department had a DEA agent follow him and then obtain a search warrant on the basis of his observations and the anonymous letter.

RULE OF LAW

An informant's veracity, reliability, and basis of knowledge are closely intertwined issues useful in determining probable cause to believe contraband or evidence is located in a particular place.

FACTS: An anonymous letter was sent to the Bloomingdale Police Department stating that Gates (D) and his wife made their living as drug dealers and detailing how it was their custom for Mrs. Gates to drive the family car to Florida to be loaded with drugs and for Mr. Gates (D) to then fly down, pick up the car, and drive it back to Illinois. The police put a detective on the case who made arrangements to have surveillance conducted, which indicated Mr. Gates (D) was following the above-described pattern. An agent from the Drug Enforcement Administration (DEA) followed Gates (D) and signed an affidavit that was used in connection with the anonymous letter in obtaining a search warrant for the residence and vehicle of Gates (D). The search uncovered substantial amounts of marijuana. However, the trial court suppressed such evidence on the grounds that the affidavit submitted failed to support a determination of probable cause. In affirming, the Illinois Supreme Court concluded that the anonymous letter had to meet a two-pronged test: first, it had to adequately reveal the "basis of knowledge" of the letter writer (the particular means by which he came by the information given in his report); and second, it had to provide facts sufficiently establishing either the "veracity" of the affiant's informant or, alternatively, the "reliability" of the informant's report in this particular case.

ISSUE: Are an informant's veracity, reliability, and basis of knowledge closely intertwined issues useful in determining probable cause to believe contraband or evidence is located in a particular place?

HOLDING AND DECISION: (Rehnquist, J.) Yes. In issuing a search warrant, an informant's veracity, reliability, and basis of knowledge are closely intertwined issues useful in determining probable cause to believe contraband or evidence is located in a particular place. If, on

review, it appears that the magistrate had a substantial basis for concluding that there was such a fair probability, his decision will not be tampered with. Probable cause is a fluid concept, one not readily, or even usefully, reduced to a neat set of legal rules. While the informant's "veracity" and his "basis of knowledge" are two relevant factors to be considered in determining if probable cause existed to issue a search warrant, they should not be given independent status. It is wise to abandon the "two-pronged test" in which, according to this Court's decisions in *Aguilar*, 378 U.S. 108 (1964), and *Spinelli*, 393 U.S. 410 (1969), these two factors were given such independent status. It is better to revert to a totality-of-circumstances analysis, which permits a balanced assessment of the relative weights of all the various indicia of reliability (and unreliability) attending an informant's tip. The veracity of persons supplying anonymous tips is by hypothesis largely unknown and unknowable. As a result, such tips would seldom survive a rigorous application of the two-pronged test utilized by the courts below. Yet when supplemented by independent police investigation, such tips frequently contribute to the solution of otherwise "perfect crimes." While a conscientious assessment of the basis for crediting such tips is required by the Fourth Amendment, a standard that leaves virtually no place for anonymous citizen information is not. Applying the totality-of-circumstances analysis to this case, it is clear that the judge issuing the search warrant had a "substantial basis" for concluding that probable cause existed to search the Gateses' (D) car and residence. Reversed.

CONCURRENCE: (White, J.) Here, it is undisputed that the anonymous tip, by itself, did not furnish probable cause. The lower court's characterization of the Gateses' (D) activity as totally innocent is dubious. In fact, the behavior was quite suspicious. The critical issue is not whether the activities observed by the police are innocent or suspicious. Instead, the proper focus should be whether the actions of the suspects, whatever their nature, give rise to an inference that the informant is credible and that the informant obtained his information in a reliable manner.

DISSENT: (Brennan, J.) If the conclusory allegations of a presumptively reliable police officer are insufficient to establish probable cause, there is no conceivable reason why the conclusory allegations of an anonymous informant should not be insufficient as well. It is no reason for rejecting the rules set forth in *Aguilar* and *Spinelli* that some courts may have employed an overly technical version of those standards.

Continued on next page.

DISSENT: (Stevens, J.) The activities in this case did not stop when the magistrate issued the warrant. The Gateses (D) drove all night to Bloomingdale, the officers searched the car, found 400 pounds of marijuana, and then searched the house. However, none of these subsequent events may be considered in evaluating the warrant, and the search of the house was legal only if the warrant were valid. The Court's casual conclusion that, before the Gateses (D) arrived in Bloomingdale, there was probable cause to justify a valid entry and search of a private home is not acceptable. No one knows who the informant in this case was, or what motivated him to write the note. Given that the note's predictions were faulty in one significant respect, and were corroborated by nothing except ordinary innocent activity, it is obvious that the Court's evaluation of the warrant's validity has been colored by subsequent events.

▶ *ANALYSIS*

The rigidness of some of the lower courts in applying the two-pronged test abandoned by the Court's decision is well-illustrated in *People v. Palanza*, 55 Ill. App. 3d 1028, 13 Ill. Dec. 752, 371 N.E.2d 687 (1978). There, an affidavit submitted to support issuance of a search warrant indicated that an informant of proven and uncontested reliability had seen in a particular premises "a quantity of a white crystalline substance that was represented to the informant by a white male occupant of the premises to be cocaine. Informant has observed cocaine on numerous occasions in the past and is thoroughly familiar with its appearance. The informant states that the white crystalline powder he observed in the above described premises appeared to him to be cocaine." In holding the warrant issued to be invalid, the lower court reasoned "(t)here is no indication as to how the informant or for that matter any other person could tell whether a white substance was cocaine and not . . . sugar or salt."

■══■

Quicknotes

AFFIDAVIT A declaration of facts written and affirmed before a witness.

MODUS OPERANDI Characteristic method employed by a criminal in committing a particular crime so as to identify the crime as having been committed by that person.

PROBABLE CAUSE A reasonable basis for believing that a crime has been committed.

■══■

Payton v. New York

Home arrestee (D) v. State (P)

445 U.S. 573 (1980).

NATURE OF CASE: Appeal from criminal convictions.

FACT SUMMARY: In appealing their criminal convictions, Payton (D) and Riddick (D) alleged that their warrantless arrests in their respective homes were prohibited by the Fourth Amendment and that the evidence seized pursuant thereto was thus improperly admitted into evidence.

🏛 RULE OF LAW
The Fourth Amendment prohibits the police, absent exigent circumstances, from making a warrantless and nonconsensual entry into a suspect's home to make a routine felony arrest.

FACTS: Payton (D) and Riddick (D) both appealed from criminal convictions and based their challenge on the constitutionality of New York statutes authorizing police to enter a private residence without a warrant and without consent to make a routine felony arrest. Both had unsuccessfully moved to suppress the evidence introduced in their individual trials. It had been seized pursuant to precisely such an unconsented-to, warrantless in-home arrest. The convictions were affirmed on appeal.

ISSUE: Absent exigent circumstances, are warrantless in-home arrests unconstitutional?

HOLDING AND DECISION: (Stevens, J.) Yes. Under the Fourth Amendment, police are prohibited, in the absence of exigent circumstances, from making a warrantless and nonconsensual entry into a suspect's home to effect a routine felony arrest. That amendment draws a firm line at the entrance to the house, in terms that apply equally to seizures of property and to seizures of persons. Absent exigent circumstances, that threshold may not reasonably be crossed without a warrant. This issue is not one that was definitively settled by the common law at the time the Fourth Amendment was adopted. Furthermore, although a majority of states have permitted this type of action, it is a declining trend and is being rejected by most state courts squarely facing the issue. Reversed and remanded.

DISSENT: (White, J.) A rule comporting with the common law, traditional practice in the states, and the history and policies of the Fourth Amendment should be adopted. After knocking and announcing, police could make a daytime entry to arrest without a warrant whenever there is probable cause to believe the one to be arrested committed a felony and is present in the house.

▶ ANALYSIS

By 1931, some 24 of 29 state codes of criminal procedure specifically authorized this type of warrantless entry to arrest, and by 1975, this had grown to 31 of 37. Further indication of the previous acceptance of this practice is the fact that the American Law Institute included such authority in its model legislation in 1931 and again in 1975.

Quicknotes

EXIGENT CIRCUMSTANCES Circumstances requiring an extraordinary or immediate response; an exception to the prohibition on a warrantless arrest or search when police officers believe probable cause to exist and there is no time for obtaining a warrant.

PROBABLE CAUSE A reasonable basis for believing that a crime has been committed.

Lo-Ji Sales, Inc. v. New York

Adult bookstore owner (D) v. State (P)

442 U.S. 319 (1979).

NATURE OF CASE: On petition from conviction of defendant for violation of state obscenity laws.

FACT SUMMARY: Investigators, accompanied by the Town Justice, conducted a general search of Lo-Ji Sales's (D) bookstore for obscene materials.

🏛 RULE OF LAW
A search warrant must particularly describe the things to be seized, and may not be used to justify a general and open-ended search of the premises.

FACTS: A police investigator purchased two films from Lo-Ji Sales (D), an adult bookstore, and took them to the Town Justice, who viewed them and concluded they were obscene. Upon a warrant application alleging that "similar" items could be found at Lo-Ji Sales (D), the Town Justice signed a warrant and accompanied police to the store, where he viewed numerous films without paying, inspected numerous magazines after police officers had removed their plastic wrappings, and seized numerous film reels contained in boxes depicting obscene acts. The warrant was then completed, describing the items found and seized during the search, and signed by the Town Justice. Lo-Ji Sales (D) appealed its obscenity conviction to the U.S. Supreme Court.

ISSUE: May a warrant support a general search for items not particularly described in the warrant?

HOLDING AND DECISION: (Burger, C.J.) No. A search warrant must particularly describe the things to be seized and may not be used to justify a general and open-ended search of the premises. The conclusory statement of the police officer that "similar" materials could be found at the Lo-Ji Sales (D) left it to the discretion of the officers conducting the search to decide what materials were obscene. This is not permitted under the Fourth Amendment; nor may a warrant be completed after an illegal general search is carried out. At most, there existed probable cause for the magistrate to authorize a search for additional copies of the two films initially obtained by police. Reversed.

▶ ANALYSIS

Chief Justice Burger also criticized the conduct of the Town Justice in accompanying the officers, noting that the warrant requirement of a "neutral and detached judicial officer" was not observed. Not only was the warrant completed after the unlawful search, in violation of the Lo-Ji Sales' (D) Fourth Amendment rights, but the Town Justice who signed it was the leader of the search party.

Quicknotes

PROBABLE CAUSE A reasonable basis for believing that a crime has been committed.

Richards v. Wisconsin

Hotel room drug dealer (D) v. State (P)

520 U.S. 385 (1997).

NATURE OF CASE: Appeal of denial of motion to suppress evidence in felony drug trial.

FACT SUMMARY: Richards (D), under investigation for dealing drugs out of his hotel room, filed a motion to suppress evidence obtained by officers serving a search warrant who he alleges forcibly entered his hotel room without knocking and announcing their presence.

🏛 RULE OF LAW
To justify a "no-knock" entry when executing a search warrant, the police must have a reasonable suspicion that knocking and announcing their presence, under the circumstances, would be dangerous or futile, or that it would inhibit the effective investigation of the crime.

FACTS: Officers in Madison, Wisconsin, obtained a warrant to search Richards's (D) hotel room for drugs and related paraphernalia following an investigation that led them to believe that he was dealing drugs out of the hotel room. The officers requested a warrant that would have given them advance authorization for a "no-knock" entry into the hotel room, but the magistrate chose not to include such a provision. An officer dressed as a maintenance worker knocked on Richards's (D) hotel room door, while several plainclothes officers and one officer in uniform stood behind him. When Richards (D) cracked the door open and saw the uniformed officer, he quickly slammed the door closed. The officers announced themselves as police officers, kicked and rammed the door to gain entry, captured Richards (D) as he tried to escape through a window, and confiscated cash and cocaine hidden above the bathroom ceiling tiles. At a pretrial hearing, Richards (D) sought to have the evidence from the hotel room suppressed on the ground that the officers had failed to knock and announce their presence prior to forcibly entering the room. The trial court denied the motion, stating that the officers had reason to suspect from Richards's (D) behavior that he might try to escape or destroy evidence. The Wisconsin Supreme Court affirmed, holding that police in Wisconsin may dispense with the knock-and-announce requirement in all felony drug cases. Richards (D) appealed and the U.S. Supreme Court granted review.

ISSUE: To justify a "no-knock" entry when executing a search warrant, must the police have a reasonable suspicion that knocking and announcing their presence, under the circumstances, would be dangerous or futile, or that it would inhibit the effective investigation of the crime?

HOLDING AND DECISION: (Stevens, J.) Yes. To justify a "no-knock" entry when executing a search warrant, the police must have a reasonable suspicion that knocking and announcing their presence, under the circumstances, would be dangerous or futile, or that it would inhibit the effective investigation of the crime. Although felony drug cases may frequently involve one or both of these circumstances, the Wisconsin court erred in holding that the Fourth Amendment permits a blanket exception to the knock-and-announce requirement for the entire category of criminal activity. A search could be conducted at a time when the only individuals present at a residence have no connection with the drug activity under investigation, or the drugs in question could be of a type that would make them impossible to destroy quickly. Therefore, it is the duty of a court to determine whether the facts and circumstances of a particular entry justifies dispensing with the knock-and-announce requirement. Although the Wisconsin court's blanket exception must be rejected, the officers' no-knock entry into Richards's (D) hotel room did not violate the Fourth Amendment. The circumstances clearly showed that the officers had a reasonable suspicion that Richards (D) might have destroyed evidence if given further opportunity to do so, given the easily disposable nature of the drugs. The fact that the judge issuing the warrant to the officers deleted the portion that would have given the officers permission to enter without knocking is irrelevant at this point. The reasonableness of the officers' decision to enter Richards's (D) hotel room must be evaluated as of the time they entered the room. The Wisconsin court's blanket exception is rejected; however, the judgment is affirmed.

▶ ANALYSIS
The Court was justified in its concern over the establishment of a blanket no-knock rule. When constitutional rights are threatened, even if only minimally, so begins an upward battle on a slippery slope. Nevertheless, the Court upheld the Wisconsin court's judgment and rationale in allowing a no-knock entry given the facts at hand, which should make obtaining no-knock warrants in similar situations easier.

■━━■

Quicknotes

EXIGENT CIRCUMSTANCES Circumstances requiring an extraordinary or immediate response; an exception to the

Continued on next page.

prohibition on a warrantless arrest or search when police officers believe probable cause to exist and there is no time for obtaining a warrant.

KNOCK AND ANNOUNCE Requirement that a police officer must first knock and announce his intention before he enters an individual's home in the execution of a valid warrant.

■══■

Warden v. Hayden

State (P) v. Convicted robber (D)

387 U.S. 294 (1967).

NATURE OF CASE: Appeal from a federal habeas writ of relief from a robbery conviction based on a warrantless search.

FACT SUMMARY: Officers followed a fleeing suspect into his home and subsequently discovered evidence in the washing machine, toilet tank and underneath a mattress, tying the suspect to a recent robbery.

🏛 RULE OF LAW
The Fourth Amendment does not distinguish between mere evidence and instrumentalities, fruits, and contraband pertaining to a crime.

FACTS: An armed robber took $363 from the Diamond Cab Company in Baltimore, Maryland, and then fled. He was spotted and followed by two cab drivers, attracted by the shouts of "Holdup," who radioed their dispatcher that a 5′8″ black man wearing a light cap and dark jacket had entered the house at 2111 Cocoa Lane. The dispatcher relayed the information to the police, who arrived at that address within minutes. Officers advised Mrs. Hayden that they believed a robber had entered the house and asked to search the house. Mrs. Hayden did not object. Hayden (D) was found in an upstairs bedroom pretending to be asleep and was arrested. A shotgun and pistol were found in a toilet flush tank. Clothing fitting the description of those worn by the fleeing man was found in a washing machine. Ammunition for a pistol and for the shotgun was found under the mattress of Hayden's (D) bed and in a bureau drawer in Hayden's (D) room, respectively. All the items were introduced as evidence at trial.

ISSUE: Does the Fourth Amendment distinguish between mere evidence and instrumentalities, fruits, and contraband pertaining to a crime?

HOLDING AND DECISION: (Brennan, J.) No. The Fourth Amendment does not distinguish between mere evidence and instrumentalities, fruits, and contraband pertaining to a crime. Both the entry without a warrant and the search were valid based on the existence of exigent circumstances. Delay would have endangered the lives of others. The seizures at issue occurred prior to or contemporaneously with Hayden's (D) arrest. The permissible scope of the search must therefore be as broad as necessary to prevent the danger of the suspect's escape, or danger posed to officers by the suspect. Because weapons could have been hidden in the washing machine, the officer was within the permissible scope of the search. The law does not distinguish between what was found and what an officer was initially searching for while permissible search occurred. Affirmed.

▶ ANALYSIS

The "mere evidence" rule was based on notions of proprietary interest. It is strange that this concept crept into Fourth Amendment analysis, as the Fourth Amendment, unlike the Fifth Amendment, is concerned less with property than with government intrusion. Where the rule had its exact beginning is unclear.

■══■

Quicknotes

FOURTH AMENDMENT Provides that persons be secure as to their person and private belongings against unreasonable searches and seizures.

■══■

Chimel v. California

Burglar (D) v. State (P)

395 U.S. 752 (1969).

NATURE OF CASE: Appeal from burglary conviction.

FACT SUMMARY: Police officers, after lawfully arresting Chimel (D) in his house, conducted a search, over his objections, of his entire house, that produced evidence used to obtain his conviction on two charges of burglary.

🏛 RULE OF LAW
Under the Fourth and Fourteenth Amendments, a warrantless search conducted incident to a lawful arrest may only extend to a search of the arrestee's person and to the area "within his immediate control" (i.e., the area within which he might obtain a weapon or destructible evidence).

FACTS: Late one afternoon, police officers arrived at Chimel's (D) home with a warrant authorizing his arrest for the burglary of a coin shop. Chimel's (D) wife allowed the officers to enter the house and wait for Chimel (D) to return from work. When Chimel (D) entered his home, the officers arrested him and then conducted a search, over his objection, of his entire three-bedroom house, including the attic, the garage, and a small workshop. During this search, the officers seized a number of coins, several metal tokens, and other objects, used subsequently at Chimel's (D) trial to obtain his conviction on two charges of burglary. Upon affirmance of this conviction, Chimel (D) brought a petition for certiorari to the U.S. Supreme Court.

ISSUE: When a suspect is lawfully arrested in one room of his house, can a search of his entire house be constitutionally justified as incident to that arrest?

HOLDING AND DECISION: (Stewart, J.) No. Under the Fourth and Fourteenth Amendments, a warrantless search conducted incident to a lawful arrest may only extend to a search of the arrestee's person and to the area "within his immediate control" (i.e., the area within which he might obtain a weapon or destructible evidence). The past decisions of this Court on such searches have been far from consistent, and this case marks the final determination of which one of two divergent lines of cases applies. On one hand, the *Harris v. United States*, 331 U.S. 145 (1947), and *United States v. Rabinowitz*, 339 U.S. 56 (1950), cases had given a broad scope to warrantless searches conducted incident to arrest. Under these cases, anything within the "possession" of the arrestee (as broadly defined to include a search of the arrestee's entire apartment in *Harris* and to include a search of the arrestee's one-room business office in *Rabinowitz*) may be searched at the time

of his arrest in order to seize any evidence connected with his suspected crime. On the other hand, the *Go-Bart Importing Co. v. United States*, 282 U.S. 344 (1931), *United States v. Lefkowitz*, 285 U.S. 452 (1932), and *Trupiano v. United States*, 334 U.S. 699 (1948) line of cases limits warrantless searches incident to arrest. In both *Go-Bart* and *Lefkowitz*, such searches were limited to evidence that was "visible and accessible and in the offender's immediate custody." In *Trupiano*, the Court stated that a search warrant is always required absent some showing of "necessity," and there must be something more of a necessity for a warrantless search than mere arrest. The decision of this Court today is an attempt to define along the line of the *Trupiano* case, when such necessity exists. As this Court stated in *Trupiano*, the burden is upon those seeking an exemption from the warrant requirement to show that it is justified by necessity. Such justification in the case of warrantless searches incident to arrest may extend no further than the arrestee's person and the area within his immediate control. It is reasonable for an officer to search the arrestee's person for his own safety since the arrestee may have concealed weapons, and it is reasonable to search the area within the arrestee's control to prevent him from reaching a weapon or destroying evidence. But, any extension beyond such an area would lead to the "evaporation" of the Fourth Amendment's right against unreasonable searches and seizures. Here, the search of Chimel's (D) house was far beyond that area considered reasonable. As such, the judgment below must be reversed.

DISSENT: (White, J.) The justifications that make a search reasonable obviously do not apply to the search of areas to which the accused does not have ready physical access. This is not enough, however, to prove such searches unconstitutional. The Court has always held, and does not today deny, that when there is probable cause to search and it is "impracticable" for one reason or another to get a search warrant, then a warrantless search may be reasonable. This reasonableness exists whether an arrest was made at the time of the search or not. This is not to say that a search can be reasonable without regard to the probable cause to believe that seizable items are on the premises. However, when there are exigent circumstances and probable cause, then the search may be made without a warrant, reasonably. This case provides a good illustration that it is unreasonable to require police to leave the scene of an arrest to obtain a search warrant when they already have probable cause to search and there is a clear danger that the items for which they may reasonably search will be

Continued on next page.

removed before they return with a warrant. When, as here, the existence of probable cause is independently established and would justify a warrant for a broader search for evidence, I would follow past cases and permit such a search to be carried out without a warrant since the fact of arrest supplies an exigent circumstance justifying police action before the evidence can be removed and also alerts the suspect to the search so that he can immediately seek both judicial determination of probable cause in an adversary proceeding and appropriate redress.

ANALYSIS

This case illustrates the limited scope of a warrantless search conducted incident to a lawful arrest. Whenever police take an arrested person into custody, it is "reasonable" to make a "full search" of his person, regardless of the reason for his arrest. But this decision leaves open the question of whether a "full search," or only a limited search for weapons, may be conducted when the person is not taken into custody after his arrest. Note, however, that after a lawful arrest, when the suspect is taken into custody, a warrantless search of his clothing and the property in his immediate possession may be done "after he has been brought to the station house" and "after a substantial period of time during his incarceration"—at least when there is probable cause linking the clothes to his crime.

Quicknotes

CERTIORARI A discretionary writ issued by a superior court to an inferior court in order to review the lower court's decisions; the Supreme Court's writ ordering such review.

FOURTH AMENDMENT Provides that persons be secure as to their person and private belongings against unreasonable searches and seizures.

LAWFUL ARREST The lawful deprivation of a person's liberty pursuant to a valid warrant, probable cause that he has committed a criminal offense, or pursuant to some other authority conferred by law.

United States v. Robinson

Federal government (P) v. Car driver (D)

414 U.S. 218 (1973).

NATURE OF CASE: Appeal from reversal of a conviction for heroin possession.

FACT SUMMARY: Robinson (D), who was stopped by police for driving without a license, was discovered to be in possession of heroin hidden in a crumpled cigarette package in his coat pocket.

🏛 RULE OF LAW
In the case of a lawful custodial arrest, a warrantless full search of the person is permissible and reasonable under the Fourth Amendment.

FACTS: Robinson (D) was stopped by Jenks, a policeman, on suspicion of driving a motor vehicle without a valid license. Jenks's cause for making the stop was based on the fact that he had made a check of Robinson's (D) license only four days earlier. Immediately upon Robinson's (D) exiting the vehicle, Jenks informed him that he was under arrest on the vehicle code charge. (It was later conceded by Robinson (D) and confirmed by the court of appeals that Jenks had probable cause to arrest Robinson (D) and at that point had effected a full custody arrest.) Jenks then conducted a pat-down search of Robinson (D) and—while so doing—he felt an object in the breast pocket of Robinson's (D) heavy coat. Removing the object, Jenks found it to be a crumpled cigarette package containing heroin capsules. Robinson (D) was convicted of heroin possession. However, the court of appeals reversed, reasoning that the search was unreasonable under *Terry v. Ohio* in that it should have been limited to a weapons search. The Government (P) appealed.

ISSUE: In the case of a lawful custodial arrest, is a warrantless full search of the person permissible and reasonable under the Fourth Amendment?

HOLDING AND DECISION: (Rehnquist, J.) Yes. In the case of a lawful custodial arrest, a warrantless full search of the person is permissible and reasonable under the Fourth Amendment. A search incident to a lawful arrest is a traditional exception to the Fourth Amendment's warrant requirement and has been historically formulated into two distinct propositions: First, that a search may be made of the arrestee's person by virtue of the lawful arrest, and, second, that a search may be made of the area within the arrestee's control. The "protective frisk" in *Terry v. Ohio*, 392 U.S. 1 (1968), was not a search incident to an arrest and could be conducted without probable cause to make an arrest but a search incident to an arrest serves an entirely different purpose. Thus *Terry* affords no basis to carry over to a probable cause arrest the limitations placed on a stop-and-frisk search permissible without probable cause. A search incident to a lawful arrest is not only to disarm the arrestee but is also to preserve evidence on his person for later use at trial, and it does not matter that there may be an absence of probable fruits of further evidence of the particular crime for which the arrest was made. Nor must it be litigated in each case the issue of whether or not there was present one of the reasons supporting the authority for a search of the person incident to a lawful arrest. It is the fact of the lawful arrest that establishes the authority to search, and the lawfulness of the search does not depend on a court's later determination of the probability of weapons or evidence in a particular fact situation. Having in the course of a lawful search found a crumpled cigarette pack, Jenks, here, was entitled to open it and seize the heroin as contraband probative of criminal conduct. Reversed.

CONCURRENCE: (Powell, J.) An individual lawfully subjected to a custodial arrest retains no significant Fourth Amendment interest in the privacy of his person. If the arrest is lawful, the Fourth Amendment privacy interest is subordinate to a legitimate and overriding governmental concern. No reason then exists to frustrate law enforcement by requiring some independent justification for a search incident to a lawful custodial arrest.

DISSENT: (Marshall, J.) A warrantless search does not preclude judicial inquiry into the reasonableness of that search. It is the rule of the judiciary, not the police, to delimit the scope of exceptions to the warrant requirement. While not impugning the integrity of the police, it is possible that an officer, lacking probable cause, will use a traffic arrest as a pretext to conduct a search, and, so, it will be always necessary to adjudicate the reasonableness of the search on a case-by-case basis. Here, the search went beyond its protective purpose and continued to the contents of personal effects, which was an unreasonable step beyond the bounds of the needs for the search.

▶ ANALYSIS

There "is little reason to doubt that search of an arrestee's person and premises is as old as the institution of arrest itself. . . . Neither in the reported cases nor the legal literature is there any indication that search of the person of an arrestee, or the premises in which he was taken; was ever challenged in England until the end of the nineteenth century and . . . the English courts gave the point short

Continued on next page.

shrift." T. Taylor, Two Studies in Constitutional Interpretation, 44–45 (1969).

■■■■

Quicknotes

CERTIORARI A discretionary writ issued by a superior court to an inferior court in order to review the lower court's decisions; the Supreme Court's writ ordering such review.

PROBABLE CAUSE A reasonable basis for believing that a crime has been committed.

■■■■

New York v. Belton

State (P) v. Jacket owner (D)

453 U.S. 454 (1981).

NATURE OF CASE: Appeal from exclusion of evidence.

FACT SUMMARY: After stopping a car for speeding, police, who smelled marijuana smoke in the car, found marijuana on the floor of the car and, after arresting the occupants, searched the pockets of Belton's (D) jacket in the back seat, there finding cocaine.

🏛 RULE OF LAW
When police have made a lawful custodial arrest of the occupant of an automobile, they may, as a contemporaneous incident of that arrest, search the passenger compartment of the automobile.

FACTS: Belton (D) and others were traveling on the New York State Thruway at an excessive rate of speed in an automobile. A State Trooper in an unmarked police car pulled the vehicle over and smelled marijuana smoke. He determined that none of the four occupants owned the car. He also noticed an envelope marked "Supergold" on the floor of the car. He arrested the four men and examined the envelope which contained marijuana. He then searched the back seat of the car, having removed the men to the police vehicle, and unzipped the pocket of Belton's (D) jacket lying there. It contained cocaine. The trial court denied Belton's (D) motion to suppress the cocaine but the New York court of appeals reversed. The U.S. Supreme Court granted certiorari.

ISSUE: When police have made a lawful custodial arrest of the occupant of an automobile, may they, as a contemporaneous incident of that arrest, search the passenger compartment of the automobile?

HOLDING AND DECISION: (Stewart, J.) Yes. No straightforward rule has emerged regarding the proper scope of a search of the interior of an automobile incident to a lawful custodial arrest of its occupants. In *Chimel v. California*, 395 U.S. 752 (1969), this Court held that a search of the passenger compartment of an automobile is justified because it is within the reach of the arrestee, who may reach somewhere within that area to grab a weapon. The jacket in this case was in the passenger compartment of the car, where Belton (D) had just been located and could have had immediate access before he was removed. When police have made a lawful custodial arrest of the occupant of an automobile, they may, as a contemporaneous incident of that arrest, search the passenger compartment of the automobile. Reversed.

DISSENT: (Brennan, J.) The Court turns back today on the careful analysis produced by *Chimel v. California* and applies an arbitrary rule extending to recent occupants of automobiles. This rule fails to reflect the policy behind *Chimel*. While in *Chimel* the arrestee was within reach of the area searched at the time of the arrest, Belton (D) in this case was handcuffed in a patrol car while the passenger compartment of the car in which he had been riding was searched. The upholding of this search is a wholesale retreat from this Court's carefully developed search-incident-to-arrest analysis.

DISSENT: (White, J.) This Court's present holding, as applied to luggage, briefcases, or other containers, is too extreme an extension of *Chimel*. Here, searches of luggage, briefcases, and other containers in the interior of a vehicle are authorized even in the absence of any suspicion whatsoever that they contain anything in which the police have a legitimate interest. More judicial caution is called for.

▶ ANALYSIS

The underlying policy for permitting the search of an area within the control of an arrestee was the protection of the arresting officers from the arrestee, who might grab a weapon and attack. A further justification announced in *Chimel v. California* was the possibility that the arrestee may quickly reach for and destroy a small piece of evidence. Neither of these reasons is furthered by the *Belton* rule, which squares neither with constitutional law history nor Justice Stewart's own opinion in *Robbins v. California*.

■=■

Quicknotes

CERTIORARI A discretionary writ issued by a superior court to an inferior court in order to review the lower court's decisions; the Supreme Court's writ ordering such review.

CONTEMPORANEOUS At the same time.

■=■

Arizona v. Gant

State (P) v. Individual (D)

556 U.S. ____, 129 S.Ct. 1710 (2009).

NATURE OF CASE: Appeal from state high court decision in favor of defendant.

FACT SUMMARY: Local police arrested Gant (D) for an outstanding warrant for driving without a license. After the police placed Gant (D) in a police vehicle, a subsequent search of Gant's (D) vehicle revealed cocaine and a handgun.

RULE OF LAW
Police may search the passenger compartment of a vehicle incident to an occupant's arrest only if the occupant may have access to the vehicle or if it is reasonable to believe the vehicle contains evidence of the offense for which the occupant was arrested.

FACTS: After receiving a tip that a house was being use to distribute drugs, Tucson police officers approached the house and spoke to Gant (D). The police then left the house and conducted a records check on Gant (D), which revealed he had an outstanding warrant for driving with a suspended license. The police went back to the house. While they were there, Gant (D) drove into the driveway. Upon recognizing Gant (D), the police immediately arrested him on the outstanding warrant. The arrest took place 10 to 15 feet away from Gant's (D) vehicle. The police then placed Gant (D) in a patrol car and searched his vehicle. The search revealed a handgun and cocaine. At trial, Gant (D) moved to suppress the evidence on the grounds police did not have probable cause for the search. The trial court denied his motion, but the Arizona Supreme Court found the search was unreasonable. The State (P) appeals.

ISSUE: May police search the passenger compartment of a vehicle incident to an occupant's arrest if the occupant may have access to the vehicle or if it is reasonable to believe the vehicle contains evidence of the offense for which the occupant was arrested?

HOLDING AND DECISION: (Stevens, J.) Yes. Police may search the passenger compartment of a vehicle incident to an occupant's arrest only if the occupant may have access to the vehicle or if it is reasonable to believe the vehicle contains evidence of the offense for which the occupant was arrested. In *New York v. Belton*, 453 U.S. 454 (1981), this Court held that searches incident to arrest may include the interior of a vehicle because of the assumption that the interior includes an area that an arrestee may reach, to either destroy evidence or retrieve a weapon. Over the past 28 years, however, *Belton* has been construed to allow all searches of a motor vehicle incident to an arrest, regardless of whether an arrestee may actually have access to the interior to the vehicle. *Belton* should not be interpreted so broadly. Rather, a search of a vehicle may only be conducted where the arrestee has actual access to the vehicle or if there is reason to believe the vehicle contains evidence related to the offense of the arrest. Here, Gant (D) was already handcuffed and in the patrol car at the time of the search. There was no way he could access the vehicle. Second, the police arrested Gant (D) for driving with a suspended license. The vehicle would not contain any additional evidence related to that offense. Accordingly, the search was unreasonable. Affirmed.

CONCURRENCE: (Scalia, J.) This case concerns only those searches conducted after police make an arrest. There is some fear that the Court's abandonment of *Belton's* bright-line rule may actually invite officers to leave a scene unsecured in order to conduct a search. *Belton* should be overruled in its entirety and the following new rule should be followed. Vehicle searches following arrests are reasonable only when the object of the search is evidence of the crime related to the arrest. Because there could be no evidence related to Gant's (D) arrest in the vehicle, the search of his vehicle was unlawful. The majority opinion will also better protect citizens from possible unlawful searches, which would likely occur if the dissent's view of the case was adopted.

DISSENT: (Breyer, J.) This is not a case of first impression. Principles of stare decisis apply, and the Court should follow the *Belton* rule and find the search reasonable. Circumstances can exist that allow the Court to overrule prior decisions, but none of those circumstances are present here.

DISSENT: (Alito, J.) The *Belton* holding was clear and unequivocal. That case held that whenever an officer makes an arrest of a person from a vehicle, the officer may search the passenger compartment of the arrestee's vehicle. The Court adopted that course because it established a bright-line rule that was easily followed by law enforcement. The Court did not limit its holding with reference to when a search was made. This Court should adhere to *Belton* because of law enforcement's reliance on the rule for the past 28 years. Circumstances have not changed since *Belton* that dictate a change in the law, nor has the *Belton* rule become unworkable. For these reasons, this Court is bound by stare decisis. The Court should have found the search of Gant's (D) vehicle reasonable and consistent with the *Belton* rule.

Continued on next page.

▶ *ANALYSIS*

This decision limited *Belton's* holding regarding the ability to search vehicles incident to arrests. However, Justice Scalia's point regarding the limited applicability of the decision is significant. This decision only applies to searches following arrests. It does not apply to those situations where officers ask an occupant to step out of a vehicle and a search is conducted without an arrest being made. Those types of searches are not implicated here.

■═■

Quicknotes

BRIGHT-LINE RULE A legal rule of decision to help resolve ambiguous issues simply and in a straightforward manner, sometimes sacrificing equity for certainty.

PROBABLE CAUSE A reasonable basis for believing that a crime has been committed.

SEARCH INCIDENT TO A LAWFUL ARREST Exception to the requirement of a valid warrant for a search or seizure so long as the officer is lawfully in the location where the evidence is obtained and it is apparent that the thing seized is evidence.

STARE DECISIS Doctrine whereby courts follow legal precedent unless there is good cause for departure.

■═■

Whren v. United States

Driver of truck (D) v. Federal government (P)

517 U.S. 806 (1996).

NATURE OF CASE: Appeal challenging determinations that a police search was constitutional under the Fourth Amendment.

FACT SUMMARY: Whren (D) challenged the constitutionality of a police search of his car, wherein narcotics were found, when the police stopped him for a traffic violation.

RULE OF LAW
The temporary detention of a motorist who the police have probable cause to believe has committed a civil traffic violation is consistent with the Fourth Amendment.

FACTS: On June 10, 1993, plainclothes vice-squad officers patrolled a "high drug area" of Washington, D.C. The police saw Whren (D) sitting at a stop sign in a truck for an unusually long time. When the police approached, Whren (D) turned right without signaling and sped off at an "unreasonable" speed. When the police stopped Whren (D), they looked in the car and saw bags of crack cocaine. When Whren (D) was arrested on narcotics charges, he challenged the legality of the stop, stating the police had no probable cause to search the car. Whren (D) claimed the police's reasons for the stop—traffic violations—were pretextual and that in this circumstance, a more strict, "objective officer" rule should govern whether the search was legal. The district court convicted Whren (D) of the narcotics charges and the appellate court affirmed. Whren (D) appealed.

ISSUE: Is the temporary detention of a motorist who the police have probable cause to believe has committed a civil traffic violation inconsistent with the Fourth Amendment's prohibition against unreasonable seizures?

HOLDING AND DECISION: (Scalia, J.) No. The temporary detention of a motorist who the police have probable cause to believe has committed a civil traffic violation is not inconsistent with the Fourth Amendment. Here, Whren (D) had violated traffic laws and, as such, the police had the right to stop him to give him a citation. The fact that such violations occur routinely does not warrant a different standard as to whether the search was constitutional. Even though the police were plainclothes officers, they still had the right to stop a motorist who violates traffic laws. An officer's motive does not automatically invalidate objectively justifiable behavior under the Fourth Amendment. Intentional discrimination in the application of a law is a Fifth Amendment Equal Protection question, not a Fourth Amendment search and seizure question, and

does not apply to the case at hand. Searches are subject to a reasonableness standard, but where probable cause has existed, balancing tests have been applied only where the search and seizure has been extraordinary. Here, the traffic violation warranted the probable cause and the police properly seized the narcotics in plain view. Affirmed.

ANALYSIS

This case highlights certain Fourth Amendment search and seizure issues in the context of automobiles. While the Fourth Amendment usually requires police to obtain search warrants before conducting a search, the easy mobility of automobiles often permits searches without warrants if the police have probable cause to search the vehicle. Occasions where warrantless searches have been allowed involved searches incident to arrest and searches to prevent the loss of evidence. See *Application of Kiser*, 419 F.2d 1134 (8th Cir. 1969); *Carroll v. U.S.*, 267 U.S. 132 (1925).

Quicknotes

AUTOMOBILE STOP A police officer may stop an automobile and conduct a search of the vehicle without a valid warrant if he has probable cause to believe the vehicle contains evidence of a crime or contraband.

PROBABLE CAUSE A reasonable basis for believing that a crime has been committed.

Chambers v. Maroney

Green sweater robbery suspect (D) v. Court (P)

399 U.S. 42 (1970).

NATURE OF CASE: Appeal from a robbery conviction.

FACT SUMMARY: Chambers (D) contended that the search of an automobile taken to the station house after his arrest was invalid.

🏛 RULE OF LAW
Where there is probable cause to believe that vehicles are carrying contraband or fruits of the crime, warrantless searches of automobiles are permissible, even where the car itself is seized and held without a warrant for whatever period is necessary to obtain a warrant for the search.

FACTS: Chambers (D) was indicted for robbing two gas stations. Partially because of a witness's statement that one of the robbers was wearing a green sweater and that the robbers were driving a station wagon, Chambers (D) was arrested, and the station wagon was taken to the police station and searched. There was no warrant. Search of the station wagon revealed evidence linking Chambers (D) with the crimes. The materials taken from the station wagon were admitted into evidence. Chambers (D) was convicted and sentenced to prison. Chambers (D) did not take a direct appeal from these convictions but applied for a writ of habeas corpus. After state and federal appeals courts denied granting the writ, the U.S. Supreme Court granted certiorari.

ISSUE: Is a warrantless search of an automobile permissible where there is probable cause to believe that the vehicle is carrying evidence and fruits of the crime, and the car itself is seized and held without a warrant for whatever period is necessary to obtain a warrant for search?

HOLDING AND DECISION: (White, J.) Yes. The warrantless search of an automobile is permissible where there is probable cause to believe that the vehicle is carrying evidence and fruits of the crime, and the car itself is seized and held without a warrant for whatever period is necessary to obtain a warrant for search. Automobiles may be searched without a warrant in circumstances where the intrusion would not be permissible for a house. The opportunity to search a car is fleeting since it is movable. Here, the station wagon could have been searched on the spot since there was probable cause to search, and it was a fleeting target for a search. Affirmed.

CONCURRENCE AND DISSENT: (Harlan, J.) Seizure of the car for the period necessary to enable the officers to obtain a warrant is the lesser intrusion and, therefore, the more desirable action. The Court's approval of a warrantless search in this instance is not consistent with the Fourth Amendment's mandate of obedience to judicial procedure. This is so where the lesser intrusion is available.

▶ ANALYSIS

This case is in accord with the proposition that the Fourth Amendment is less strict with cars than it is with homes. The movability of the car, the lesser aspect of privacy, and the plain view of the auto on the highway contribute to this.

Quicknotes

CERTIORARI A discretionary writ issued by a superior court to an inferior court in order to review the lower court's decisions; the Supreme Court's writ ordering such review.

WRIT OF HABEAS CORPUS A proceeding in which a defendant brings a writ to compel a judicial determination of whether he is lawfully being held in custody.

California v. Carney

State (P) v. Motor home drug dealer (D)

471 U.S. 386 (1985).

NATURE OF CASE: Appeal from conviction for drug trafficking.

FACT SUMMARY: Carney (D) was accused of trading drugs for sexual favors.

RULE OF LAW

The "automobile exception" to the warrant requirement applies to motor homes.

FACTS: A Drug Enforcement Agency (DEA) agent placed the motor home of Carney (D) under surveillance. When a youth exited the motor home, he was stopped by Williams, a DEA agent. The youth told him that he had received marijuana in return for sexual favors. Williams and other agents searched the motor home and found marijuana and related paraphernalia. Carney (D) was charged with possession for sale. He moved to suppress the evidence as the agents did not have a search warrant. The trial court denied the motion, but the California Supreme Court reversed.

ISSUE: Does the "automobile exception" to the warrant requirement apply to motor homes?

HOLDING AND DECISION: (Burger, C.J.) Yes. The "automobile exception" to the warrant requirement applies to motor homes. The reason for the exception is twofold. Autos are inherently mobile and can be taken away before a warrant is issued. Also, autos, unlike homes, are subject to regulations that lower the owner's expectation of privacy. The motor home here, while having homelike qualities, is also inherently mobile and is subject to the same state licensing as a regular automobile. Therefore, the rationales for the auto exception apply to mobile homes. Reversed.

DISSENT: (Stevens, J.) Where, as here, agents have the element of surprise on their side, and the motor home is parked, the exigencies justifying the auto exception do not apply.

⏵ *ANALYSIS*

While auto searches do not require warrants, probable cause is still necessary. For this reason, the scope of an auto search is limited. It may not be more intrusive than that necessary to obtain the required evidence.

◼︎═◼︎

Quicknotes

AUTOMOBILE EXCEPTION Exception to the requirement of a valid warrant if a police officer has probable cause to believe that a vehicle contains evidence of a crime or contraband; the officer may search the entire vehicle.

EXIGENT CIRCUMSTANCES Circumstances requiring an extraordinary or immediate response; an exception to the prohibition on a warrantless arrest or search when police officers believe probable cause to exist and there is no time for obtaining a warrant.

PROBABLE CAUSE A reasonable basis for believing that a crime has been committed.

United States v. Chadwick

Federal government (P) v. Accused drug trafficker (D)

433 U.S. 1 (1977).

NATURE OF CASE: Appeal from district court judgment dismissing charges of marijuana possession.

FACT SUMMARY: Chadwick (D) and his confederates were arrested by federal narcotics agents; an hour and a half later, their footlocker was opened and found to contain marijuana.

> ## 🏛 RULE OF LAW
> The "automobile exception" permitting warrantless searches of vehicles in certain narrow circumstances does not apply to searches of luggage.

FACTS: Narcotics agents in San Diego observed the suspicious behavior of two persons (D) carrying a footlocker on a train bound for Boston. They alerted agents in Boston, who had a dog sniff the footlocker upon its arrival. The dog indicated the presence of drugs without alerting the owners of the locker. Chadwick (D) then joined the two suspects (D), and they placed the footlocker in the trunk of Chadwick's (D) car. The agents then arrested the three suspects (D) and took possession of the footlocker. An hour and a half later, the agents opened the footlocker and discovered large quantities of marijuana. Prior to their trial for drug possession, Chadwick et al. (D) successfully moved to suppress the marijuana. The Government (P) sought review.

ISSUE: Does the "automobile exception" permitting warrantless searches of vehicles in certain narrow circumstances apply to searches of luggage?

HOLDING AND DECISION: (Burger, C.J.) No. The "automobile exception" permitting warrantless searches of vehicles in certain narrow circumstances does not apply to searches of luggage. Luggage and automobiles are not analogous for Fourth Amendment purposes. Luggage contents are not open to public view, and the expectation of privacy is greater in luggage than in an automobile. Once the footlocker was transferred to the agents' control, there was no longer a danger that it would be moved before a warrant could be obtained. Moreover, the search, occurring more than an hour after the arrest of Chadwick et al. (D), was not incident to their arrest. The judgment is affirmed.

CONCURRENCE: (Brennan, J.) It is not at all obvious that the agents could have legally searched the footlocker had they seized it after the suspects (D) had driven away with it in their car or at the time and place of the arrests.

DISSENT: (Blackmun, J.) A warrant is not required to search any movable object in the possession of a person arrested in a public place. Perverse circumstances control the outcome here. If the agents had waited until the suspects (D) drove away, they could have made the arrest, taken the locker to their office and searched it there. Alternatively, the agents could lawfully have searched the footlocker at the scene of the arrest.

▶ ANALYSIS

The dissent is clearly suggesting that the automobile exception would have applied if the agents had stopped Chadwick's (D) vehicle "on the highway" rather than making the arrest before the car was started. However, a subsequent case, implicitly addressing Justice Blackmun's concerns, held that the warrantless search of the respondent's luggage was not lawful merely because the luggage happened to be in respondent's vehicle when it was stopped on the highway.

■■■

Quicknotes

SEARCH INCIDENT TO LAWFUL ARREST Exception to the requirement of a valid warrant for a search or seizure so long as the officer is lawfully in the location where the evidence is obtained and it is apparent that the thing seized is evidence.

■■■

California v. Acevedo

State (P) v. Paper bag owner (D)

500 U.S. 565 (1991).

NATURE OF CASE: Appeal from the grant of a motion to suppress.

FACT SUMMARY: Without first obtaining a warrant, police officers searched a closed container that Acevedo (D) placed in his trunk.

RULE OF LAW
Police officers may search closed containers within an automobile without a warrant, pursuant to a valid search of the vehicle.

FACTS: Drug enforcement agents intercepted a package of marijuana being sent to Daza and notified Daza when it arrived at Federal Express. Officers followed Daza when he picked up the package and drove it to his apartment. Acevedo (D) arrived at Daza's apartment and left shortly thereafter carrying a paper bag of the same size as the marijuana package. Acevedo (D) placed the bag in the trunk of his car and started to drive away. The officers stopped him and opened the trunk and the bag and found the marijuana. Acevedo (D) claimed that the search of the bag was illegal. The appeals court agreed, and the State (P) appealed.

ISSUE: May police officers search closed containers within an automobile without a warrant, pursuant to a valid search of the vehicle?

HOLDING AND DECISION: (Blackmun, J.) Yes. Police officers may search closed containers within an automobile without a warrant, pursuant to a valid search of the vehicle. Two previous cases decided by this Court have raised some confusion in this area. In *United States v. Chadwick*, 433 U.S. 1 (1977), the Court held that a closed container placed in a car could not be searched without a warrant when there was probable cause only as to the container. On the other hand, in *United States v. Ross*, 456 U.S. 798 (1982), we found that a warrantless search of an automobile could include a search of containers inside when there was probable cause to search the car. The contradiction between these cases could result in officers conducting more intrusive searches as they seek to generate probable cause to search an entire car rather than just a container within the car. Furthermore, the rule in *Chadwick* has not protected privacy and has confused courts and police officers. It is better to adopt a single clear-cut rule to govern auto searches. Thus, the warrant requirement for closed containers set forth in *Chadwick* is overruled. Reversed.

CONCURRENCE: (Scalia, J.) While the dissent makes the correct point that the new rule will produce anomalous results, the Fourth Amendment does not require a prior warrant for searches; it requires only that the search not be unreasonable. This is the concept that should govern this area of the law.

DISSENT: (White, J.) The judgment below should be confirmed for the reason stated by Justice Stevens.

DISSENT: (Stevens, J.) When the police have probable cause to search a particular container, they can seize that container and have no need to search an entire vehicle. The majority opinion creates a situation in which a search of a container is prohibited while the owner is carrying it in the open, but allowed once the owner has placed the container in a locked trunk.

ANALYSIS

This decision does not eliminate challenges based on an excessive search under the auto exception. A defendant may still claim that a search of other areas of a car was invalid if the officers had probable cause with regard to the container only. Lower courts have not been consistent in interpreting the new rule.

━━■

Quicknotes

MOTION TO SUPPRESS Motion to exclude the introduction of evidence in a criminal prosecution that was unlawfully obtained.

PROBABLE CAUSE A reasonable basis for believing that a crime has been committed.

━━■

Horton v. California

Home owner (D) v. State (P)

496 U.S. 128 (1990).

NATURE OF CASE: Appeal from conviction of robbery.

FACT SUMMARY: When the police searched Horton's (D) apartment for proceeds of an armed robbery, they found weapons used in the robbery lying in plain view.

🏛 RULE OF LAW
Inadvertence is not a necessary condition of "plain view" seizures.

FACTS: Walker was accosted by two masked men who threatened him with weapons and robbed him. Walker identified Horton's (D) voice as that of one of the robbers. A search warrant was issued authorizing a search for the proceeds of the robbery, but not for the weapons allegedly used in the commission of the robbery. While searching Horton's (D) apartment, the police found the weapons in question in plain view and seized them. The trial court refused to suppress the evidence found in Horton's (D) home, and he was convicted of armed robbery. The California court of appeal affirmed, rejecting Horton's (D) argument that suppression of the evidence that had not been listed in the warrant was required because its discovery was not inadvertent. The California Supreme Court affirmed. The U.S. Supreme Court granted certiorari.

ISSUE: Is inadvertence a necessary condition of "plain view" seizures?

HOLDING AND DECISION: (Stevens, J.) No. Inadvertence is not a necessary condition of "plain view" seizures. Evenhanded law enforcement is best achieved by application of the objective standards of conduct, rather than standards that depend upon the subjective state of mind of the officer. The fact that an officer is interested in an item of evidence and expects to find it in the course of a search should not invalidate its seizure if the search is confined in area and duration by the terms of the warrant or a valid exception to the warrant requirement. The suggestion that the inadvertence requirement is necessary to prevent the police from conducting general searches is not persuasive because that interest is already served by the requirements that no warrant issue unless it particularly describes the place to be searched and the persons or things to be seized. Here, the scope of the search was not enlarged in the slightest by the omission of any reference to the weapons in the warrant. Affirmed.

DISSENT: (Brennan, J.) In eschewing the inadvertent discovery requirement, the majority ignores the Fourth Amendment's express command that warrants particularly describe not only the places to be searched, but also the things to be seized.

▌ ANALYSIS

In *Arizona v. Hicks*, 480 U.S. 321 (1987), police, during the execution of a search, moved stereo equipment that they suspected (but lacked probable cause to believe) was stolen in order to gain access to the serial numbers on the back of the equipment. The Supreme Court rejected the argument that the plain view doctrine authorized police to move the stereo equipment. It found that if an object is unrelated to the justification for the search and if police do not have probable cause to seize the object, they cannot use the plain view doctrine as an excuse for meddling with the object.

■━■

Quicknotes

AFFIDAVIT A declaration of facts written and affirmed before a witness.

EXIGENT CIRCUMSTANCES Circumstances requiring an extraordinary or immediate response; an exception to the prohibition on a warrantless arrest or search when police officers believe probable cause to exist and there is no time for obtaining a warrant.

PLAIN VIEW Exception to the requirement of a valid warrant for a search or seizure so long as the officer is lawfully in the location where the evidence is obtained and it is apparent that the thing seized is evidence.

■━■

Arizona v. Hicks

State (P) v. Accused robber (D)

480 U.S. 321 (1987).

NATURE OF CASE: On certiorari from appellate court decision reversing robbery conviction.

FACT SUMMARY: Police conducted a search of Hicks's (D) apartment, moving stereo equipment in order to observe the serial numbers.

🏛 RULE OF LAW
Physically moving a suspicious object in an individual's home to determine if it is incriminating evidence, without probable cause, during an unrelated warrantless search, is violative of the Fourth Amendment.

FACTS: Police entered Hicks's (D) apartment after a bullet was fired through the floor of the apartment, injuring a man below. One of the officers observed expensive stereo equipment that seemed out of place in the shabby surroundings. He moved the equipment in order to observe and record its serial numbers. It was later determined that the serial numbers matched those on equipment taken in an armed robbery, and a search warrant was issued and executed.

ISSUE: May a suspicious object in an individual's home be physically moved to determine if it is incriminating evidence, without probable cause, during an unrelated warrantless search?

HOLDING AND DECISION: (Scalia, J.) No. Physically moving a suspicious object in an individual's home to determine if it is incriminating evidence, without probable cause, during an unrelated warrantless search, is violative of the Fourth Amendment. The moving of the turntable constituted an invasion of privacy unrelated to the objectives of the search for the shooter. Although the movement was slight, the difference between looking at a suspicious object in plain view and moving it even a few inches is more than trivial for purposes of the Fourth Amendment. Without probable cause, the officer may not search beyond what is already exposed to view. The judgment of the court of appeals is affirmed.

DISSENT: (Powell, J.) The distinction between looking at a suspicious object in plain view and moving it a few inches trivializes the Fourth Amendment.

DISSENT: (O'Connor, J.) On reasonable suspicion that an object is contraband, officers ought to be permitted to conduct a cursory inspection, such as was done here. Probable cause should be required in order to conduct a full-blown search.

▶ ANALYSIS

Justice Scalia rejected Justice O'Connor's "cursory inspection" theory, saying that such a vague standard would plunge police and judges into a "new thicket of Fourth Amendment law." He indicated that society's interests in privacy and the consistent administration of justice required a bright-line rule.

■=■

Quicknotes

CONTRABAND Items that are illegal to have in one's possession or to trade or produce.

PROBABLE CAUSE A reasonable basis for believing that a crime has been committed.

REASONABLE SUSPICION That which would cause an ordinary prudent person under the circumstances to suspect that a crime has been committed based on specific and articulable facts.

SEIZURE The removal of property from one's possession due to unlawful activity or in satisfaction of a judgment entered by the court.

■=■

Schneckloth v. Bustamonte

Court (P) v. Passenger of car (D)

412 U.S. 218 (1973).

NATURE OF CASE: Appeal of writ of habeas corpus from a trial for theft.

FACT SUMMARY: Evidence obtained by a vehicle search after the driver consented to the search by a police officer was used to convict Bustamonte (D), a passenger in the vehicle.

🏛 RULE OF LAW
Whether a consent to a search was "voluntary" or was the product of duress or coercion, express or implied, is a question of fact to be determined from the totality of all the circumstances.

FACTS: During the course of a consent search of a car that had been stopped for traffic violations, evidence was discovered that was used to convict Bustamonte (D), a passenger in the car, of unlawfully possessing a check. The police officer who had stopped the car asked the driver if he could search the car and was told, "Sure, go ahead." Evidence from the search (stolen checks found under the rear seat) resulted in Bustamonte's (D) conviction. The officer had initially stopped the car because he noticed that a headlight and the vehicle's license plate light were burned out. Bustamonte (D) brought a petition for habeas corpus. The federal district court denied the petition, and Bustamonte (D) appealed. The Ninth Circuit Court of Appeals vacated the order of the district court and remanded, and certiorari was granted by the U.S. Supreme Court.

ISSUE: Is the question whether a consent to a search was "voluntary" or was the product of duress or coercion, express or implied, a question of fact to be determined from the totality of all the circumstances?

HOLDING AND DECISION: (Stewart, J.) Yes. Whether a consent to a search was "voluntary" or was the product of duress or coercion, express or implied, is a question of fact to be determined from the totality of all the circumstances. Knowledge of the right to refuse consent to a search is one factor to be taken into account, but the government need not establish such knowledge as the sine qua non of an effective, voluntary consent. Two competing concerns must be accommodated in determining the meaning of a "voluntary" consent to a search: the legitimate need for such searches and the equally important requirement of assuring the absence of coercion. The Fourth and Fourteenth Amendments require that a consent to a search not be coerced, by explicit or implicit means, by implied threat or covert force. Furthermore, in examining all the surrounding circumstances to determine if, in fact, consent to a search were coerced, account must be taken of subtly coercive police questions, as well as the possibly vulnerable subjective state of the person who consents. Our decision today is a narrow one. We hold only that when the subject of a search is not in custody and the state attempts to justify a search on the basis of his or her consent, the Fourth and Fourteenth Amendments require that it demonstrate that the consent was in fact voluntarily given, and not the result of duress or coercion, express or implied. Voluntariness is a question of fact to be determined from all the circumstances, and while the subject's knowledge of a right to refuse is a factor to be taken into account, the prosecution is not required to demonstrate such knowledge as a prerequisite to establishing a voluntary consent. Here, because the California court followed these principles in affirming Bustamonte's (D) conviction, and because the Ninth Circuit Court of Appeals in remanding for an evidentiary hearing required more, its judgment must be reversed.

DISSENT: (Marshall, J.) This Court is authorizing law enforcement personnel to take advantage of lack of knowledge of citizens to achieve by ploy what they could not accomplish by relying only on the knowing relinquishment of constitutional rights. Of course it would be "practical" for the police to ignore the commands of the Fourth Amendment, if by practicality we mean that more criminals will be apprehended, even though the constitutional rights of innocent people also are ignored. Such advantage is achieved, however, at the cost of permitting the police to ignore constitutional limitations on their conduct.

▌ ANALYSIS

In *Schneckloth*, the Supreme Court noted that a strict standard of waiver has been applied to those rights guaranteed to criminal defendants to insure that they will be accorded the greatest possible opportunity to utilize every facet of the constitutional model of a fair criminal trial. Any trial conducted in derogation of that model leaves open the possibility that the trial reached an unfair result precisely because all the protections specified in the Constitution were not provided. A prime example, said the Court, is the right to counsel since without that right, wholly innocent accuseds face the real and substantial danger that simply because of their lack of legal expertise they may be convicted.

■=■

Continued on next page.

Quicknotes

CERTIORARI A discretionary writ issued by a superior court to an inferior court in order to review the lower court's decisions; the Supreme Court's writ ordering such review.

COERCION The overcoming of a person's free will as a result of threats, promises, or undue influence.

DURESS Unlawful threats or other coercive behavior by one person that causes another to commit acts that he would not otherwise do.

EVIDENTIARY HEARING Hearing pertaining to the evidence of the case.

FOURTEENTH AMENDMENT Declares that no state shall make or enforce any law that shall abridge the privileges and immunities of citizens of the United States. No state shall deny to any person within its jurisdiction the equal protection of the laws.

FOURTH AMENDMENT Provides that persons be secure as to their person and private belongings against unreasonable searches and seizures.

SINE QUA NON Without which not; a necessary element or requirement.

WRIT OF HABEAS CORPUS A proceeding in which a defendant brings a writ to compel a judicial determination of whether he is lawfully being held in custody.

Georgia v. Randolph

State (P) v. Cocaine suspect (D)

547 U.S. 103 (2006).

NATURE OF CASE: Appeal from the state supreme court's ruling that suppressed an illegal warrantless search.

FACT SUMMARY: Police conducted a warrantless search of a premises based on consent by a co-occupant. When the other occupant arrived at the premises, he refused the warrantless search alleging his Fourth Amendment rights were violated. He subsequently sought to have the evidence excluded.

🏛 RULE OF LAW
A physically present co-occupant's stated refusal to permit a warrantless entry renders the warrantless search unreasonable and invalid as to such co-occupant.

FACTS: Scott Randolph (D) and his wife were separated. One morning the wife called the police to report domestic violence and that Randolph (D) had taken away their son. When the police responded, she told the police Randolph (D) was a cocaine user. She gave permission to search the house. Randolph (D) returned to the premises before the search and expressly refused a warrantless search. The police, nevertheless, conducted a search based on the wife's permission and discovered cocaine. Randolph (D) was indicted for possession of cocaine and moved to suppress the evidence as the product of an illegal warrantless search. The trial court denied the motion, however the court of appeals reversed the denial. The state supreme court affirmed the court of appeals, and the state took a writ of certiorari to the U.S. Supreme Court.

ISSUE: Does a physically present co-occupant's stated refusal to permit a warrantless entry render the warrantless search unreasonable and invalid as to such co-occupant?

HOLDING AND DECISION: (Souter, J.) Yes. A physically present co-occupant's stated refusal to permit a warrantless entry renders the warrantless search unreasonable and invalid as to such co-occupant. The instant case calls for straightforward application of the rule that a physically present inhabitant's express refusal to give the police consent to a search is dispositive as to that occupant, regardless of the consent of any fellow occupant. The record here reveals no indication the consenter (the wife) indicated any need for her protection inside the house that might have justified a police entry into the area where the cocaine was found, nor were any exigent circumstances shown, such as entry to prevent evidence destruction. This case has no bearing on the capacity of the police to protect victims of domestic violence. The undoubted right of the police to enter premises to protect a victim is clear and is not before the Court. In the balancing of competing individual and governmental interests involved

with unreasonable searches, a cooperative occupant's invitation to police to enter or search adds nothing as to co-occupants. Accordingly, disputed permission is no match for the Fourth Amendment. Affirmed.

CONCURRENCE: (Stevens, J.) Assuming they are both competent, neither of two spouses is a master who possesses power to override the constitutional right of the other to deny police entry onto their premises.

CONCURRENCE: (Breyer, J.) Here, the totality of the circumstances fails to justify abandonment of the Fourth Amendment's long-established hostility to entry by law enforcement officers into a home without a warrant.

DISSENT: (Roberts, C.J.) Today's rule serves not to interpret the Fourth Amendment to protect privacy but rather to afford its protections on a random and happenstance basis. Great is the cost of providing such random protection.

DISSENT: (Scalia, J.) The issue here is what to do when there is a conflict between two equals. Now that women have authority to consent, it does not follow that the spouse who refuses consent should be the winner of the contest.

▶ ANALYSIS

As the Supreme Court notes in its *Randolph* decision, the constant element in assessing Fourth Amendment reasonableness in consent cases is the great significance given to widely shared social expectations that are naturally influenced by property law, but not totally controlled by its rules.

■■■

Quicknotes

CERTIORARI A discretionary writ issued by a superior court to an inferior court in order to review the lower court's decisions; the Supreme Court's writ ordering such review.

EXIGENT CIRCUMSTANCES Circumstances requiring an extraordinary or immediate response; an exception to the prohibition on a warrantless arrest or search when police officers believe probable cause to exist and there is no time for obtaining a warrant.

FOURTH AMENDMENT Provides that persons be secure as to their person and private belongings against unreasonable searches and seizures.

■■■

Illinois v. Rodriguez

State (P) v. Apartment owner (D)

497 U.S. 177 (1990).

NATURE OF CASE: Appeal from acquittal for possession of controlled substance.

FACT SUMMARY: Rodriguez (D) was arrested after Gail Fischer gave the police entry to Rodriguez's (D) apartment.

🏛 RULE OF LAW
A warrantless entry is valid when based upon the consent of a third party who the police at the time of the entry reasonably believe has common authority over the premises.

FACTS: Rodriguez (D) was arrested in his apartment by the police and charged with possession of illegal drugs. The police gained entry to Rodriguez's (D) apartment with the assistance of one Gail Fischer. Fischer had referred to the residence as "our" apartment. The police did not obtain an arrest warrant for Rodriguez (D) or seek a search warrant for the apartment. After Fischer let them in, the police found cocaine. The officers arrested Rodriguez (D). Rodriguez (D) was charged with possession of a controlled substance. Rodriguez (D) attempted to suppress all evidence seized at the apartment, claiming that Fischer had vacated the apartment several weeks earlier and had no authority to consent to the police entry. The Cook county court found that Fischer was not a usual resident but rather an infrequent visitor. The court rejected Illinois's (P) contention that, even if Fischer did not possess common authority over the premises, there was no Fourth Amendment violation if the police reasonably believed that Fischer possessed the authority to consent. The appellate court affirmed. The U.S. Supreme Court granted certiorari.

ISSUE: Is a warrantless entry valid when based upon the consent of a third party who the police at the time of the entry reasonably believe has common authority over the premises?

HOLDING AND DECISION: (Scalia, J.) Yes. A warrantless entry is valid when based upon the consent of a third party who the police at the time of the entry reasonably believe has common authority over the premises. Common authority rests on mutual use of property by persons generally having joint access to the premises. In order to satisfy the "reasonableness" standard of the Fourth Amendment, it is not that the magistrate issuing a warrant or the police officer conducting a search always be correct, but that they always be reasonable. Here, the appellate court found it unnecessary to determine whether the officers reasonably believed Fischer had the authority to consent because it ruled as a matter of law that a reasonable

belief could not validate the entry. Remanded for reconsideration of that question.

DISSENT: (Marshall, J.) In the absence of an exigency, warrantless home searches and seizures are unreasonable under the Fourth Amendment. The weighty constitutional interest in preventing unauthorized intrusions into the home overrides any law enforcement interest in relying on the reasonable but potentially mistaken belief that a third party has authority to consent to such a search or seizure.

▶ ANALYSIS

A Wisconsin regulation allowing a probation officer to search a probationer's residence without a warrant if there are reasonable grounds to believe that he has contraband does not violate the Fourth Amendment. The special needs of the probation system justify departure from the requirements of a warrant and probable cause. *Griffin v. Wisconsin*, 483 U.S. 868 (1987).

◼══◼

Quicknotes

CONSENT A voluntary and willful agreement by an individual possessing sufficient mental capacity to undertake an action suggested by another.

EXIGENT CIRCUMSTANCES Circumstances requiring an extraordinary or immediate response; an exception to the prohibition on a warrantless arrest or search when police officers believe probable cause to exist and there is no time for obtaining a warrant.

EXPECTATION OF PRIVACY Requirement that in order to invoke the Fourth Amendment's protection against unreasonable searches and seizures, the individual must have a reasonable expectation of privacy in respect to the location searched or thing seized.

◼══◼

Terry v. Ohio

Criminal defendant (D) v. State (P)

392 U.S. 1 (1968).

NATURE OF CASE: Review of order denying motion to suppress in prosecution for carrying concealed weapons.

FACT SUMMARY: Terry (D), who was frisked by a police officer, contended that such a procedure could not have been performed absent probable cause to arrest.

🏛 RULE OF LAW
Police may stop and frisk an individual who they reasonably suspect may be armed and dangerous, even if probable cause to arrest is not present.

FACTS: McFadden, a police detective of 35 years' experience, was patrolling his beat on foot when he observed Terry (D) and another man repeatedly strolling by a store, looking in, and then walking away. This continued for over ten minutes. McFadden formed the opinion that they were casing the store. He approached them and asked for identification. When their responses proved evasive, McFadden spun Terry (D) against a wall. Frisking him, he found a gun. Terry (D) was charged with carrying a concealed weapon. His motion to suppress was denied, and the state supreme court affirmed. The U.S. Supreme Court granted review.

ISSUE: May police stop and frisk an individual who they reasonably suspect may be armed and dangerous, even if probable cause to arrest is not present?

HOLDING AND DECISION: (Warren, C.J.) Yes. Police may stop and frisk an individual who they reasonably suspect may be armed and dangerous, even if probable cause to arrest is not present. Competing values are at issue here. On the one hand, the rapidly increasing dangerousness on city streets has created the need for flexible responses on the part of law enforcement. On the other hand, the authority of the police to search a person must be limited to situations when probable cause is present for the Fourth Amendment to have any meaning. Superimposed on this analysis is the limited ability of the judiciary to control day-to-day situations on city streets. The exclusionary rule can only go so far in controlling police conduct. When it cannot do so, its reasons for existence cease. The point of departure for analysis is that the Fourth Amendment's reasonableness requirement remains central. The reasonableness of a stop and frisk depends upon weighing the governmental interest in police and bystander security against a possibly armed criminal and every citizen's interest against police interference. This Court believes that a proper balance between these interests is struck by a rule allowing the minimally intrusive stop and frisk for weapons when an officer suspects, on an objectively reasonable level, that a person may be armed and dangerous. Here, Terry's (D) conduct was sufficiently suggestive of an intent to rob that McFadden's belief in this regard was reasonable. The stop, therefore, did not constitute a Fourth Amendment violation. Affirmed.

CONCURRENCE: (Harlan, J.) Once circumstances justify a confrontation with a citizen, the right to frisk naturally flows therefrom.

CONCURRENCE: (White, J.) A person cannot be compelled to cooperate if addressed by an officer, and such refusal cannot in itself furnish a basis for arrest.

DISSENT: (Douglas, J.) Nothing less than probable cause can justify forcible detention of an individual.

▶ ANALYSIS

The exclusionary rule is found nowhere in the Constitution. It was created by the Court as a prophylactic measure to advance the rights found in the Fourth Amendment. In the present case, the Court reasoned that when the rule could no longer serve its prophylactic purpose, which is believed to be the case here, it should not be imposed.

■=■

Quicknotes

FOURTH AMENDMENT Provides that persons be secure as to their person and private belongings against unreasonable searches and seizures.

TERRY STOP A search of a person suspected of intending to commit a crime that is conducted by patting down the clothes of the person; the search must be limited to the reason for which the individual was lawfully stopped.

■=■

Dunaway v. New York

Attempted robbery suspect (D) v. State (P)

442 U.S. 200 (1979).

NATURE OF CASE: Review of conviction obtained after custodial interrogation.

FACT SUMMARY: An inmate provided information insufficient to constitute probable cause that Dunaway (D) was involved in an attempted robbery, and police took Dunaway (D) in and held him where he gave incriminating statements after a *Miranda* warning.

RULE OF LAW
Under the Fourth Amendment, a seizure and transport of a suspect against his will is sufficiently intrusive to require probable cause that the suspect has committed a crime.

FACTS: A police officer told a colleague assigned to an attempted robbery case that he had obtained information that Dunaway (D) had committed the attempt. The investigating officer questioned the source but did not obtain sufficient information to have probable cause that Dunaway (D) was involved in the crime. Nonetheless, the officer had Dunaway (D) arrested from the home of a neighbor and brought in for questioning. Dunaway (D) was advised of his *Miranda* rights and then waived counsel and gave incriminating evidence against himself in the absence of any attorney. Dunaway's (D) motions to suppress the statements and sketches he made were denied, and he was convicted. The court of appeals affirmed, and the U.S. Supreme Court granted certiorari and remanded the case. The county court found on remand that the motions should have been granted. The appellate division reversed, and the U.S. Supreme Court granted certiorari.

ISSUE: Under the Fourth Amendment, is a seizure and transport of a suspect sufficiently intrusive to require probable cause that the suspect has committed a crime?

HOLDING AND DECISION: (Brennan, J.) Yes. Under the Fourth Amendment, a seizure and transport of a suspect against his will is sufficiently intrusive to require probable cause that the suspect has committed a crime. A suspect may be stopped on less than probable cause if the intrusion into his privacy is less than an arrest. But the stop and frisk exception does not apply in this case. The intrusion upon Dunaway (D) was indistinguishable from arrest. He was taken from his neighbor's home into a car and required to go to the station and be interrogated. He was not "free to go," and physical restraint would have been used to prevent him from going. Under the Fourth Amendment, a seizure and transport of a suspect is sufficiently intrusive to require probable cause that the subject has committed a crime. Here, there was no such probable cause, and the conviction based on evidence obtained by this method must be overturned. Reversed.

CONCURRENCE: (White, J.) The key principle of the Fourth Amendment is reasonableness, namely, the balancing of competing interests. If governmental officials are to have practical rules, this balancing must be properly accomplished, not on a case-by-case basis by individual police officers. It is here sufficient that the police conduct is comparable enough to an arrest that the ordinary level of probable cause is necessary before interests of privacy and personal security be required to yield.

DISSENT: (Rehnquist, J.) The defendant voluntarily accompanied the police to the station to answer their questions. Although a police request to come to the station may be an "awesome experience," such fact alone does not indicate that in every occurrence when a citizen agrees to a police request to come to headquarters, there has been a Fourth Amendment "seizure." The issue turns on whether the officer's conduct is objectively coercive or physically threatening, not on the fact that a person might to some degree be intimidated by an officer's request.

ANALYSIS

The stop and frisk exception to the general rule that probable cause is required for an intrusion into a suspect's privacy depends upon a determination of what is an arrest and what is a mere detention. A detention must be brief and not unreasonably inconvenient under the circumstances. When a person is moved against his will, an arrest has usually taken place.

Quicknotes

CUSTODIAL INTERROGATION The questioning of a suspect by police while in custody.

PROBABLE CAUSE A reasonable basis for believing that a crime has been committed.

STOP AND FRISK A brief, nonintrusive stop, requiring the police officer to have a reasonable suspicion that a crime has been committed based on specific and articulable facts, and involving a search for a concealed weapon that is conducted by patting down the clothes of the person.

United States v. Mendenhall

Federal government (P) v. Accused drug trafficker (D)

446 U.S. 544 (1980).

NATURE OF CASE: On petition from judgment of court of appeals overturning conviction for drug possession.

FACT SUMMARY: Drug Enforcement Administration (DEA) agents conducted a search of Mendenhall (D) without a warrant or probable cause based on her apparent consent.

🏛 RULE OF LAW
A person is "seized" within the meaning of the Fourth Amendment only when, in light of all the circumstances, a reasonable person would believe he was not free to leave.

FACTS: Mendenhall (D) was observed by agents of the DEA at the Detroit Metropolitan Airport exhibiting characteristics of persons unlawfully carrying narcotics. The agents stopped her and identified themselves, and asked to see her airline ticket and identification. The ticket and identification bore different names. One agent asked her to accompany him to the airport DEA office. Once at the office, the agent asked Mendenhall (D) if she would consent to a search of her person and handbag. A policewoman arrived and asked Mendenhall (D) to disrobe. Mendenhall (D) removed her clothes, handed two small packages to the police-woman, and was placed under arrest for possessing heroin.

ISSUE: Is a person "seized" within the meaning of the Fourth Amendment only when, in light of all the circumstances, a reasonable person would believe he was not free to leave?

HOLDING AND DECISION: (Stewart, J.) Yes. A person is "seized" within the meaning of the Fourth Amendment only when, in light of all the circumstances, a reasonable person would believe he was not free to leave. Here, the agents approached Mendenhall (D) in public; they wore no uniforms and displayed no weapons. They asked, but did not demand, to see her identification. Our conclusion that no seizure occurred is not affected by the fact that the agents did not expressly tell Mendenhall (D) she was free to go. The judgment is reversed and remanded to the court of appeals for further proceedings.

CONCURRENCE: (Powell, J.) This Court should not hold that no seizure occurred; rather, that the agents had reasonable and articulable suspicion that Mendenhall (D) was engaging in criminal activity. They therefore did not violate the Fourth Amendment when they stopped her for routine questioning.

DISSENT: (White, J.) The Government (P) never questioned in the lower courts that a seizure occurred. Having failed to convince the court of appeals that the seizure was justified by reasonable suspicion, the Government (P) now seeks reversal here by claiming no seizure occurred. To the contrary, here the accused's Fourth Amendment interests were indeed implicated, and she was undoubtedly "seized" when the DEA agents escorted her from the public area of the terminal to the DEA office for questioning and a strip-search of her person. Such conduct of the DEA agents was in all important respects indistinguishable from a traditional arrest. She was not free to refuse to go to the DEA office and, once inside, was not permitted to leave.

▶ *ANALYSIS*

As the dissent observes, five justices held that Mendenhall (D) was lawfully stopped and questioned. However, the justices in the majority disagreed fundamentally on their reasoning. Two justices, announcing the opinion of the Court, decided that no seizure had taken place—and thus did not address the issue of whether such a seizure was justified; the other three justices in the "majority" wrote that Mendenhall (D) was properly seized on reasonable suspicion.

■═■

Quicknotes

APPARENT CONSENT The manifestation by actions, or by the failure to act, of an agreement of the minds or of the acquiescence by one party to the will of another.

■═■

United States v. Drayton

Federal government (P) v. Drug possessor (D)

536 U.S. 194 (2002).

NATURE OF CASE: Appeal by Government from suppression of drug evidence.

FACT SUMMARY: When a police officer conducted a pat-down search of his person during a "bus sweep," Christopher Drayton (D) argued that any purported consent he may have given was vitiated in the absence of some positive indication that consent could have been refused.

RULE OF LAW

Law enforcement officers do not violate the Fourth Amendment prohibition of unreasonable searches merely by approaching individuals on the street or in other public places and putting questions to them if they are willing to listen.

FACTS: Christopher Drayton (D) was traveling on a Greyhound bus. As part of a routine drug and weapons interdiction effort, police officers, dressed in plain clothes and with concealed weapons but visible badges, entered the bus, and randomly asked passengers, "Do you mind if I check your bags?" and "Do you mind if I check your person?" When Officer Lang asked Drayton (D) if he minded a search of his baggy pants, Drayton (D) responded by lifting his hands about eight inches from his legs, and Lang conducted a pat-down search, found bundles of cocaine, and arrested Drayton (D). Drayton (D) was charged with drug crimes, and the federal district court denied his motion to suppress the drugs on the ground that the entire procedure was a consensual encounter. The court of appeals reversed, and the Government (P) appealed.

ISSUE: Do law enforcement officers violate the Fourth Amendment prohibition of unreasonable searches merely by approaching individuals on the street or in other public places and putting questions to them if they are willing to listen?

HOLDING AND DECISION: (Kennedy, J.) No. Law enforcement officers do not violate the Fourth Amendment prohibition of unreasonable searches merely by approaching individuals on the street or in other public places and putting questions to them if they are willing to listen. Even when law enforcement officers have no basis for suspecting a particular individual, they may pose questions, ask for identification, and request consent to search luggage provided they do not induce cooperation by coercive means. If a reasonable person would feel free to terminate the encounter, as here, then he or she has not been seized. Here, the officers gave the passengers no

reason to believe that they were required to answer the officers' questions. When Officer Lang approached Drayton (D), he did not brandish a weapon or make any intimidating movements. He left the aisle free so that Drayton (D) could exit. He spoke to passengers one by one and in a polite, quiet voice. Nothing he said would suggest to a reasonable person that he or she was barred from leaving the bus or otherwise terminating the encounter. There was no application of force, no intimidating movement, no overwhelming show of force, no blocking of exits, no command, not even an authoritative tone of voice. It is beyond question that had this encounter occurred on the street, it would be constitutional. The fact that an encounter takes place on a bus does not on its own transform standard police questioning of citizens into an illegal seizure. Furthermore, even the presence of a holstered firearm is unlikely to contribute to the coerciveness of the encounter absent active brandishing of the weapon. Reversed and remanded.

DISSENT: (Souter, J.) Although anyone who travels by air today clearly submits to searches of the person and luggage as a condition of boarding the aircraft, the commonplace precautions of air travel have not, thus far, been justified for ground transportation. There is therefore "an air of unreality" about the majority's explanation that bus passengers consent to searches of their luggage to enhance their own safety and the safety of those around them. Furthermore, a police officer who is certain to get his way has no need to shout.

ANALYSIS

In *Drayton,* the Supreme Court notes that although Officer Lang did not inform Drayton (D) of his right to refuse the search, he did request permission to search and that the totality of the circumstances indicated that the consent was voluntary, hence the search was admissible. In a society based on law, said the court, the concept of agreement and consent should be given "a weight and dignity of its own."

Quicknotes

FOURTH AMENDMENT Provides that persons be secure as to their person and private belongings against unreasonable searches and seizures.

California v. Hodari D.

State (P) v. Running cocaine possession suspect (D)

499 U.S. 621 (1991).

NATURE OF CASE: Review of order suppressing evidence pursuant to a criminal prosecution.

FACT SUMMARY: Hodari (D) sought to suppress contraband tossed away after a police officer came upon him but prior to his personal restraint.

🏛 RULE OF LAW
A defendant's rights against unlawful arrest will not operate to suppress evidence found prior to physical restraint.

FACTS: Two police officers came upon several persons, including Hodari (D), acting in a suspicious manner. When they approached, all took flight. Hodari (D) inadvertently ran in the direction of one officer, whom he did not see until he was almost upon the officer. As soon as he saw the officer, he tossed away an object that later proved to be rock cocaine. Charged with possession, Hodari (D) moved to suppress the evidence on the grounds that the evidence was obtained in an unlawful seizure in violation of the Fourth and Fourteenth Amendments. The trial court denied the motion, but the state court of appeal reversed. The U.S. Supreme Court granted certiorari.

ISSUE: Will a defendant's right against unlawful arrest operate to suppress evidence found prior to physical restraint?

HOLDING AND DECISION: (Scalia, J.) No. A defendant's right against unlawful arrest will not operate to suppress evidence found prior to physical restraint. The Fourth Amendment protects against unlawful seizure. "Seizure," when applied to the person, as it must be in the context of arrest, can only refer to physical restraint. The term "seizure," as it is commonly understood, implies some form of custody or control. Consequently, any evidence found prior to such custody or control cannot be said to be the fruit of an illegal seizure. Here, Hodari (D) had not been placed under physical restraint when he attempted to conceal the incriminating evidence, so the evidence should not have been suppressed. Reversed.

DISSENT: (Stevens, J.) The Court has essentially concluded that the unlawful attempt at an arrest does not implicate the Fourth Amendment. This is at odds with precedent and logic. Here, the show of force on the part of the police officer, constituting an actual chase, made clear that the accused was not free to leave. This Court should insist on greater rewards to society before sacrificing constitutional protections. Today's holding fails to recognize the coercive and intimidating nature of much current-day police behavior.

▶ ANALYSIS

United States v. Mendenhall, 446 U.S. 544 (1980), had held that a person is seized only if a person's freedom of movement is restrained. Hodari (D) argued that the presence of an officer alone could work to constitute such a restraint. The Court disagreed, noting that *Mendenhall* did not say an arrest was necessarily effected when movement is restrained, but rather that an arrest cannot occur absent such restraint. The dissent declared this a distinction without a difference.

■=■

Quicknotes

ARREST The lawful deprivation of a person's liberty pursuant to a valid warrant, probable cause that he has committed a criminal offense, or pursuant to some other authority conferred by law.

CERTIORARI A discretionary writ issued by a superior court to an inferior court in order to review the lower court's decisions; the Supreme Court's writ ordering such review.

EXCLUSIONARY RULE A rule precluding the introduction at trial of evidence unlawfully obtained in violation of the federal constitutional safeguards against unreasonable searches and seizures.

SEIZURE The removal of property from one's possession due to unlawful activity or in satisfaction of a judgment entered by the court.

■=■

Alabama v. White

State (P) v. Cocaine dealer (D)

496 U.S. 325 (1990).

NATURE OF CASE: Review of order reversing conviction for possession of narcotics.

FACT SUMMARY: Acting on an anonymous phone tip, police stopped Vanessa White (D) and searched her car after corroborating her noncriminal behavior predicted by the informant.

🏛 RULE OF LAW
Reasonable suspicion can be established with information different in quantity or content than that required to establish probable cause, and can arise from information that is less reliable than that required to show probable cause.

FACTS: On the afternoon of April 22, 1987, Officer Davis received an anonymous telephone tip stating that Vanessa White (D) would leave 235-C Lynwood Terrace Apartments at a particular time later that day in a brown Plymouth station wagon with a broken right taillight lens, that she would drive to Dobey's Motel, and that she would be in possession of a brown attaché case containing an ounce of cocaine. Davis proceeded to the apartment and observed White (D) leave the building empty-handed, enter the described station wagon, and drive by a route involving many turns to Dobey's Motel. Davis stopped the vehicle just short of the motel. Pursuant to a consensual search, marijuana was discovered in a brown attaché case found in the car. Three milligrams of cocaine were later found in White's (D) purse. The trial court denied White's (D) motion to suppress, and she was convicted of possession of narcotics. The state court of appeals reversed the conviction on the grounds that White's (D) detention was unconstitutional. The state supreme court denied certiorari, and Alabama (P) appealed.

ISSUE: Can reasonable suspicion be established with information different in quantity or content than that required to establish probable cause, and arise from information that is less reliable than that required to show probable cause?

HOLDING AND DECISION: (White, J.) Yes. Reasonable suspicion can be established with information different in quantity or content than that required to establish probable cause, and can arise from information that is less reliable than that required to show probable cause. Reasonable suspicion, like probable cause, is dependent upon both the content of information possessed by police and its degree of reliability as determined by the "totality of circumstances" test. The only difference is that the level of suspicion required to establish "reasonable suspicion" is

less than that required to establish "probable cause." Although this is a close case, the range of details actually corroborated by the officers imparted some degree of reliability to the informant's other allegations. The caller's ability to predict White's (D) future behavior demonstrated the possession of inside information, in this case White's (D) itinerary, normally restricted to a small number of people. The totality of these facts established the requisite reasonable suspicion to stop White (D). Reversed.

DISSENT: (Stevens, J.) The common activity of leaving one's apartment at the same time every day carrying an attaché case does not establish reasonable suspicion of illegal activity. It is an activity engaged in daily by millions of lawful citizens. Today's decision makes a mockery of the protections of the Fourth Amendment.

▶ ANALYSIS

White presents one of the weakest factual scenarios held to satisfy the reasonable suspicion standard. The majority quoted the statement in *Gates*, 462 U.S. 213 (1983), that "the anonymous [tip] contained a range of details relating not just to easily obtained facts and conditions existing at the time of the tip, but to future actions of third parties ordinarily not easily predicted." The dissent expressed unease with the record's silence on the issue of whether police made any attempt to determine the identity, motivation, and basis of knowledge of the anonymous phone caller.

■=■

Quicknotes

CERTIORARI A discretionary writ issued by a superior court to an inferior court in order to review the lower court's decisions; the Supreme Court's writ ordering such review.

PROBABLE CAUSE A reasonable basis for believing that a crime has been committed.

REASONABLE SUSPICION That which would cause an ordinary prudent person under the circumstances to suspect that a crime has been committed based on specific and articulable facts.

■=■

Illinois v. Wardlow

State (P) v. Convicted weapons felon (D)

528 U.S. 119 (2000).

NATURE OF CASE: Appeal from conviction for unlawful use of a weapon by a felon.

FACT SUMMARY: Wardlow (D) sought to suppress introduction of a .38-caliber handgun at trial on the basis that the gun was recovered during an unlawful stop and frisk.

🏛 RULE OF LAW
Flight from police is sufficient to support a finding of reasonable suspicion and to justify a police officer's further investigation.

FACTS: Officers Nolan and Harvey were working as uniformed officers in the special operations section of the Chicago Police Department. They observed Wardlow (D) standing next to a building holding an opaque bag. When he saw the officers, he fled. The officers eventually cornered him and conducted a pat-down search for weapons. During the frisk, Nolan felt a hard object and opened the bag to discover a .38-caliber handgun with five live rounds of ammunition. The officers arrested Wardlow (D). The trial court denied Wardlow's (D) motion to suppress, concluding the gun was recovered during a lawful stop and frisk and convicted Wardlow (D) of unlawful use of a weapon by a felon. The appellate court reversed on the basis that Nolan did not have reasonable suspicion sufficient to justify an investigative stop under *Terry v. Ohio.* The Illinois Supreme Court agreed.

ISSUE: Is flight from police sufficient to support a finding of reasonable suspicion justifying a police officer in further investigation?

HOLDING AND DECISION: (Rehnquist, C.J.) Yes. Flight from police is sufficient to support a finding of reasonable suspicion justifying a police officer in further investigation. This case is governed by this Court's analysis in *Terry.* Nolan and Harvey were among eight other officers in a four-car caravan converging on an area known for drug trafficking. While an individual's presence in an area of expected criminal activity is not sufficient, without more to support a reasonable, particularized suspicion that the person is committing a crime, the officers may take into consideration the relevant characteristics of a location in determining whether the circumstances are sufficiently suspicious to warrant further investigation. Moreover, nervous, evasive behavior is another pertinent factor in determining reasonable suspicion, such as Wardlow's (D) unprovoked flight upon seeing the police. Thus Nolan was justified in suspecting Wardlow (D) was involved in criminal activity and in investigating further. Reversed.

CONCURRENCE AND DISSENT: (Stevens, J.) The State (P) asks the Court to announce a per se rule authorizing the temporary detention of anyone who flees at the mere sight of a police officer, while Wardlow (D) asks the Court to adopt the opposite per se rule—that the fact that a person flees upon seeing the police can never justify a temporary investigative stop. While the Court's rejection of both per se rules is appropriate, the testimony of the officer who seized Wardlow (D) does not support the conclusion that he had reasonable suspicion to make the stop.

▶ ANALYSIS

Compare the result in this case with that in *Florida v. J.L.,* 529 U.S. 266 (2000). There the police responded to an anonymous call that a young black male would be at a particular location, wearing particular clothing and carrying a gun. While nothing in the youth's behavior aroused suspicion, the police officer frisked him and discovered a gun. The Court held that an "anonymous tip" was insufficient to establish reasonable suspicion justifying the police to make an investigatory stop.

■■■

Quicknotes

PER SE By itself; not requiring additional evidence for proof.

REASONABLE SUSPICION That which would cause an ordinary prudent person under the circumstances to suspect that a crime has been committed based on specific and articulable facts.

STOP AND FRISK A brief, non-intrusive stop, requiring the police officer to have a reasonable suspicion that a crime has been committed or is contemplated being committed based on specific and articulable facts, and involving a search for a concealed weapon that is conducted by patting down the clothes of the person.

■■■

Maryland v. Buie

State (P) v. Red-suited robber (D)

494 U.S. 325 (1990).

NATURE OF CASE: Review of order reversing denial of motion to suppress in a robbery prosecution.

FACT SUMMARY: A police officer, after having arrested Buie (D) in his residence, searched the basement for possible accomplices.

▥ RULE OF LAW
After an arrest is made in a residence, a search of the house for accomplices requires articulable facts warranting a belief that the presence of an accomplice is likely.

FACTS: An armed robbery occurred in which one of the robbers was wearing a red running suit. Police obtained an arrest warrant for Buie (D). The officers went to his house and entered it. An officer yelled for anyone in the basement to come out. Buie (D) did and was arrested. An officer, who then descended into the basement to check for possible confederates hiding there, instead found a red running suit. Prior to a trial, the court denied Buie's (D) motion to suppress admission of the running suit as evidence. The state court of appeals reversed, holding probable cause for such a search to be required. The U.S. Supreme Court granted review.

ISSUE: After an arrest is made in a residence, does a search of the house for accomplices require articulable facts warranting a belief that the presence of an accomplice is likely?

HOLDING AND DECISION: (White, J.) Yes. After an arrest is made in a residence, a search of the house for accomplices requires articulable facts warranting a belief that the presence of an accomplice is likely. As an incident to arrest, police may search the house, as a precautionary measure, without a warrant or probable cause. As long as there is some articulable reason for an officer to believe that there might be an accomplice hiding who might pose a threat, a search for such an individual is legitimate. [The Court, rather than ruling on the facts of the present case, vacated the appellate court order and remanded for a factual determination of the issue.]

CONCURRENCE: (Stevens, J.) That Buie (D) offered no resistance when he emerged from the basement is somewhat inconsistent with the hypothesis that the danger of an attack by a hidden confederate persisted after the arrest. All of the evidence suggests that no reasonable suspicion of danger justified the entry into the basement.

DISSENT: (Brennan, J.) A planned arrest in the home is very different from a *Terry* search, which is an exception

to probably cause designed to protect officers from unavoidable confrontations. A protective search of the home is not minimally intrusive, in light of the sanctity of the home. The nature and scope of the search in this case are widely different from a *Terry* search. In light of the "special sanctity of a private residence" and the highly intrusive nature of a protective sweep, police officers must have probable cause to fear that their personal safety is threatened by a hidden confederate of an arrestee before they may sweep through the entire home.

▶ ANALYSIS

The present case can be seen as a fairly direct descendant of *Terry v. Ohio*, 392 U.S. 1 (1968). There, officers were allowed to stop and pat down a suspect on only a reasonable suspicion of wrongdoing. The standard here, although phrased differently, would appear to be essentially the same.

■=■

Quicknotes

ACCOMPLICE An individual who knowingly, purposefully or voluntarily combines with the main actor in the commission or attempted commission of a criminal offense.

PROBABLE CAUSE A reasonable basis for believing that a crime has been committed.

■=■

Michigan Department of State Police v. Sitz

State police (D) v. Automobile drivers (P)

496 U.S. 444 (1990).

NATURE OF CASE: Appeal from order prohibiting state's use of sobriety checkpoints.

FACT SUMMARY: When Police (D) began operation of a sobriety checkpoint in Saginaw, Michigan, Sitz (P), a licensed Michigan driver, filed a complaint seeking relief from potential subjection to the checkpoint.

🏛 RULE OF LAW
A state's use of highway sobriety checkpoints does not violate the Fourth and Fourteenth Amendments.

FACTS: The Police (D) established a sobriety checkpoint pilot program in 1986. All vehicles passing through a checkpoint would be stopped and the drivers briefly examined for signs of intoxication. In cases where signs were detected, the officer would check the driver's license and registration, and if warranted, would conduct further sobriety tests. If the tests indicated the driver's intoxication, the driver would be arrested. All other drivers would be allowed to resume their journey. The only checkpoint operated was conducted in Saginaw County. The 126 vehicles passing through the checkpoint were delayed an average of approximately 25 seconds. Two drivers were detained for field tests, and one was arrested for driving under the influence. A third driver who drove through without stopping was pulled over and arrested for driving under the influence. Sitz (P), and other Michigan drivers, filed a complaint seeking declaratory and injunctive relief from potential subjection to the checkpoints. The court held that the program violated the Fourth Amendment and the Michigan Constitution. The Michigan Supreme Court affirmed. The U.S. Supreme Court granted certiorari.

ISSUE: Does a state's use of highway sobriety checkpoints violate the Fourth and Fourteenth Amendments?

HOLDING AND DECISION: (Rehnquist, C.J.) No. A state's use of highway sobriety checkpoints does not violate the Fourth and Fourteenth Amendments. No one can dispute the magnitude of the drunken driving problem and the state's interest in stopping it. Conversely, the measure of the intrusion on motorists stopped briefly at sobriety checkpoints is slight. The motorist can see that other vehicles are being stopped so he is less likely to be frightened or annoyed by the intrusion. The balance of the state's interest in preventing drunken driving, the extent to which this system can reasonably be said to advance this interest, and the degree of intrusion upon individual motorists who are briefly stopped weighs in favor of the state program. Reversed.

DISSENT: (Brennan, J.) Here, by holding that no level of suspicion is required prior to a police stop to prevent drunk driving, the Court subjects the public to police conduct which may be arbitrary or harassing. The public must be protected against even the so-called "minimally intrusive" seizures in the instant case.

DISSENT: (Stevens, J.) The Court here ignores the interest of the citizen in liberty from seizures that are suspicionless, unannounced, and investigatory. The effect of sobriety checkpoints on traffic safety is extremely small. Any relationship between sobriety checkpoints and the actual reduction in highway fatalities is even less substantial than the negligible effect on arrest rates. A police officer who questions a driver at a checkpoint has almost limitless discretion to detain a driver on the basis of the slightest suspicion.

▶ ANALYSIS

In *Bostick v. State*, 554 So. 2d 1153 (Fla. 1989), the case involved the constitutionality of a police practice of boarding buses and asking passengers at random for permission to search their luggage. The Florida Supreme Court held that boarding a bus during a brief layover and questioning passengers constituted a "seizure" of the person, which, if not based on an articulable suspicion, violated the passengers' rights guaranteed under the Fourth Amendment. The U.S. Supreme Court, in *Florida v. Bostick*, 501 U.S. 429 (1991), reversed, saying the action did not violate Fourth Amendment rights because no seizure occurred (i.e., passengers were free to leave).

■=■

Quicknotes

CHECKPOINT AUTOMOBILE STOP Exception to the requirement that a police officer have a reasonable suspicion that an automobile contains illegal evidence or contraband for automobile stops made at a fixed checkpoint for the purpose of questioning the occupants of the vehicle; however, the officers must have probable cause or consent of the occupants prior to conducting a search of the vehicle.

EXPECTATION OF PRIVACY Requirement that in order to invoke the Fourth Amendment's protection against unreasonable searches and seizures, the individual must have a reasonable expectation of privacy in respect to the location searched or thing seized.

FOURTH AMENDMENT Provides that persons be secure as to their person and private belongings against unreasonable searches and seizures.

■=■

City of Indianapolis v. Edmond
City (D) v. Class action plaintiffs (P)

531 U.S. 32 (2000).

NATURE OF CASE: Class action challenging constitutionality of vehicle checkpoints.

FACT SUMMARY: Motorists (P) challenged the constitutional validity of city-imposed vehicle checkpoints as violative of the Fourth Amendment's prohibition against unlawful searches and seizures.

RULE OF LAW
Where a vehicle checkpoint program is designed primarily to uncover evidence of criminal wrongdoing, such program constitutes an unlawful search and seizure in violation of the Fourth Amendment.

FACTS: The City of Indianapolis (D) began to operate vehicle checkpoints in an effort to intercept unlawful drugs. Checkpoint locations were selected weeks in advance, based on certain considerations such as area crime statistics and traffic flow. Edmond (P) and Palmer (P) were each stopped at such a narcotics checkpoint. They filed a lawsuit on behalf of themselves and the class of all motorists who had been stopped or were subject to being stopped in the future at the checkpoints. They claimed the roadblocks violated the Fourth Amendment and the search and seizure provision of the state constitution, and they moved for a preliminary injunction. The district court denied, holding the Fourth Amendment was not violated. The court of appeals reversed, and the U.S. Supreme Court granted certiorari.

ISSUE: When a vehicle checkpoint program is designed primarily to uncover evidence of criminal wrongdoing, does such program constitute an unlawful search and seizure in violation of the Fourth Amendment?

HOLDING AND DECISION: (O'Connor, J.) Yes. When a vehicle checkpoint program is designed primarily to uncover evidence of criminal wrongdoing, such program constitutes an unlawful search and seizure in violation of the Fourth Amendment. Our checkpoint cases have recognized only limited exceptions to the general rule that a seizure must be accompanied by some measure of individualized suspicion. When law enforcement authorities pursue primarily general crime-control purposes at checkpoints such as these, such stops may only be justified because of some measure of individualized suspicion. Because the primary purpose of the program was indistinguishable from its general interest in crime control, the checkpoints violate the Fourth Amendment. Affirmed.

DISSENT: (Rehnquist, C.J.) The program in issue here complies with previous decisions regarding roadblock seizures. It is constitutionally irrelevant that the law enforcement also hoped to intercept narcotics.

DISSENT: (Thomas, J.) Prior decisions compel upholding the program at issue here, although those cases may not have been correctly decided. A program of indiscriminate stops of individuals not suspected of wrongdoing is not consistent with the intent of the Fourth Amendment.

ANALYSIS
The Fourth Amendment requires that searches be "reasonable" in order to be held valid. A search is presumptively unreasonable if there is a lack of probable cause. A special category of searches are excluded from the reasonable requirement where they are required to serve "special needs, beyond the normal need for law enforcement." The Court has upheld such special needs as border control and sobriety checkpoints, while rejecting discretionary, suspicionless spot checks of drivers' licenses and registrations. The constitutionality of any such program is based on a balancing test between the interests at stake and the program's effectiveness.

Quicknotes
CERTIORARI A discretionary writ issued by a superior court to an inferior court in order to review the lower court's decisions; the Supreme Court's writ ordering such review.

FOURTH AMENDMENT Provides that persons be secure from unreasonable searches and seizures as regards their person and private belongings.

PROBABLE CAUSE A reasonable basis for believing that a crime has been committed.

SEIZURE The removal of property from one's possession due to unlawful activity or in satisfaction of a judgment entered by the court.

Remedies for Fourth Amendment Violations

Quick Reference Rules of Law

Rakas v. Illinois

Auto passengers (D) v. State (P)

439 U.S. 128 (1978).

NATURE OF CASE: Appeal from a conviction for armed robbery.

FACT SUMMARY: Rakas (D) was not allowed to object to the introduction of evidence obtained by a search of the car in which he was riding as a passenger and was convicted of armed robbery.

RULE OF LAW
Since a car passenger has no legitimate expectation of privacy as to the car, he cannot object to a search of the car or to the introduction of evidence thereby obtained.

FACTS: After hearing a description of the getaway car used in a robbery, police stopped the vehicle in which Rakas (D) was riding as a passenger. A search of the car revealed rifle shells in the locked glove compartment and a sawed-off rifle under the front passenger seat. Contending that the search had been in violation of the Fourth Amendment, Rakas (D) sought to suppress this evidence, but the trial court held he had no standing to make such a motion, and the appellate court agreed. On appeal from his conviction of armed robbery, Rakas (D) argued that anyone at whom a search was "directed" should have standing to contest the legality of that search and object to the admission at trial of evidence obtained as a result thereof.

ISSUE: Does a car passenger have a legitimate expectation of privacy as to the car so that he cannot object to a search of the car or to the introduction of evidence thereby obtained?

HOLDING AND DECISION: (Rehnquist, J.) No. A car passenger has no legitimate expectation of privacy as to the car so that he cannot object to a search of the car or to the introduction of evidence thereby obtained. Until now, many decisions in this area have been couched in terms of whether or not a defendant had "standing" to object to the introduction of evidence obtained by an allegedly unconstitutional search, but this was simply another way of addressing what should now be considered the single guiding standard: whether or not the one making the motion to suppress has had his own Fourth Amendment rights infringed upon by the search and seizure he challenges. As measured by the legitimate expectation of privacy standard, the Fourth Amendment protections offered Rakas (D) were simply not involved when the car was searched. He, therefore, has no basis to object to the evidence obtained. Affirmed.

CONCURRENCE: (Powell, J.) The Fourth Amendment clearly distinguishes between a person's expectation of privacy in a vehicle and his expectation when in other types of locations. Here, none of the vehicle's occupants controlled vehicle or keys. The passengers had no reasonable expectation the car in which they had been riding would not be searched. Their negligible privacy is not similar to the privacy of a person in their place of abode or who hides in a telephone booth or of a traveler who hides possessions in a container that is locked.

DISSENT: (White, J.) The majority opinion so limits the concept of what is a legitimate expectation of privacy as to make it nearly impossible to have such an expectation without having a property interest in the place searched, and the Fourth Amendment was not intended to protect property interests but privacy interests. It is now open season on automobiles.

ANALYSIS

A number of courts have determined that one's reasonable expectation of privacy is abandoned when he puts his garbage out for collection. Thus, the government is free to rummage through it without obeying the strictures of the Fourth Amendment.

Quicknotes

CERTIORARI A discretionary writ issued by a superior court to an inferior court in order to review the lower court's decisions; the Supreme Court's writ ordering such review.

FOURTH AMENDMENT Provides that persons be secure as to their person and private belongings against unreasonable searches and seizures.

PROPRIETARY INTEREST An owner's interest and rights in property.

Minnesota v. Carter

State (P) v. Household visitors (D)

525 U.S. 83 (1998).

NATURE OF CASE: Appeal from an order holding that an illegal search had occurred.

FACT SUMMARY: When a police officer saw people packaging cocaine through a window and later arrested the occupants of the apartment, they alleged that their Fourth Amendment rights had been violated, and sought to have the evidence excluded.

RULE OF LAW
An overnight guest in a home may claim the protection of the Fourth Amendment, but one who is merely present with the consent of the householder may not.

FACTS: A confidential informant told the police that when walking by the window of a ground floor apartment, he had seen people putting a white powder into bags. The police officer looked through the same window and saw the men, and notified headquarters to prepare affidavits for a search warrant. When Carter (D) and Johns (D) left the building, they were arrested while in a motor vehicle, and cocaine was later found in the vehicle and in the apartment. Carter (D) and Johns (D) had never been in that apartment before and had been there for 2½ hours to package the cocaine. Carter (D) and Johns (D) were convicted of state drug offenses. The trial court held that since they were only temporary out-of-state visitors, they could not challenge the legality of the government intrusion into the apartment, and that the police officer's observation through the window was not a "search" within the meaning of the Fourth Amendment. The state supreme court reversed, holding that Carter (D) and Johns (D) did have "standing" because they had a legitimate expectation of privacy in the invaded place, and that the officer's observation constituted an unreasonable "search" of the apartment. Minnesota (P) appealed.

ISSUE: If an overnight guest in a home may claim the protection of the Fourth Amendment, may one who is merely present with the consent of the householder also do so?

HOLDING AND DECISION: (Rehnquist, C.J.) No. An overnight guest in a home may claim the protection of the Fourth Amendment, but one who is merely present with the consent of the householder may not. The purely commercial nature of the transaction engaged in here, the relatively short time on the premises, and the lack of any previous connection between Carter (D) and the householder, all lead to the conclusion that their situation is closer to that of one simply permitted on the premises, rather than that of an overnight guest. Therefore, any search that may have occurred did not violate their Fourth Amendment rights. Reversed.

CONCURRENCE: (Scalia, J.) This Court would go beyond its proper power were it to restrict the ability of the people to govern themselves by use of the full choice of policy decisions that the Constitution provides to them. Whereas it is plausible to regard a person's overnight lodging as at least his "temporary" residence, it is entirely impossible to give that characterization to an apartment that he uses to package cocaine.

CONCURRENCE: (Kennedy, J.) Almost all social guests have a legitimate expectation of privacy, and hence protection against unreasonable searches, in their host's home. In this case, Carter (D) and Johns (D) have established nothing more than a fleeting and insubstantial connection with Thompson's home.

CONCURRENCE: (Breyer, J.) The police officer's observation made from a public area outside the curtilage of the residence did not violate Carter's (D) Fourth Amendment rights. The officer did not engage in what the constitution forbids, namely, an unreasonable search.

DISSENT: (Ginsburg, J.) The Court's decision undermines not only the security of short-term guests, but also the security of the home resident herself. When a homeowner chooses to share the privacy of her home and her company with a short-term guest, both host and guest have exhibited an actual (subjective) expectation of privacy, and that expectation is one that our society is prepared to recognize as reasonable.

▶ ANALYSIS

Property used for commercial purposes is treated differently for Fourth Amendment purposes than residential property. While Carter (D) and Johns (D) were present in a "home," it was not their home. Only the Dissent argued that a short-term guest in a home should share his host's shelter against unreasonable searches and seizures. Since there was no violation of the Fourth Amendment, the evidence seized by the police was used against Carter (D) and Johns (D).

Quicknotes

EXPECTATION OF PRIVACY Requirement that in order to invoke the Fourth Amendment's protection against unreasonable searches and seizures, the individual must have a reasonable expectation of privacy in respect to the location searched or thing seized.

FOURTH AMENDMENT Provides that persons be secure as to their person and private belongings against unreasonable searches and seizures.

Continued on next page.

SEARCH An inspection conducted in order to obtain evidence to be utilized for the prosecution of a crime.

SEIZURE The removal of property from one's possession due to unlawful activity or in satisfaction of a judgment entered by the court.

United States v. Leon

Federal government (P) v. Cocaine conspirators (D)

468 U.S. 897 (1984).

NATURE OF CASE: Appeal from order granting motion to suppress evidence.

FACT SUMMARY: The district court held that although the police acted in good faith, they seized evidence showing Leon's (D) involvement in illegal drug activities pursuant to a search warrant that was not based on probable cause, and, therefore, the evidence had to be excluded under the Fourth Amendment.

🏛 RULE OF LAW
The Fourth Amendment exclusionary rule does not bar the use of evidence obtained by officers acting in good faith in reasonable reliance on a facially valid search warrant ultimately found to be unsupported by probable cause.

FACTS: The Burbank police obtained a facially valid search warrant to search Leon's (D) premises for narcotics. The information in the supporting affidavit was obtained from a confidential informant whose credibility and reliability were not substantiated. The police found narcotics, and Leon (D) was charged with conspiracy to possess and distribute cocaine. The district court granted Leon's (D) motion to suppress the evidence, holding the information in the affidavit was stale and derived from an unsubstantiated source. Therefore, the court held, the warrant was not based on probable cause, and the search was illegal. The court further held that the Fourth Amendment's exclusionary rule required suppression of the evidence even though the police admittedly acted in good faith. The court of appeals affirmed, refusing to recognize a good-faith exception to the exclusionary rule, and the U.S. Supreme Court granted certiorari.

ISSUE: Does the exclusionary rule bar the use of evidence illegally obtained in good faith by law enforcement officers?

HOLDING AND DECISION: (White, J.) No. The Fourth Amendment exclusionary rule does not bar the use of evidence obtained by officers acting in good faith in reasonable reliance on a facially valid search warrant which is subsequently found to be unsupported by probable cause. The exclusionary rule is not mandated by the Fourth Amendment. The Amendment contains no provision that expressly precludes the use of illegally obtained evidence. It is a judicially created remedy to deter illegal law enforcement conduct. Because of its deterrent purpose, the rule cannot be justifiably applied to cases in which the police have acted in good faith under a facially valid warrant. Therefore, it is clear that exclusion of evidence must be determined on a case-by-case basis and only where such exclusion furthers the purpose of the exclusionary rule. As a

result, the evidence, obtained in good faith, should not have been suppressed. Reversed.

CONCURRENCE: (Blackmun, J.) The decision to recognize a good-faith exception to the exclusionary rule comports with the legitimate interests of the criminal justice system without unduly burdening individual Fourth Amendment rights.

DISSENT: (Brennan, J.) The Court's decision to allow illegally obtained evidence in the prosecution's case-in-chief signals the end of the exclusionary rule. The abandonment of the rule shows the Court sacrificing sound principles of individual rights out of fear and frustration caused by an ever-increasing crime rate. The purpose of the Fourth Amendment was to insure that such sacrifice not be made. The rule is based on the protection of Fourth Amendment rights, not exclusively on deterring police conduct. The decision, therefore, denies constitutionally protected rights.

DISSENT: (Stevens, J.) The Fourth Amendment renders unconstitutional seizures made upon a warrant unsupported by probable cause. Such searches are defined as unreasonable, thus rendering them unconstitutional. The Court in this case comes to the completely invalid conclusion that an unreasonable search will not taint resulting evidence if it was reasonable for the police to conduct it. A search cannot be both reasonable and unreasonable. The rule allows automatic reliance of the police on search warrants, which is clearly contrary to the intent of the Fourth Amendment.

▌ ANALYSIS

The court in this case recognized that the issuance of a facially valid search warrant by a neutral magistrate provides sufficient Fourth Amendment protection against unreasonable searches. The exclusionary rule was viewed as having no deterrent effect on the issuing magistrate. Such judicial officers, therefore, will not, as a result of this decision, have any increased incentive to make a reasoned decision concerning the existence of probable cause to search.

■■■

Quicknotes

EXCLUSIONARY RULE A rule precluding the introduction at trial of evidence unlawfully obtained in violation of the federal constitutional safeguards against unreasonable searches and seizures.

FOURTH AMENDMENT Provides that persons be secure as to their person and private belongings against unreasonable searches and seizures.

Continued on next page.

GOOD-FAITH RELIANCE Honest reliance on the representations of another.

PROBABLE CAUSE A reasonable basis for believing that a crime has been committed.

■━■

Silverthorne Lumber Company v. United States

Contemnor (D) v. United States (P)

251 U.S. 385 (1920).

NATURE OF CASE: Writ of error to reverse fine and order of imprisonment for refusal to obey subpoena.

FACT SUMMARY: The United States Marshal (P) seized papers of the Silverthorne Lumber Co. (D) without a warrant, made copies, and returned the originals; the district court then issued a subpoena for production of the originals.

🏛 RULE OF LAW
Knowledge gained by the federal government in violation of the Fourth Amendment cannot be used directly or indirectly as evidence in its case.

FACTS: Silverthorne (D) and his son (D) were arrested for violation of a federal statute. Without a warrant, the United States Marshal (P) then went to the offices of the Silverthorne Lumber Co. (D) and seized incriminating evidence. Copies were made of the papers seized and a new indictment drawn. The district court ordered the return of the illegally seized documents, but kept the copies and issued a subpoena for production of the originals. The Silverthornes (D) refused to comply with the subpoena and were cited for contempt of court. The U.S. Supreme Court granted review.

ISSUE: May knowledge gained by the federal government in violation of the Fourth Amendment be used against a criminal defendant?

HOLDING AND DECISION: (Holmes, J.) No. Knowledge gained by the federal government in violation of the Fourth Amendment cannot be used directly or indirectly as evidence in its case. Such conduct reduces the Fourth Amendment to mere words. For the Fourth Amendment to have any meaning, it must stand for the proposition that not only cannot illegally obtained evidence be admitted, but that it cannot be used at all. Reversed.

▶ ANALYSIS

This is the essence of the "fruit of the poisonous tree" doctrine. Justice Holmes noted that it did not act as a complete bar to the use of illegally seized evidence, only insofar as the evidence would not have been available to prosecutors but for the illegality. If, for example, an independent source obtained the same evidence and provided it to the police in a lawful manner, it would be admissible.

■═■

Quicknotes

WRIT OF ERROR A writ issued by an appellate court, ordering a lower court to deliver the record of the case so that it may be reviewed for alleged errors.

■═■

Murray v. United States

Driver from warehouse (D) v. Federal government (P)

487 U.S. 533 (1988).

NATURE OF CASE: Appeal from a conviction for marijuana possession.

FACT SUMMARY: Murray (D) contended that marijuana seized in his warehouse, initially discovered during an illegal search but subsequently acquired through an independent and lawful search warrant, should be excluded.

🏛 RULE OF LAW
Evidence found for the first time during the execution of a valid and untainted search warrant is admissible if it is discovered pursuant to an independent source.

FACTS: Police officers made an illegal warrantless entry into a warehouse where they observed bales of marijuana. Some officers stayed at the warehouse, keeping it under surveillance, while others obtained a search warrant. In seeking the warrant, the officers made no mention of the illegal entry and did not rely on any observations made during the entry. After obtaining the warrant, the officers searched the warehouse and seized the marijuana. Murray (D) and the other defendants unsuccessfully objected to the use of the evidence against them on the grounds that the officers should have told the magistrate of the illegal entry and that the illegal entry tainted the warrant. Following his conviction, Murray (D) appealed.

ISSUE: Is evidence found for the first time during the execution of a valid and untainted search warrant admissible if it is discovered pursuant to an independent source?

HOLDING AND DECISION: (Scalia, J.) Yes. Evidence found for the first time during the execution of a valid and untainted search warrant is admissible if it is discovered pursuant to an independent source. If the officers' decision to seek the warrant was prompted by what they had seen during the initial entry, or if information obtained during that entry was presented to the magistrate and affected his decision to issue the warrant, the search pursuant to the warrant would not have been an independent source. The district court found that the officers did not reveal their warrantless entry or their observations of the marijuana to the magistrate. The Court did not, however, explicitly find that the agents would have sought a warrant if they had not earlier entered the warehouse. This was error; a determination of whether the warrant-authorized search was an independent source of the challenged evidence should have been made. Vacated and remanded.

DISSENT: (Marshall, J.) Here, no demonstrated historical facts are set forth to show that the subsequent warrant search was wholly unaffected by the prior search which was illegal. In both searches, the same investigators were used, and no effort was first made to acquire a warrant. Today's Court ruling lends itself to easy abuse and provides police encouragement to bypass constitutional requirements.

▸ ANALYSIS

Justice Marshall argued that where the police cannot point to some historically verifiable fact demonstrating that the subsequent search pursuant to a warrant was wholly unaffected by the prior illegal search, a per se rule of inadmissibility should be adopted. It would be difficult for the trial court to verify, or the defendant to rebut, an assertion by officers that they always intended to obtain a warrant, regardless of the results of the illegal search. The testimony of the officers conducting the illegal search is the only direct evidence of intent, and the defendant will be relegated simply to arguing that the officers should not be believed.

Quicknotes

FRUIT OF POISONOUS TREE Doctrine that evidence obtained as a result of illegal procedures is inadmissible at trial.

INDEPENDENT SOURCE Pertaining to facts derived from another source, independent of those contained in a defective warrant.

PROBABLE CAUSE A reasonable basis for believing that a crime has been committed.

Wong Sun v. United States

Drug dealer (D) v. Federal government (P)

371 U.S. 471 (1963).

NATURE OF CASE: On certiorari from appellate court judgment upholding conviction for dealing in heroin.

FACT SUMMARY: Wong Sun's (D) co-defendant was unlawfully arrested and made incriminating statements to police.

🏛 RULE OF LAW
Statements made by a defendant directly as the result of lawless police conduct are inadmissible against the defendant.

FACTS: Federal agents went to the Chinese laundry operated by Wong Sun's (D) co-defendant, James Wah Toy. Toy told the agent that he was not open for business and to come back. The agent identified himself as a narcotics agent, and Toy ran into his living quarters at the back of the laundry. The agents broke open the door, followed Toy into his bedroom, and arrested him. A search of the premises revealed no narcotics. Toy told the agents that he and another man had been smoking the drug the night before, and told him where the other man lived. Toy and two others were indicted on drug charges, and his statements to the agents in his bedroom were admitted against him.

ISSUE: May statements made by a defendant directly as the result of lawless police conduct be admitted against the defendant?

HOLDING AND DECISION: (Brennan, J.) No. Statements made by a defendant directly as the result of lawless police conduct are inadmissible against the defendant. The court of appeals held that there was neither reasonable grounds nor probable cause for Toy's arrest. We have held that physical evidence obtained during an unlawful invasion must be excluded. Today we hold that verbal evidence that derives so immediately from an unlawful entry is no less the fruit of official illegality than the more tangible fruits of the unwarranted intrusion. There was no intervening independent act to purge the illegality of its taint; therefore the judgment of the court of appeals is reversed.

▶ ANALYSIS

Wong Sun (D) made a confession as well, but his confession took place when he voluntarily returned several days after being arraigned to make the statement. Given his independent intervening voluntary act, the Court held that the taint of Toy's unlawful arrest was purged as to Wong Sun's (D) confession.

Quicknotes

EXCLUSIONARY RULE A rule precluding the introduction at trial of evidence unlawfully obtained in violation of the federal constitutional safeguards against unreasonable searches and seizures.

Hudson v. Michigan

Convicted felon (D) v. State (P)

547 U.S. 586 (2006).

NATURE OF CASE: Appeal of lower court refusal to exclude evidence obtained following a knock-and-announce violation.

FACT SUMMARY: Police (P) entered and searched a home after failing to knock and announce. They found drugs and a firearm in their search, and Booker Hudson (D) moved at trial to exclude the evidence based on the knock-and-announce violation.

🏛 RULE OF LAW
Violation of the knock-and-announce rule does not require the suppression of all evidence found in a warranted search.

FACTS: Police (P) entered and searched Booker Hudson's (D) home with a warrant but failed to knock first, and only waited three to five seconds after announcing themselves before entering. Hudson (D) was convicted in state court for possessing cocaine and a firearm. Hudson (D) argued that the evidence against him was seized in violation of the "knock and announce" rule of the Fourth Amendment, which requires the police to knock, announce their presence, and wait 20 to 30 seconds before executing a search warrant, except in exigent circumstances. The trial judge granted Hudson's (D) motion to suppress the evidence on the basis of the knock-and-announce rule. The Michigan Court of Appeals reversed, holding that it was bound by two cases decided by the Michigan Supreme Court that created an "exception" to the suppression of evidence obtained in violation of the knock-and-announce rule when the evidence would inevitably have been discovered.

ISSUE: Does violation of the knock-and-announce rule require the suppression of all evidence found in a warranted search?

HOLDING AND DECISION: (Scalia, J.) No. Violation of the knock-and-announce rule does not require the suppression of all evidence found in a warranted search. Evidence seized in violation of the knock-and-announce rule can be used against a defendant in a later criminal trial without violating the Fourth Amendment, and judges cannot suppress such evidence for a knock-and-announce violation alone. The purpose of the knock-and-announce rule is to protect police officers from surprising residents who might retaliate in presumed self-defense, to protect private property from damage, and to protect the privacy and dignity of residents. The knock-and-announce rule has never purported to protect one's interest in preventing the government from seeing or taking evidence described in a warrant. In addition, the cost of excluding evidence based on knock-and-announce violations would be serious, amounting to providing dangerous criminals with a get-out-of-jail-free card. Affirmed.

CONCURRENCE: (Kennedy, J.) The knock-and-announce requirement protects rights and expectations linked to ancient principles in our constitutional order. The majority opinion does not suggest that violations of the knock-and-announce requirement are trivial or beyond the law's concern. In addition, the decision determines only that in the specific context of the knock-and-announce requirement, a violation is not sufficiently related to the later discovery of evidence to justify suppression.

DISSENT: (Breyer, J.) Settled case law by this Court established that the Fourth Amendment normally requires police officers to knock and announce their presence before entering a dwelling. The majority opinion holds that evidence seized from a home following a violation of this requirement need not be suppressed. As a result, the Court destroys the strongest legal incentive to comply with the Constitution's knock-and-announce requirement. At the very least, eliminating the exclusionary rule from consideration for knock-and-announce violations will cause some government agents to find it less risky to violate the rule.

▶ ANALYSIS

This case is premised on the insufficient connection between the failure by the police to knock and announce and the evidence found in the house, thus rendering exclusion of that evidence based on the violation unjustifiable. The case might stand for a broader application of the rule, which might curb altogether the exclusionary rule based on knock-and-announce violations.

Quicknotes

EXIGENT CIRCUMSTANCES Circumstances requiring an extraordinary or immediate response; an exception to the prohibition on a warrantless arrest or search when police officers believe probable cause to exist and there is no time for obtaining a warrant.

FOURTH AMENDMENT Provides that persons be secure as to their person and private belongings against unreasonable searches and seizures.

KNOCK AND ANNOUNCE Requirement that a police officer must first knock and announce his intention before he enters an individual's home in the execution of a valid warrant.

Herring v. United States

Individual (D) v. Federal government (P)

555 U.S. _____ , 129 S.Ct. 172 (2009).

NATURE OF CASE: Appeal from Eleventh Circuit Court of Appeals in favor of government.

FACT SUMMARY: After receiving information from a neighboring county that Herring (D) had an outstanding warrant against him, police officers in Coffee County arrested Herring (D). A search of his vehicle revealed a gun and illegal drugs. The police then learned the warrant had previously been recalled.

🏛 RULE OF LAW
When police mistakes leading to an unlawful search are the result of isolated negligence attenuated from the search, rather than systemic error or reckless disregard of constitutional requirements, the exclusionary rule does not apply.

FACTS: Police in Coffee County investigated whether Herring (D) had any outstanding warrants against him. A search of a neighboring county's database initially revealed that Herring (D) had a warrant against him for failure to appear for a felony charge. Acting on the information, the police officers arrested Herring (D). A search of his vehicle incident to his arrest turned up a gun and illegal drugs. Shortly after the search, police dispatch informed the arresting officers that the warrant had actually been recalled five months earlier and was no longer valid. Federal charges were subsequently brought against Herring (D) and he moved to suppress the evidence from the search on the grounds the arrest and search were in violation of his Fourth Amendment rights. The trial court and Eleventh Circuit Court of Appeals found that because the mistake was caused by the mere negligence of the police record keeping system, the exclusionary rule did not apply. Herring (D) appealed.

ISSUE: When police mistakes leading to an unlawful search are the result of isolated negligence attenuated from the search, rather than systemic error or reckless disregard of constitutional requirements, does the exclusionary rule apply?

HOLDING AND DECISION: (Roberts, J.) No. When police mistakes leading to an unlawful search are the result of isolated negligence attenuated from the search, rather than systemic error or reckless disregard of constitutional requirements, the exclusionary rule does not apply. The mere fact that a search is unreasonable does not mean the exclusionary rule automatically applies. The Court has previously held the rule does not apply when police reasonably relied upon an invalid warrant issued by a court. The only issue here is whether negligence by the police, as opposed to others, will lead to the suppression of evidence. The Court holds that it should not. The exclusionary rule was created to deter police misconduct. The conduct must have a deliberate or indifferent nature to invoke the exclusionary rule. Those circumstances are not present here. An error arising from nonrecurring negligence, as opposed to systemic negligence, does not implicate the concerns the exclusionary rule was designed to protect. Affirmed.

DISSENT: (Ginsburg, J.) The Court's decision may lead to the arrest of innocent persons based upon information that is negligently maintained. Police departments across the country will have little incentive to ensure the accuracy of their warrant databases. The exclusionary rule is the only remedy Herring (D) and others in his situation have. A subsequent lawsuit against the police for wrongful arrest will be barred by qualified immunity. Just as in tort law, the risk of exclusion of evidence would encourage police departments at the state and federal level to monitor the warrant databases and ensure their accuracy.

DISSENT: (Breyer, J.) In addition to Justice Ginsburg's arguments, an additional factor to apply the exclusionary rule is that the police were responsible for the error. Prior cases have allowed evidence when the police rely in good faith on the incorrect information provided by third parties. This court has never held that evidence may be allowed when the police are themselves responsible for the incorrect information.

▶ ANALYSIS

A debate has ensued over the scope of this five to four decision. Some commentators believe the scope is limited to police errors in regards to record keeping only. However, others believe police departments may rely on the decision to argue that any of their good-faith mistakes will prohibit the application of the exclusionary rule. It does appear though that the holding concerns only those isolated and negligent mistakes that are "attenuated from the search." The precise contours of this "attenuation" factor have yet to be defined.

━═▪

Quicknotes

EXCLUSIONARY RULE A rule precluding the introduction at trial of evidence unlawfully obtained in violation of the federal constitutional safeguards against unreasonable searches and seizures.

WARRANT An order issued by a court directing an officer to undertake a certain act (e.g., arrest or search).

━═▪

Confessions

Quick Reference Rules of Law

Hector (A Slave) v. State

State (P) v. Burglary suspect (D)

Mo. Sup. Ct., 2 Mo. 166 (1829).

NATURE OF CASE: Appeal from trial court ruling that failed to exclude confessions extorted by use of torture.

FACT SUMMARY: When a burglary suspect, Hector (D), confessed to a crime while being flogged, his attorney argued the confession should be excluded.

🏛 **RULE OF LAW**
A confession not freely given but made under torture should be excluded.

FACTS: Hector (D) was caught "by certain persons" for suspected burglary and flogged all night, screaming under the lash, until he confessed. At one point Hector (D) said if they would stop flogging him, he would go and find the money. Hector's (D) attorney moved to exclude the confession and others and the ground they were not freely and voluntarily made but were extorted by pain and torture. The trial court overruled the motion, and Hector's (D) attorney appealed.

ISSUE: Should a confession not freely given but made under torture be excluded?

HOLDING AND DECISION: (M'Girk, C.J.) Yes. A confession not freely given but made under torture should be excluded. The record revealed Hector (D) was under the lash nearly all night. Of itself, such circumstance would have been sufficient to cause him to confess to any crime charged. When he did ultimately confess, such confession most probably was to prevent further torture and to gain respite from the pain. The trial court further erred in leaving it to the jury to determine which confessions were voluntary and which were not. As a matter of law, this is a court decision. In this case, all confessions should have been excluded. Reversed.

▶ *ANALYSIS*

The record in *Hector* indicated that all of the several confessions appear to have been given either during torture, fear of torture, or to prevent further torture.

■━■

Quicknotes

COERCED CONFESSION A statement made by a person charged with the commission of a criminal offense, acknowledging his guilt in respect to the charged offense, that was made when the confessor's free will was overcome as a result of threats, promises, or undue influence, and that is inadmissible at trial.

■━■

Lisenba v. California

Convicted murderer (D) v. State (P)

314 U.S. 219 (1941).

NATURE OF CASE: On certiorari from state supreme court judgment upholding murder conviction.

FACT SUMMARY: Lisenba (a.k.a. James) (D) married a woman, took out a life insurance policy on her, then murdered her in a manner to give the appearance of an accident.

🏛 RULE OF LAW
Illegal acts committed in the course of procuring a confession do not automatically render the confession inadmissible as a violation of due process; all the surrounding circumstances must be evaluated to determine whether the confession was freely and voluntarily made.

FACTS: Lisenba (a.k.a. James) (D) hired a woman as a manicurist in his barber shop and subsequently married her. The marriage was invalid, as he had a living wife. While they were engaged, he took out a life insurance policy on her. After his earlier marriage was annulled, they were married in a legal ceremony. Several months later, James (D) and a confederate blindfolded his wife, tied her to a table, and allowed rattlesnakes to bite her. When that did not succeed in killing her, they took her to a pond and drowned her. When James (D) attempted to collect the insurance, an investigation was instituted, resulting in his arrest. He eventually confessed, laying the blame for planning the crime on his confederate. When the prosecution sought to introduce the confession, James (D) moved to exclude it, arguing that he had been deprived of the opportunity to consult counsel and that he had been brought to the district attorney's office for questioning without a valid court order. James (D) also claimed that he had been mistreated by police several days earlier, although at the time he was mistreated he did not confess. The confession was admitted and James (D) was convicted and sentenced to death.

ISSUE: Do illegal acts committed in the course of procuring a confession automatically render the confession inadmissible as a violation of due process?

HOLDING AND DECISION: (Roberts, J.) No. Illegal acts committed in the course of procuring a confession do not automatically render the confession inadmissible as a violation of due process; all the surrounding circumstances must be evaluated to determine whether the confession was freely and voluntarily made. We are bound to make an independent examination of the record to evaluate James's (D) claim. We disapprove of any mistreatment of James (D), and of any unlawful acts by the State including the deprivation of counsel. However, James (D) admits that no threats, promises or acts of violence were employed during the questioning when he made his confession, or for eleven days before then. He displayed a self-possession, a coolness, and an acumen during his questioning and at trial that negates the view that he had so lost his freedom of action that the statements he made were not his. The conviction is affirmed.

DISSENT: (Black, J.) Testimony of the officers was sufficient to indicate the confession was not freely and voluntarily given. The confession that convicted James (D) resulted from coercion and compulsion. Accordingly, it should be reversed.

▶ ANALYSIS

The Court considered not only the circumstances directly surrounding the confession, but also James's (D) subjective traits that would bear on the likelihood of voluntariness. Justice Roberts described James (D) as "a man of intelligence and business experience," as well as noting an apparently similar incident where James (D) had collected double indemnity for the "accidental" death of a former wife. The Court also noted that while James (D) did not have his attorney present when he confessed, he had had a full opportunity in the days before to meet with and be advised by counsel.

■■■

Quicknotes

COERCED CONFESSION A statement made by a person charged with the commission of a criminal offense, acknowledging his guilt in respect to the charged offense, that was made when the confessor's free will was overcome as a result of threats, promises, or undue influence, and that is inadmissible at trial.

DUE PROCESS The constitutional mandate requiring the courts to protect and enforce individuals' rights and liberties consistent with prevailing principles of fairness and justice and prohibiting the federal and state governments from such activities that deprive its citizens of a life, liberty, or property interest.

■■■

Spano v. New York

Bar-fighting murderer (D) v. State (P)

360 U.S. 315 (1959).

NATURE OF CASE: Appeal from a conviction for first-degree murder.

FACT SUMMARY: After prolonged interrogation, Spano (D) confessed to a murder and was thereafter convicted of murder over his objection that the confession was involuntary.

RULE OF LAW

If a confession is obtained by overbearing the will of the accused, it is involuntary and inadmissible.

FACTS: Spano (D), who was a derivative citizen born in Italy, was 25, a junior high school graduate, and regularly employed. On the day of the shooting in question, Spano (D) was drinking in a bar. The decedent took some of Spano's (D) money from the bar. A fight ensued, and the decedent kicked Spano (D) in the head several times. Later, Spano (D) secured a gun, entered a store where the decedent was frequently found, and shot him to death. Spano (D) then disappeared. Later, Spano (D) informed a friend, Bruno, who was a fledgling police officer, that he was giving himself up. Spano (D), accompanied by counsel, turned himself in. Thereafter, the police questioned Spano (D), without his attorney, for over eight hours. Using Bruno to gain his sympathy, Spano (D) was worn down physically and mentally until he finally confessed by answering leading questions in a question-and-answer confession. At the trial, the confession was introduced in evidence over appropriate objections. The jury was instructed that it could rely on it only if it was found to be voluntary. The jury returned a guilty verdict, and Spano (D) was sentenced to death. The court of appeals affirmed, and the U.S. Supreme Court granted certiorari.

ISSUE: If a confession is obtained by overbearing the will of the accused, is it involuntary and inadmissible?

HOLDING AND DECISION: (Warren, C.J.) Yes. If a confession is obtained by overbearing the will of the accused, it is involuntary and inadmissible. Spano (D) was a foreign-born young man of 25 with no past history of law violation or of subjection to official interrogation. Spano (D) was not highly educated and had a history of emotional instability. Spano (D) did not make a narrative statement but was subject to the leading questions of a skillful prosecutor in a question-and-answer confession. He was subjected to questioning by many men. Spano (D) was questioned for virtually eight straight hours. The questioners persisted in the face of his repeated refusals to answer on the advice of his attorney, and they ignored his reasonable requests to contact his attorney. Spano's

(D) will was overborne by official pressure, fatigue, and sympathy falsely aroused, and, thus, his confession was involuntary and cannot stand under the Fourteenth Amendment. Reversed.

CONCURRENCE: (Stewart, J.) The Constitution provides to an accused the right to assistance of counsel at every stage of the criminal process. Here the police were questioning a suspect in investigating an unsolved crime. When Spano (D) surrendered to the New York authorities, he had already been indicted for first degree murder. He was at that time constitutionally entitled to be represented by an attorney.

ANALYSIS

The abhorrence of society to the use of involuntary confessions does not turn alone on their inherent untrustworthiness. It also turns on the deep-rooted notion that the police must obey the law while enforcing the law, that in the end life and liberty can be as much endangered from illegal methods used to convict those thought to be criminals as from the actual criminals themselves. See *Brown v. Mississippi*, 297 U.S. 278 (1936), and *Ashcraft v. Tennessee*, 322 U.S. 143 (1944).

Quicknotes

COERCED CONFESSION A statement made by a person charged with the commission of a criminal offense, acknowledging his guilt in respect to the charged offense, that was made when the confessor's free will was overcome as a result of threats, promises, or undue influence, and that is inadmissible at trial.

CUSTODIAL INTERROGATION The questioning of a suspect by police while in custody.

EXCLUSIONARY RULE A rule precluding the introduction at trial of evidence unlawfully obtained in violation of the federal constitutional safeguards against unreasonable searches and seizures.

CHAPTER 7

Police Interrogation: The Self-Incrimination Clause

Quick Reference Rules of Law

Chavez v. Martinez

Police officer (D) v. Initiator of § 1983 suit (P)

538 U.S. 760 (2003).

NATURE OF CASE: Appeal from refusal of federal court of appeals to grant qualified immunity to police officer in a § 1983 suit against him.

FACT SUMMARY: Martinez (P) brought a § 1983 suit against Chavez (D), a police officer, for interrogating him in the hospital during emergency medical treatment for life-threatening gunshot wounds, arguing that such conduct violated his Fifth Amendment protection against self-incrimination.

RULE OF LAW

The Fifth Amendment protection against self-incrimination applies only in criminal cases.

FACTS: During a police altercation, an officer shot Martinez (P) five times, causing life-endangering injuries. Chavez (D), a police officer, arrived on the scene and accompanied Martinez (P) to the hospital where he continuously interrogated Martinez (P) during medical treatment, despite Martinez's (P) statements to the officer, "I don't know," "I am choking," "I am dying, please," and "I don't want to die." Although Martinez (P) was never charged with a crime and his answers were never used against him in any criminal prosecution, he brought a § 1983 suit, arguing, inter alia, that Chavez (D) had violated his Fifth Amendment privilege against self-incrimination. The federal court of appeals held that Chavez (D) was not entitled to a defense of qualified immunity because he violated Martinez's (P) clearly established constitutional rights. Chavez (D) appealed.

ISSUE: Does the Fifth Amendment protection against self-incrimination apply only in criminal cases?

HOLDING AND DECISION: (Thomas, J.) Yes. The Fifth Amendment protection against self-incrimination applies only in criminal cases. Although some judicial decisions permit assertion of the Fifth Amendment privilege against self-incrimination in certain noncriminal situations, such fact does not alter the Court's conclusion that violation of such constitutional right results only if an individual has been compelled to be a witness against himself in a criminal case. Here, it has not been shown that Martinez (P) ever had a constitutional right violated or that he was ever even prosecuted for a crime, let alone compelled to be a witness in a criminal case. A "criminal case" at the very least requires initiation of criminal proceedings. Although conduct by law enforcement officials prior to trial may ultimately impair that right, a constitutional violation occurs only at trial. Here, Martinez (P) was never made to be a "witness" against himself because his statements were never admitted as testimony against him in a criminal case. Nor was he ever placed under oath and exposed to the cruel "trilemma" of self-accusation, perjury, or contempt. Rules designed to safeguard a constitutional right do not extend the scope of the constitutional right itself, just as violations of judicially crafted prophylactic rules do not violate the constitutional rights of any person. Reversed.

CONCURRENCE: (Souter, J.) Martinez (P) has not here been able to make the "powerful showing," subject to a realistic assessment of costs and risks, necessary to expand protection of the privilege against compelled self-incrimination to the point of the civil liability he asks this Court to recognize.

DISSENT IN PART: (Kennedy, J.) A constitutional right arises the moment torture or its close equivalents are brought to bear. Constitutional protection for a tortured suspect is not held in abeyance until some later criminal proceeding takes place. To tell the legal system that public officials, when conducting a criminal investigation, can use severe compulsion or even torture without violating constitutional rules, diminishes the Bill of Rights.

DISSENT IN PART: (Ginsburg, J.) The Self-Incrimination Clause applies at the time and place police use severe compulsion to extract a statement from a suspect.

ANALYSIS

As the *Chavez* decision makes clear, the text of the Self-Incrimination Clause cannot support a view that the mere use of compulsive questioning, without more, violates the Constitution.

Quicknotes

FIFTH AMENDMENT Provides that no person shall be compelled to serve as a witness against himself, or be subject to trial for the same offense twice, or be deprived of life, liberty, or property without due process of law.

INTER ALIA Among other things.

LIBERTY INTEREST A right conferred by the Due Process Clauses of the state and federal constitutions.

Bram v. United States

Murder suspect (D) v. Federal government (P)

168 U.S. 532 (1897).

NATURE OF CASE: Appeal from conviction for murder.

FACT SUMMARY: Bram (D) contended that his conversation with a detective was erroneously admitted as a confession because it was not shown to be voluntary.

RULE OF LAW
In the context of the Fifth Amendment privilege against self-incrimination, a confession will be suppressed if any degree of influence is exerted by the police.

FACTS: A shipboard murder occurred. The initial suspect was Brown. When the ship arrived at port, a second suspect named Bram (D) was stripped to search his clothes for evidence. During the interrogation, an official named Power told Bram (D) that Brown stated that he allegedly saw Bram (D) commit the murder. Bram (D) replied that Brown could not have seen him from where he was. The statement was used at trial as a confession. Bram (D) was convicted and appealed.

ISSUE: In the context of the Fifth Amendment privilege against self-incrimination, will a confession be suppressed if any degree of influence is exerted by the police?

HOLDING AND DECISION: (White, J.) Yes. In the context of the Fifth Amendment privilege against self-incrimination, a confession will be suppressed if any degree of influence is exerted by the police. A statement must not be extracted by any sorts of threat or violence nor obtained by any direct or implied promises, however slight, nor by the exertion of any improper influence. The situation of the accused, and the nature of the communication made to him by the detective, necessarily overthrows any possible implication that Bram's (D) reply to the detective could have been the result of a purely voluntary mental action. Error was committed by the trial court in admitting the confession. Reversed.

DISSENT: (Brewer, J.) Power testified that there were no threats nor inducements made to Bram (D). Accordingly, the trial court properly allowed Power's testimony as to Bram's (D) statements. There is nothing in the conversation between Power and Bram (D) that can be construed as a threat or an inducement. Bram's (D) replies to Power were given freely.

▶ ANALYSIS

The *Bram* decision had little immediate impact for two reasons. First, it was not until 1964 that the U.S. Supreme Court ruled that the Fifth Amendment privilege was applicable to the states. Thus, the rule was limited to federal cases. Second, although Bram (D) invoked the Fifth Amendment, without dissent on this point, the standard actually employed was the voluntariness standard of the common law.

Quicknotes

FIFTH AMENDMENT Provides that no person shall be compelled to serve as a witness against himself, or be subject to trial for the same offense twice, or be deprived of life, liberty, or property without due process of law.

Miranda v. Arizona

Coerced confessor (D) v. State (P)

384 U.S. 436 (1966).

NATURE OF CASE: Appeal from convictions for murder.

FACT SUMMARY: In this consolidation of several cases, Miranda (D) and others appealed from their convictions, claiming that their confessions were elicited through violation of their constitutional rights.

🏛 RULE OF LAW
The prosecution may not use statements stemming from custodial interrogation of the defendant, unless it demonstrates the use of procedural safeguards effective to secure the privilege against self-incrimination.

FACTS: In *Miranda v. Arizona,* the police arrested Miranda (D) and took him to a special room where they secured a confession. In *Vignera v. New York,* Vignera (D) made oral admissions to the police after interrogation. In *Westover v. United States,* Westover (D) was handed over to the FBI by local authorities after they had detained and interrogated him for a lengthy period. The FBI obtained signed statements from Westover (D). Lastly, in *California v. Stewart,* the local police held Stewart (D) for five days in the station, interrogating him until they secured his inculpatory statement. In none of these cases was the defendant given a full and effective warning of his rights at the outset of the interrogation process. In all the cases, the questioning elicited oral admissions, and in three of them, signed statements as well which were admitted at their trials. Miranda (D) and the others appealed from their convictions on the ground that their admissions were secured through means that violated their constitutional rights.

ISSUE: May the prosecution use statements stemming from custodial interrogation of the defendant where it does not demonstrate the use of procedural safeguards effective to secure the privilege against self-incrimination?

HOLDING AND DECISION: (Warren, C.J.) No. The prosecution may not use statements, whether exculpatory or inculpatory, stemming from custodial interrogation of the defendant unless it demonstrates the use of procedural safeguards effective to secure the privileges against self-incrimination. Prior to any questioning, the person must be warned that he has a right to remain silent, that any statement he does make may be used as evidence against him, and that he has a right to the presence of an attorney. The defendant may waive effectuation of these rights, provided the waiver is made voluntarily, knowingly and intelligently. Likewise, if the individual is alone and indicates in any manner that he does not wish to be interrogated, the police may not question him. In each of the cases at bar, Miranda (D) and the others were subjected to

menacing custodial interrogation without the benefits of any procedural safeguards in derogation of their Fifth Amendment rights against self-incrimination. Reversed.

DISSENT: (Harlan, J.) The decision of the Court today in abandoning its historical case-by-case approach represents poor constitutional law. The Court's new rules are designed to "ultimately discourage any confession at all." Such an approach cannot be sustained by constitutional or policy considerations. First, constitutionally, there is no basis for extending the Fifth Amendment to the police station. Historically, the ban against self-incrimination has applied only in criminal proceedings, not in "extra-legal" situations, such as interrogations. Furthermore, even if it can be applied to custodial interrogations, it has never been held to forbid all pressures on an accused, as the Court today attempts to do. Similarly, there is no constitutional basis for applying the right to counsel to custodial interrogations. The danger of injustice by allowing an untrained person to defend himself in a technical court situation is the basis for this right, and that rationale is not applicable to custodial situations. Second, in considering policy issues, although it is true that police questioning will inherently entail some pressure on the suspect, until today the role of the Constitution has been to "sift out" only "undue pressure." The inflexible rules today, however, ignore this. Those who use coercive tactics may simply lie in court about having given the required warnings. Nothing is gained and many voluntary confessions will be lost. In conclusion, neither the constitutional interpretations nor the consequences of today's ruling is justifiable.

DISSENT: (White, J.) First, the Fifth Amendment forbids self-incrimination only if it is "compelled." Yet, the Court today has no factual basis for concluding that custodial interrogations are so inherently coercive as to make any statements arising from them, if there is no warning of rights, compelled. In fact, the Court has not examined a single transcript of any police interrogation. Furthermore, even if it is assumed that "all" such interrogations are coercive, the rule adopted today is irrational. If such interrogations are so "coercive," how can a suspect ever voluntarily waive his rights as the Court indicates he can? Second, and more importantly, the Court overlooks the ominous consequences of its decision. Although the Court states that the rule adopted is necessary to preserve the "integrity" of the individual, it overlooks the fact that without effective prevention of crime (or personal violence), there can be no human dignity. The most basic function of any government is to provide for the security of an individual and his property but after today's decision, effective law enforcement will be impaired, both by

Continued on next page.

the fact that more who are guilty may go free and many who could easily explain their innocence will waste police time while waiting for their attorneys.

▶ *ANALYSIS*

In *Michigan v. Mosley,* 423 U.S. 96 (1975), detectives gave the defendant the *Miranda* warnings and then questioned him about the robbery charges for which he had been arrested. When he said he did not want to be questioned any further, the questioning stopped. A few hours later, after repeating the warnings, other detectives questioned the defendant about a homicide for which he had not been arrested. His answers incriminated him and he was prosecuted for murder. The Court held that the resumption of questioning, each session being independent of the other and accompanied by warnings, did not violate *Miranda*; that is to say, *Miranda* did not create a per se proscription of indefinite duration.

■━━■

Quicknotes

CUSTODIAL INTERROGATION   The questioning of a suspect by police while in custody.

EXCULPATORY CLAUSE   A clause in a contract relieving one party from liability for certain unlawful conduct.

FIFTH AMENDMENT   Provides that no person shall be compelled to serve as a witness against himself, or be subject to trial for the same offense twice, or be deprived of life, liberty, or property without due process of law.

INCULPATORY   Evidence tending to show a person's guilt in committing a criminal act.

PER SE   By itself; not requiring additional evidence for proof.

■━━■

New York v. Quarles

State (P) v. Gun owner (D)

467 U.S. 649 (1984).

NATURE OF CASE: Appeal from order to suppress evidence.

FACT SUMMARY: The trial court granted Quarles's (D) motion to suppress a statement he made to police before being given his *Miranda* warnings.

🏛 RULE OF LAW
Police need not give *Miranda* warnings where the need for such warnings is outweighed by the need to protect the public safety.

FACTS: Two New York police officers were approached by a woman who said she had just been raped by a large black man who was armed and who had just entered a supermarket. The police entered the market and apprehended Quarles (D) after a short chase. Officer Kraft frisked him, while three other officers surrounded him and discovered he was wearing an empty shoulder holster. After handcuffing him, Kraft asked Quarles (D) where the gun was. Quarles (D) told him, and after the gun was retrieved, he was placed under arrest and given his *Miranda* rights. In his trial for criminal possession of a weapon, Quarles (D) successfully moved to suppress the gun and the statement on the basis that at the time the statement was made he had not been given his *Miranda* warning. The State (P) appealed, contending the need to protect public safety outweighed the need to protect Quarles's (D) *Miranda* rights, thereby eliminating the need to read them in this case. The court of appeals affirmed, and the U.S. Supreme Court granted certiorari.

ISSUE: Must *Miranda* warnings be given when the need for them is outweighed by public safety concerns?

HOLDING AND DECISION: (Rehnquist, J.) No. Police need not give *Miranda* warnings where concern for the public safety outweighs the need for the warnings. In this case, the police were placed in a situation where, in order to protect the people in the supermarket, they had to find a gun they had reason to believe was in the vicinity of the suspect. Under these circumstances, concern for public safety outweighed Quarles's (D) immediate invocation of his Fifth Amendment right against compelled self-incrimination. Therefore, the evidence should not have been suppressed. Reversed and remanded.

CONCURRENCE AND DISSENT: (O'Connor, J.) *Miranda* is now the law and the Court has not provided sufficient justification for departing from it or for blurring its now clear strictures. Accordingly, the initial statement taken from Quarles (D) should be repressed. A "public safety" exception unnecessarily blurs the edges of the clear line heretofore established and makes *Miranda*'s requirements more

difficult to understand. In some cases, police will benefit because a reviewing court will find that an exigency excused their failure to administer the required warnings. But in other cases, police will suffer because, though they thought an exigency excused their noncompliance, a reviewing court will view the "objective" circumstances differently and require exclusion of admissions thereby obtained. The end result will be a fine-spun new doctrine on public safety exigencies incident to custodial interrogation, complete with the hair-splitting distinctions that currently plague our Fourth Amendment jurisprudence.

DISSENT: (Marshall, J.) Quarles (D) clearly was in custody and was interrogated without being advised of his *Miranda* rights. Therefore, the evidence must be suppressed. The questioning of Quarles (D) was coercive. The police questioned him in the middle of the night in the rear of an empty supermarket. His hands were handcuffed behind his back, and he was surrounded by four armed officers. The irony of today's majority decision is that safety of the public can be protected without Fifth Amendment abridgement.

▶ ANALYSIS

This case illustrates the Court's adoption of a public safety exception to the requirement that a suspect in custody be informed of his rights to remain silent and to have counsel present during questioning. Even if the evidence were suppressed under *Miranda v. Arizona*, 384 U.S. 436 (1966), it could be admissible under the inevitable discovery doctrine of *Nix v. Williams*, 467 U.S. 431 (1984).

■■■■

Quicknotes

CERTIORARI A discretionary writ issued by a superior court to an inferior court in order to review the lower court's decisions; the Supreme Court's writ ordering such review.

CUSTODIAL INTERROGATION The questioning of a suspect by police while in custody.

MIRANDA WARNINGS Specified warnings that must be communicated to a person prior to a custodial interrogation; in the absence of the communication of such warnings, any communications made during the interrogation is inadmissible at trial.

PRIVILEGE AGAINST SELF-INCRIMINATION A privilege guaranteed by the Fifth Amendment to the federal Constitution in a criminal proceeding for communications made by an

Continued on next page.

accused and protecting an accused or witness from having to give testimony that may incriminate himself.

STOP AND FRISK   A brief, nonintrusive stop, requiring the police officer to have a reasonable suspicion that a crime has been committed based on specific and articulable facts, and involving a search for a concealed weapon that is conducted by patting down the clothes of the person.

■══■

Oregon v. Elstad

State (P) v. Convicted burglar (D)

470 U.S. 298 (1985).

NATURE OF CASE: Appeal from conviction for burglary.

FACT SUMMARY: Oregon (P) appealed from a decision of the Oregon Court of Appeals, which reversed Elstad's (D) conviction for burglary, holding that the initial failure of police officers to administer *Miranda* warnings tainted the subsequent confession of Elstad (D) made after he had been advised of and waived his *Miranda* rights.

🏛 RULE OF LAW
A voluntary signed confession, made after being fully advised of *Miranda* rights, is not rendered inadmissible by a prior remark made in response to questioning without benefit of *Miranda* warnings.

FACTS: A witness implicated Elstad (D) in the burglary of a local home. Officers Burke and McAllister went to Elstad's (D) home with an arrest warrant. While McAllister advised Elstad's (D) mother of what was happening, Burke told Elstad (D) that they had a warrant for his arrest, and he felt Elstad (D) had been involved. Elstad (D) replied, "Yes, I was there." He was then transported to sheriff headquarters, where, after being fully advised of his *Miranda* rights, he voluntarily made and signed a confession. At his trial, the trial court excluded the statement made at Elstad's (D) home, but admitted the confession. He was convicted and he appealed. The Oregon Court of Appeals reversed, finding that the confession, though voluntarily made after being warned of his *Miranda* rights, was tainted by the earlier remark, which the State (P) conceded was made in violation of *Miranda*. It held the confession inadmissible and overturned Elstad's (D) conviction, and from this decision, the State (P) appealed.

ISSUE: Is a voluntary, signed confession, made after being fully advised of *Miranda* rights, rendered inadmissible by a prior remark made in response to questioning without benefit of *Miranda* warnings?

HOLDING AND DECISION: (O'Connor, J.) No. A voluntary, signed confession, made after being fully advised of *Miranda* rights, is not rendered inadmissible by a prior remark made in response to questioning without the benefit of *Miranda* warnings. A procedural *Miranda* violation differs significantly from a Fourth Amendment exclusionary rule violation, whose purpose to deter improper conduct justifies application of the "fruit of the poisonous tree doctrine." The *Miranda* exclusionary rule serves the Fifth Amendment, and the failure to administer *Miranda* warnings raises a presumption of compulsion; this presumption, however, does not necessarily require that the statement and its fruits are irreparably tainted. If such evidence is to be suppressed, one must consider whether this action will deter improper police conduct or will ensure the truthfulness of the evidence admitted. The statement made in the absence of *Miranda* warnings should be suppressed, but absent any evidence of coercion, the admissibility of subsequent statements should turn solely on whether they were knowingly or voluntarily made. Whatever the reason was that Burke failed to give *Miranda* warnings at the outset, it is clear that there was no element of coercion involved, and the subsequent waiver of the right to remain silent was made voluntarily and knowingly. The reading of *Miranda* rights at this later stage was complete and should serve to remove the presumption of compulsion. The contention that the police were required to tell Elstad (D) that the earlier remark could not have been used is neither practical nor constitutionally mandated. Reversed.

DISSENT: (Brennan, J.) Most federal courts have rejected the rule adopted today. There should be a presumption that a statement obtained in violation of *Miranda* taints subsequent statements, particularly when the second confession is obtained as a result of confronting the defendant with the earlier illegal confession.

▌ ANALYSIS

Justice Brennan's fears that the present case may be used to obtain confessions may be unfounded. There appears to be a view that few officers are sophisticated enough to make the attempt, and that if an officer is confronted with a suspect who wants to talk, the confession can probably be obtained after giving *Miranda* rights.

■═■

Quicknotes

EXCLUSIONARY RULE A rule precluding the introduction at trial of evidence unlawfully obtained in violation of the federal constitutional safeguards against unreasonable searches and seizures.

FRUIT OF THE POISONOUS TREE Doctrine that evidence obtained as a result of illegal procedures is tainted and is usually inadmissible at trial.

MIRANDA WARNINGS Specified warnings that must be communicated to a person prior to a custodial interrogation; in the absence of the communication of such warnings, any communications made during the interrogation is inadmissible at trial.

■═■

Dickerson v. United States

Bank robber (D) v. Federal government (P)

530 U.S. 428 (2000).

NATURE OF CASE: Appeal from denial of motion to suppress statement based on *Miranda* violation.

FACT SUMMARY: Dickerson (D) sought to suppress a statement he made while in an FBI field office prior to being given his *Miranda* warnings.

🏛 RULE OF LAW
When a decision of the Court involves interpretation and application of the Constitution, Congress may not legislatively supersede such decision.

FACTS: Dickerson (D) was indicted for bank robbery and conspiracy to commit bank robbery. Before trial he moved to suppress a statement he made at an FBI field office, on the grounds that he had not received *Miranda* warnings before being interrogated. The district court granted the motion, and the Government (P) took an interlocutory appeal to the court of appeals, which reversed, stating that § 3501 was satisfied since the statement was made voluntarily. Dickerson (D) appealed.

ISSUE: Where a decision of the Court involves interpretation and application of the Constitution, may Congress legislatively supersede such decision?

HOLDING AND DECISION: (Rehnquist, C.J.) No. Where a decision of the Court involves interpretation and application of the Constitution, Congress may not legislatively supersede such decision. *Miranda* and its progeny govern the admissibility of statements made during custodial interrogation in both state and federal courts. Section 3501 provides that the admissibility of a custodial suspect's statements should depend on whether they are voluntarily made. Prior to *Miranda*, the admissibility of a suspect's confession was evaluated under a voluntariness test. The requirement of voluntariness was based on the Fifth Amendment right against self-incrimination and the Due Process Clause of the Fourteenth Amendment. The Court's decisions in *Miranda* and *Malloy* changed the focus of the due process inquiry. In *Malloy*, the Court held that the Fifth Amendment's self-incrimination clause is incorporated into the Due Process Clause of the Fourteenth Amendment and this applies to the states. In *Miranda*, the Court recognized that the coercion inherent in custodial interrogation makes it difficult to determine whether a statement is voluntary or involuntary and heightens the risk of self-incrimination. Section 3501 was enacted two years after the decision in *Miranda* and was intended by Congress to overrule the Court's decision in that case. The issue is whether Congress has the constitutional authority to do so. While Congress retains the ultimate authority to modify or set aside any judicially created rules of evidence and procedure that are not required by the

Constitution, it may not legislatively supersede the Court's decisions that interpret and apply the Constitution. *Miranda* is a constitutional decision. The Court specifically stated that it was intended "to explore some facets of the problems of applying the privilege against self-incrimination to in-custody interrogation and to give concrete constitutional guidelines for law enforcement agencies and courts to follow." The decision is otherwise replete with references to constitutional rules and standards. *Miranda* announced a constitutional rule that Congress may not supersede legislatively.

DISSENT: (Scalia, J.) To justify the majority's result, the Court is adopting a significant new, if not entirely comprehensible, principle of constitutional law. The majority has held that statutes of Congress can be disregarded, not only when what they prescribe violates the Constitution, but when what they prescribe contradicts a decision of the Supreme Court. What this means is that the Supreme Court has the power, not merely to apply the Constitution, but to expand it, imposing what it regards as useful "prophylactic" restrictions upon Congress and the states. "That is an immense and frightening antidemocratic power, and it does not exist."

▶ ANALYSIS

The Court also relies on the principle of stare decisis as weighing heavily against overruling *Miranda*, since *Miranda* warnings have become "embedded in routine police practice to the point where the warnings have become part of our national culture." Justice Scalia rejects such rationale on the basis that the court rules are both "mutable and modifiable" and that they "must make sense."

■══■

Quicknotes

DUE PROCESS CLAUSE Clauses found in the Fifth and Fourteenth Amendments to the United States Constitution providing that no person shall be deprived of "life, liberty, or property, without due process of law."

MIRANDA WARNINGS Specified warnings that must be communicated to a person prior to a custodial interrogation; in the absence of the communication of such warnings, any communications made during the interrogation is inadmissible at trial.

STARE DECISIS Doctrine whereby courts follow legal precedent unless there is good cause for departure.

■══■

Missouri v. Seibert

State (P) v. Murder suspect (D)

542 U.S. 600 (2004).

NATURE OF CASE: Appeal from reversal of a murder conviction.

FACT SUMMARY: Patrice Seibert (D) argued that since her murder confession was obtained by the police technique of interrogating in successive, unwarned and warned phases, known as "question-first," the requirements of *Miranda* were violated.

🏛 RULE OF LAW
The police technique of interrogating in successive, unwarned and warned phases violates the requirements of *Miranda.*

FACTS: In questioning Patrice Seibert (D), a murder suspect, the police interrogator employed a widely used interrogation technique known as "question-first" in which the interrogator questions the suspect first, then gives the *Miranda* warnings, and then repeats the questioning until the interrogator obtains the confession or incriminating statement that the suspect has already previously provided. After employing this technique of interrogating in successive, unwarned and warned phases, Seibert (D) confessed to murder prior to her warnings and then again after being given the warnings. The trial court suppressed Seibert's (D) prewarning confession but admitted her postwarning confession. She was convicted of murder. The Missouri Supreme Court reversed, holding that here where the interrogation was "nearly continuous," the second statement was clearly "the product of the invalid first statement and should have been suppressed. Missouri (P) appealed.

ISSUE: Does the police technique of interrogating in successive, unwarned and warned phases violate the requirements of *Miranda*?

HOLDING AND DECISION: (Souter, J.) Yes. The police technique of interrogating in successive, unwarned and warned phases violates the requirements of *Miranda*. *Miranda* addressed interrogation practices likely to disable an individual from making a free and rational choice about speaking and held that a suspect must be "adequately and effectively" advised of the choice the Constitution guarantees. The object of the "question-first" technique here utilized against Seibert (D) was to render *Miranda* warnings ineffective by waiting for a particularly opportune time to give them, after the suspect had already confessed. Just as no talismanic incantation is required to satisfy *Miranda*'s strictures, it would be absurd to think that mere recitation of the litany suffices to satisfy *Miranda* in every conceivable circumstance. The issue when interrogators question first and warn later is thus whether the warnings reasonably convey to a suspect his *Miranda* rights.

Unless the warnings could place a suspect who has just been interrogated in a position to make an informed choice as to whether to speak, there is no practical justification for accepting the formal warnings as compliance with *Miranda*, or for treating the second stage of interrogation as distinct from the first, unwarned and inadmissible segment. By any objective measure, applied to circumstances exemplified here, it is likely that if the interrogators employ the technique of withholding warnings until after interrogation succeeds in eliciting a confession, the warnings will be ineffective in preparing the suspect for successive interrogation, close in time and similar in content. Accordingly, the question-first tactic effectively threatens to thwart *Miranda*'s purpose of reducing the risk that a coerced confession would be admitted. Affirmed.

CONCURRENCE: (Breyer, J.) Courts should exclude the "fruits" of the initial unwarned questioning unless the failure to warn was in good faith.

CONCURRENCE: (Kennedy, J.) Not every violation of *Miranda* requires suppression of the evidence obtained. The scope of the *Miranda* suppression remedy depends on a consideration of whether admission of the evidence under the circumstances would frustrate *Miranda*'s "central concerns and objectives."

DISSENT: (O'Connor, J.) Because here the isolated fact of the interrogating officer's intent could not have had any bearing on Seibert's (D) capacity to comprehend and knowingly relinquish her right to remain silent, it could not by itself affect the voluntariness of her confession.

▶ ANALYSIS

As the U.S. Supreme Court makes clear in *Seibert*, the reason for the increased popularity of the question-first method of interrogation is to obtain a confession the suspect would not make if he understood his rights at the outset. The underlying police assumption, which is accurate, is that with one confession in hand before the warnings, the interrogator can usually count on getting a duplicate. It is unrealistic, explained the Court, to treat two bouts of integrated and proximately conducted questioning as independent interrogations subject to independent evaluation simply because *Miranda* warnings formally punctuate them in the middle.

■=■

Quicknotes

CUSTODIAL INTERROGATION The questioning of a suspect by police while in custody.

Continued on next page.

MIRANDA RULE   A required warning given before any questioning by law enforcement authorities can take place. Individuals in custody receive warnings regarding their privilege against self incrimination, right to remain silent, and right to be represented by an attorney.

MIRANDA WARNINGS   Specified warnings that must be communicated to a person prior to a custodial interrogation; in the absence of the communication of such warnings, any communications made during the interrogation are inadmissible at trial.

Oregon v. Mathiason

State (P) v. Convicted burglar (D)

429 U.S. 492 (1977).

NATURE OF CASE: Petition to review reversal of a burglary conviction.

FACT SUMMARY: Mathiason (D) argued that his burglary confession during questioning at the police station was inadmissible because he had not been given his *Miranda* warnings.

🏛 RULE OF LAW
Miranda warnings must be given only if a person has been taken into custody or otherwise deprived of his freedom of action in any significant way.

FACTS: Mathiason (D) had been suggested as a possible suspect in a theft at the home of the mother of one of his friends. A policeman left a card at his apartment asking him to call, which he did. He agreed to meet the officer at the patrol some two blocks from his home. He was told, when he met the officer in the hallway, that he was not under arrest. They went into a room and closed the door, sitting across a desk from each other. The officer said he wanted to talk to Mathiason (D) about a burglary, that his truthfulness could possibly be considered by the district attorney or judge, and that his fingerprints had been found at the scene (which was a lie). Mathiason (D) sat a few minutes and then admitted he had taken the property. All this took about five minutes from the time he had entered the station. The officer then advised Mathiason (D) of his *Miranda* rights and took a taped confession, which was admitted at the trial in which Mathiason (D) was convicted of burglary. The Oregon Supreme Court reversed the conviction, finding the interrogation took place in the type of "coercive" environment that made issuance of the *Miranda* warnings mandatory.

ISSUE: Are *Miranda* warnings required where one is not in custody or deprived of his freedom of action?

HOLDING AND DECISION: (Per curiam) No. *Miranda* warnings are not required where one is not in custody or deprived of his freedom of action. *Miranda* warnings need be given only in circumstances of "custodial interrogation," which exists if a person has been taken into custody or has been otherwise deprived of his freedom of action in any significant way. The circumstances in this case do not evidence any such restraint on Mathiason's (D) freedom of action, so failure to give the *Miranda* warnings prior to his confession is of no consequence to its admissibility at trial. Reversed and remanded.

DISSENT: (Marshall, J.) Even if Mathiason (D) were not in custody, the coercive elements in this case were so pervasive as to require *Miranda*-type warnings.

▶ ANALYSIS

This case is best viewed as part of the general *Miranda* backlash that has taken place in more recent years. There is no doubt that the Court that decided *Miranda* would most likely have sided with the more liberal opinion of the Oregon Supreme Court in this case. However, the changed Court has, in a series of cases, been slowly nipping away at the *Miranda* decision by narrowing its scope in the manner illustrated in this case.

■═■

Quicknotes

CUSTODIAL INTERROGATION The questioning of a suspect by police while in custody.

***MIRANDA* WARNINGS** Specified warnings that must be communicated to a person prior to a custodial interrogation; in the absence of the communication of such warnings, any communications made during the interrogation is inadmissible at trial.

PER CURIAM Denotes a decision that represents the opinion of the entire court.

■═■

Berkemer v. McCarty

Drunk driver (D) v. Court (P)

468 U.S. 420 (1984).

NATURE OF CASE: Appeal of conviction for driving under the influence of alcohol and/or drugs.

FACT SUMMARY: When stopped by a traffic officer, Berkemer (D) admitted prior use of alcohol and marijuana.

🏛 RULE OF LAW
Miranda warnings do not have to be given during a routine traffic stop.

FACTS: A highway patrol officer noticed Berkemer (D) to be driving erratically. He pulled him over and subjected him to a field sobriety test, which he failed. Upon being asked if he had been drinking, Berkemer (D) admitted consumption of alcohol and marijuana. He was then arrested. At trial, his statement was admitted against him, over objections that the *Miranda* warnings have to be given during a routine traffic stop.

ISSUE: Do *Miranda* warnings have to be given during a routine traffic stop?

HOLDING AND DECISION: (Marshall, J.) No. *Miranda* warnings do not have to be given during a routine traffic stop. *Miranda* is concerned with the inherently coercive nature of custodial interrogation. A roadside stop differs from custodial interrogation in several respects. First, usually only one or two officers are present. Second, such detentions are usually open to public view. Finally, the duration is generally rather short. For these reasons, the Court finds a routine traffic stop not to be so coercive that *Miranda* is implicated. Affirmed.

▶ ANALYSIS

The Court likened routine traffic stops to the situation in *Terry v. Ohio,* 392 U.S. 1 (1968). In *Terry,* incriminating evidence was found on a person during a "pat down." The Court declined to extend *Miranda* to this situation, holding it not to be inherently coercive.

■━■

Quicknotes

CUSTODIAL INTERROGATION The questioning of a suspect by police while in custody.

MIRANDA WARNINGS Specified warnings that must be communicated to a person prior to a custodial interrogation; in the absence of the communication of such warnings, any communications made during the interrogation is inadmissible at trial.

TRAFFIC STOP A police officer may stop an automobile and conduct a search of the vehicle without a valid warrant if he has probable cause to believe the vehicle contains evidence of a crime or contraband.

■━■

Rhode Island v. Innis

State (P) v. Convict with conscience (D)

446 U.S. 291 (1980).

NATURE OF CASE: Review of reversal of conviction for murder.

FACT SUMMARY: Murder suspect Innis (D) directed police officers, who were driving him to the police station following his arrest, to his hidden murder weapon after listening to the officers discuss the risk of harm to nearby children if the weapon were not found quickly.

RULE OF LAW

The term "interrogation" under *Miranda* refers not only to express questioning, but also to any words or actions on the part of the police (other than those normally attendant to arrest and custody) that the police should know are reasonably likely to elicit an incriminating response.

FACTS: On January 16, 1975, the body of a Providence, Rhode Island, taxicab driver killed by a shotgun blast was found. On January 17, 1975, a taxicab driver at Providence police headquarters identified Innis (D) from a photograph as the man who had used a shotgun to rob him in his taxicab earlier that night. Later that night, a police officer spotted Innis (D) standing in the street unarmed, arrested him, and advised him of his *Miranda* rights. Innis (D) stated that he wanted to speak with his lawyer. Patrolmen Gleckman, Williams, and McKenna drove Innis (D) to the police station in a patrol car while other officers searched the arrest scene for the shotgun. En route to the police station, Gleckman expressed his concern to McKenna that a school for handicapped children stood near the arrest scene, and "God forbid one of them might find a weapon with shells, and they might hurt themselves." McKenna concurred in the apprehension expressed by Gleckman. Innis (D) interrupted the conversation to direct the officers to the shotgun, which was hidden nearby. Innis (D) was tried and convicted of murder. The Rhode Island Supreme Court reversed the conviction on the grounds that the officers' dialogue constituted "subtle compulsion" and was therefore equivalent to interrogation under *Miranda*. The State (P) appealed.

ISSUE: Does the term "interrogation" under *Miranda* refer not only to express questioning, but also to any words or actions on the part of the police (other than those normally attendant to arrest and custody) that the police should know are reasonably likely to elicit an incriminating response?

HOLDING AND DECISION: (Stewart, J.) Yes. *Miranda* defined custodial interrogation as "questioning initiated by law enforcement officers after a person has been taken into custody." The *Miranda* proscriptions were designed to prevent a combination of interrogation and custody that would "subjugate the individual to the will of his examiner." The police practices that evoked this concern included several that did not involve express questioning (e.g., doctored lineups, positing the guilt of the accused, blaming the victim or society). Interrogation within the meaning of *Miranda* therefore extends to express questioning and its functional equivalent. The functional equivalent standard applies to any words or actions by the police, other than those normally attendant to arrest and custody, that the police should know are reasonably likely to elicit an incriminating response from the suspect. Since *Miranda* is concerned with protecting suspects from coercive police practices irrespective of the underlying intent of the police, reasonableness is determined by an examination of the perception of the suspect rather than the intent of the police. The conversation between the officers constituted neither express questioning nor its functional equivalent. The entire conversation consisted of a few offhand remarks in the form of a dialogue to which no response by Innis (D) was invited. Furthermore, nothing in the record suggests that they should have known that Innis (D) was particularly susceptible to an appeal to his conscience concerning the safety of the handicapped children. Vacated.

CONCURRENCE: (Burger, C.J.) *Miranda*'s meaning is reasonably clear, and the practices of law enforcement have adjusted to its confines. *Miranda* should neither be overruled, disparaged, nor extended.

DISSENT: (Marshall, J.) The Court's definition of "interrogation" is correct but its finding that Innis (D) was not interrogated in this case is wrong. Gleckman's appeal to Innis's (D) conscience was a classic interrogation technique and would have constituted interrogation if it had been directed at Innis (D). The result should not be different because the remarks were nominally addressed to another officer.

DISSENT: (Stevens, J.) From the suspect's point of view, the effectiveness of *Miranda* warnings depends on whether it appears that the police are scrupulously honoring his rights. Therefore, any statement that would normally be understood by the average listener as calling for a response is the functional equivalent of a direct question, whether or not it is punctuated by a question mark.

ANALYSIS

Justice Stewart explained that the intent of the police "may well have a bearing on whether the police should have known that their words or actions were likely to evoke an incriminating response." In *Brewer v. Williams,* 430 U.S. 387 (1977), the defendant was a mentally ill and very religious

Continued on next page.

man suspected of killing a missing child. When a police officer mentioned to the defendant that the child would need a "good, Christian burial," the defendant directed police to the child's body. His subsequent murder conviction was overturned on Sixth Amendment grounds, based on the officer's knowledge of the suspect's religious fervor and his susceptibility to appeals based on his religious beliefs.

■===■

Quicknotes

CUSTODIAL INTERROGATION   The questioning of a suspect by police while in custody.

■===■

North Carolina v. Butler

State (P) v. Mirandized confessor (D)

441 U.S. 369 (1979).

NATURE OF CASE: Appeal from a conviction for kidnapping, armed robbery, and felonious assault.

FACT SUMMARY: Butler's (D) conviction for kidnapping, etc. was overturned on the ground that no statement of a person under custodial interrogation may be admitted in evidence against him unless he had explicitly waived the right to the presence of a lawyer.

🏛 **RULE OF LAW**
An express oral or written statement of waiver is not a prerequisite to establishing that a defendant waived his *Miranda* rights.

FACTS: Having been arrested and advised of his *Miranda* rights, Butler (D) was taken to the local FBI office for interrogation. There, he was given the Bureau's "Advice of Rights" form. He read it and replied that he understood his rights when inquiry was made. However, he refused to sign the waiver of rights at the bottom of the form. He was informed he need neither speak nor sign the form but that agents would like to talk to him. Butler (D) replied, "I will talk to you but I am not signing any form." He proceeded to make incriminating statements that were used at his trial. In setting aside his conviction, the North Carolina Supreme Court held that *Miranda* required that no statement of a person under custodial interrogation be admitted into evidence against him unless, at the time the statement was made, he explicitly waived his right to presence of counsel.

ISSUE: Must there be an express oral or written statement to establish a waiver of *Miranda* rights?

HOLDING AND DECISION: (Stewart, J.) No. An express oral or written statement of waiver is not a prerequisite to establishing that a defendant waived his *Miranda* rights. While silence of a defendant after being advised of his rights cannot alone establish waiver, coupled with an understanding of his rights and a course of conduct indicating waiver, it may support a conclusion that a defendant waived his *Miranda* rights. Although the courts must presume nonwaiver and the prosecution's burden is great to show otherwise, there are some cases in which waiver can clearly be inferred from the actions and words of the person interrogated. Reversed.

DISSENT: (Brennan, J.) *Miranda* refuses to recognize a waiver unless "specifically made" after the appropriate warnings, which would require an "affirmative waiver" in the form of some express written or oral statement.

▶ **ANALYSIS**

Claims of coerced waiver have now taken the place of the once-popular claims of coerced confession in *Miranda*-type cases. In assessing the "voluntariness" of a waiver, the courts use the same "totality of circumstances" test that was previously used in determining the "voluntariness" of confessions.

■=■

Quicknotes

CUSTODIAL INTERROGATION The questioning of a suspect by police while in custody.

KNOWING AND INTELLIGENT WAIVER The intentional or voluntary forfeiture of a recognized right.

■=■

Edwards v. Arizona

Accused murder suspect (D) v. State (P)

451 U.S. 477 (1981).

NATURE OF CASE: Review of order affirming admission of incriminating statements in a murder trial.

FACT SUMMARY: After invoking his *Miranda* right to counsel, Edwards (D), without counsel, made incriminating statements during a subsequent custodial interrogation initiated by police.

🏛 **RULE OF LAW**
An accused who has expressed the desire to deal with police only through counsel may not be interrogated by police until counsel has been made available to him, unless the accused initiates further communication with the police.

FACTS: On January 19, 1976, Edwards (D) was arrested on murder charges pursuant to a warrant, and he submitted to questioning at a police station after being informed of his *Miranda* rights. During the course of the interrogation, the possibility of a plea bargain was raised. After a brief phone call by Edwards (D) to an attorney, he stated, "I want an attorney before making a deal." The questioning then ceased. On the morning of January 20, Edwards (D) was told by a detention officer that two detectives wanted to see him. When Edwards (D) replied that he did not want to talk to anyone, the officer advised him that he "had to" talk and brought Edwards (D) to the detectives. The detectives advised Edwards (D) of his *Miranda* rights. Edwards (D), with no counsel present, agreed to talk and to listen to a taped statement made by an accomplice. While listening to the tape, he made statements implicating himself in criminal activity. The trial court held these statements admissible. The state supreme court affirmed, finding the statements to have been voluntarily and knowingly made. Edwards (D) appealed.

ISSUE: May an accused who has expressed the desire to deal with police only through counsel be interrogated by police before counsel has been made available to him, if the accused does not initiate further communication with the police?

HOLDING AND DECISION: (White, J.) No. An accused who has expressed the desire to deal with police only through counsel cannot be interrogated by police before counsel has been made available to him, if the accused does not initiate further communication with the police. This Court has held that a waiver of the right to counsel must constitute a knowing and intelligent relinquishment of a known right or privilege. Where the accused actually invokes the right to counsel, additional safeguards are required to insure that subsequent waivers are valid. Edwards (D) invoked his *Miranda* right to counsel on January 19.

The police returned the next day, without making counsel available to Edwards (D), and conducted a custodial interrogation. Because this meeting was initiated not by Edwards (D), but by the police, Edwards's (D) responses to their questions did not constitute a valid waiver of his previously invoked right to counsel. The incriminating statements Edwards (D) made on January 20 were, therefore, inadmissible. Reversed.

CONCURRENCE: (Powell, J.) Once the accused has been provided the requisite warnings, and right to counsel has been requested, whether the suspect still is willing to talk to the authorities without counsel is a factual issue for determination under all the circumstances of the particular case.

▶ **ANALYSIS**

Michigan v. Mosley, 423 U.S. 96 (1975), requires police to "scrupulously honor" a suspect's assertion of the right to terminate questioning. In contrast to *Mosley, Edwards* states a far stricter "bright line" rule. The particular *Miranda* clause invoked by the accused, therefore, determines the standard of review, and often the outcome, of waiver cases.

Quicknotes

CUSTODIAL INTERROGATION The questioning of a suspect by police while in custody.

KNOWING AND INTELLIGENT WAIVER The intentional or voluntary forfeiture of a recognized right.

PRIVILEGE AGAINST SELF-INCRIMINATION A privilege guaranteed by the Fifth Amendment to the federal Constitution in a criminal proceeding for communications made by an accused and protecting an accused or witness from having to give testimony that may incriminate himself.

Police Interrogation: The Sixth Amendment Right to Counsel

Quick Reference Rules of Law

Massiah v. United States

Wiretapped narcotics suspect (D) v. Federal government (P)

377 U.S. 201 (1964).

NATURE OF CASE: Review of conviction for narcotics possession.

FACT SUMMARY: While free on bail following his indictment and arraignment, Massiah (D) made incriminating statements to an accomplice who had secretly agreed with authorities to act as an informer.

🏛 RULE OF LAW
After the accused has been indicted, the Sixth Amendment forbids the use at trial of incriminating statements deliberately elicited from the accused by government agents in the absence of counsel.

FACTS: Massiah (D) was arrested, arraigned, and indicted for possession of narcotics. He retained a lawyer, pleaded not guilty, and was released on bail. In the same indictment naming Massiah (D), Colson was charged with conspiracy to sell narcotics. Without Massiah's (D) knowledge, Colson agreed to cooperate with federal agents in their investigation of Massiah (D) and have a radio transmitter installed in his car so that federal agents could overhear conversations taking place there. During one such conversation with Colson, Massiah (D) made incriminating statements. The district court admitted the statements at trial, which resulted in Massiah's (D) conviction. The court of appeals affirmed, and Massiah (D) appealed.

ISSUE: Does the Sixth Amendment forbid the use at trial of incriminating statements deliberately elicited from an accused by government agents after the accused has been indicted and in the absence of counsel?

HOLDING AND DECISION: (Stewart, J.) Yes. The Sixth Amendment forbids the use at trial of incriminating statements deliberately elicited from an accused by government agents after the accused has been indicted and in the absence of counsel. Under the Fourteenth Amendment, the right of an accused to counsel in a state criminal adversarial proceeding commences no later than upon indictment of the accused. A contrary ruling might deny an accused "effective representation by counsel at the only stage when legal aid and advice would help him." The Sixth Amendment's specific guarantee of the right to assistance of counsel applies directly to this federal proceeding. The interrogation need not take place in a police station. For the rule to have any efficacy, it must also apply to the indirect and surreptitious interrogation conducted here. This is especially true, since Massiah (D) was more seriously imposed upon in that he did not even know he was being interrogated. The continued investigation of Massiah (D) following his indictment was within Sixth Amendment strictures. The introduction at trial of the incriminating statements deliberately elicited from Massiah (D) by authorities in the absence of his counsel was not. Reversed.

DISSENT: (White, J.) Massiah's (D) right to counsel was not interfered with because Massiah (D) was not prevented from consulting with his counsel, no meetings with counsel were disturbed or spied upon, and preparation for trial was in no way obstructed. The Fifth Amendment prohibits the use at trial of coerced incrimination. The decisive element in Fifth Amendment analysis of incriminating statements is voluntariness. The Court has expressly rejected the argument that admissions are to be deemed involuntary if made outside the presence of counsel. Exclusion is particularly inappropriate here because no evidence was presented of coercion during Massiah's (D) conversation with his partner in crime.

▶ ANALYSIS

In *Massiah,* the U.S. Supreme Court, for the first time, held that the right to counsel arises prior to trial in a criminal proceeding. The Sixth Amendment right to counsel at trial discussed in *Massiah* must be clearly distinguished from the prophylactic right to counsel during interrogation articulated in *Miranda.* In fact, *Massiah,* decided in 1964, preceded *Miranda* by two years.

■=■

Quicknotes

CONSPIRACY Concerted action by two or more persons to accomplish some unlawful purpose.

CRITICAL STAGE OF PROCEEDINGS That stage in criminal proceedings, when an accused's right to counsel arises, at which some action may be taken that will prejudice later proceedings.

PRIVILEGE AGAINST SELF-INCRIMINATION A privilege guaranteed by the Fifth Amendment to the federal Constitution in a criminal proceeding for communications made by an accused and protecting an accused or witness from having to give testimony that may incriminate himself.

■=■

Brewer v. Williams

Prosecutor (P) v. Murderer with conscience (D)

430 U.S. 387 (1977).

NATURE OF CASE: Appeal from a conviction of murder.

FACT SUMMARY: Williams (D) was convicted of murder based on a confession obtained during a custodial trip.

⚖ RULE OF LAW
The police cannot interrogate a defendant represented by known counsel after a refusal to speak without the presence of his attorney.

FACTS: Williams (D), an escaped mental patient, killed a 10-year-old girl. Williams (D) subsequently contacted a lawyer in Des Moines, informed him that he was in Davenport, and was willing to surrender to the police in Des Moines who were searching for him. The attorney informed the police and they sent a car to Waterloo to return him to Des Moines under a warrant issued for his arrest. The attorney informed both the police and his client that under no circumstances was Williams (D) to say anything. Williams (D), in the meantime, had been arrested in Davenport and hired counsel there to represent him at the arraignment on the murder charge. His attorney requested permission to accompany Williams (D) on the trip to Des Moines, but was refused. The attorney warned both Williams (D) and the police that there was to be no conversation during the trip concerning the crime as Williams (D) was represented by counsel who had informed him to remain silent. During the first part of the trip Williams (D) repeatedly refused to speak unless counsel was present. One of the detectives then began to play on Williams's (D) religious beliefs pleading with him to reveal the dead girl's whereabouts so that she could obtain a Christian burial. Williams (D) finally revealed the whereabouts of the body after confessing to the crime. Williams (D) appealed the admissibility of his confession after conviction. Williams (D) alleged, among other things, that the tactics used to obtain the confession violated his right to counsel.

ISSUE: Is questioning without the presence of known counsel during a critical stage of the proceedings violative of the Sixth and Fourteenth Amendments?

HOLDING AND DECISION: (Stewart, J.) Yes. The Sixth and Fourteenth Amendments grant an accused the right to the presence of counsel during all critical stages of the proceedings. First, this was a critical stage. Williams (D) had a warrant issued for his arrest and had already been arraigned in Davenport on the charge. The police officers knew he was represented by counsel; that he had been informed not to speak; that Williams (D) told them he would not speak without counsel present. Williams (D) had pleaded not guilty to the charge. There are no grounds present herein that establish that Williams (D) knowingly, intelligently, and voluntarily waived. The state bears a heavy burden of establishing that once rights have been invoked by the defendant/accused that they have been waived. No clear and convincing evidence of such a waiver is present herein. While the crime is abhorrent, we must reverse the conviction and remand for a new trial.

CONCURRENCE: (Marshall, J.) Good police work is something far different from catching the criminal at any price. It is equally important that the police, as guardians of the law, fulfill their responsibility to obey its commands scrupulously. In the end, life and liberty can be as much endangered from illegal methods used to convict those thought to be criminals as from the actual criminals themselves.

CONCURRENCE: (Powell, J.) Interrogation may be subtle. The thrust of the detective's efforts were to elicit information through use of psychological techniques. Such interrogation cannot be countenanced once constitutional rights have been invoked absent waiver.

CONCURRENCE: (Stevens, J.) Nothing can restore the life of the dead child herein. However, the rights of even the guilty must be protected.

DISSENT: (Burger, C.J.) After at least five warnings from two attorneys Williams (D) voluntarily lead the police to where the body was buried. There was no coercion or threats. Williams (D) was prompted solely on the simple statement by the detective. This constitutes a voluntary waiver of known rights. The exclusionary rule should not be arbitrarily applied to non-egregious police conduct.

DISSENT: (White, J.) The voluntary confession of Williams (D), made without threats or coercion, of a known right is conclusive evidence of a waiver. The very fact that Williams (D) consulted with his attorney as to whether he should speak with the officers in counsel's absence makes his later decision to talk to the police better informed and, if anything, more intelligent. Furthermore, the conduct of the officers did not jeopardize the fairness of Williams's (D) trial or risk conviction of a person who was innocent.

Continued on next page.

▶ *ANALYSIS*

Miranda warnings were not required to be given to a grand jury witness and their statements were not entitled to suppression in subsequent perjury trials. *U.S. v. Wong,* 431 U.S. 174 (1977). The same rationale applied to grand jury witnesses who were not informed that they were targets of the investigation. *U.S. v. Washington,* 431 U.S. 181 (1977). *Brewer* could probably have been reversed on *Miranda* grounds on a showing that the confession was involuntary.

■━■

Quicknotes

CUSTODIAL INTERROGATION The questioning of a suspect by police while in custody.

FOURTEENTH AMENDMENT Declares that no state shall make or enforce any law that shall abridge the privileges and immunities of citizens of the United States. No state shall deny to any person within its jurisdiction the equal protection of the laws.

KNOWING AND INTELLIGENT WAIVER The intentional or voluntary forfeiture of a recognized right.

RIGHT TO COUNSEL Right conferred by the Sixth Amendment that the accused shall be provided effective legal assistance in a criminal proceeding.

SIXTH AMENDMENT Provides the right to a speedy and public trial by impartial jury, the right to be informed of the accusation, the right to confront witnesses, and the right to have the assistance of counsel in all criminal prosecutions.

■━■

Patterson v. Illinois

Individual (D) v. State (P)

487 U.S. 285 (1988).

NATURE OF CASE: Appeal from Illinois Supreme Court in favor of the State (P).

FACT SUMMARY: After being indicted for murder, Patterson (D) voluntarily waived his right to counsel and made statements implicating himself in the murder.

🏛 RULE OF LAW
Interrogation of a criminal defendant after indictment does not violate the Sixth Amendment right to counsel as long as the defendant knowingly and voluntarily waives his right to counsel at that stage.

FACTS: Patterson (D) and two others allegedly beat a rival gang member who later died as a result of his injuries. After a jury indicted Patterson (D), Patterson (D) inquired aloud to a police officer as to why another person was not indicted, because "he did everything." The police officer then handed a *Miranda* waiver form to Patterson (D), read the form aloud to him, and had Patterson (D) initial the form. The form made Patterson (D) aware of his right to counsel and the consequences of any statement he might make to the police. Patterson (D) then gave a detailed statement to the police officer regarding his involvement with the murder. Later in the same day, Patterson (D) read, signed, and reviewed another *Miranda* form with an Assistant District Attorney assigned to the case. After this, Patterson (D) gave additional damaging statements to the prosecutor. At trial, Patterson (D) moved to suppress. The trial court and the Illinois Supreme Court found the statements were admissible and that Patterson (D) had voluntarily waived his right to counsel. Patterson (D) appealed.

ISSUE: Does interrogation of a criminal defendant after indictment violate the Sixth Amendment right to counsel where the defendant knowingly and voluntarily waives his right to counsel at that stage?

HOLDING AND DECISION: (White, J.) No. Interrogation of a criminal defendant after indictment does not violate the Sixth Amendment right to counsel as long as the defendant knowingly and voluntarily waives his right to counsel at that stage. First, Patterson's (D) argument that the police were barred from interrogating him after his indictment is incorrect. Our prior cases have held that once a defendant requests counsel, police cannot interrogate him, unless the defendant initiates further communication. That is precisely what occurred here. Second, Patterson's (D) waiver of his Sixth Amendment right to counsel was valid. For a waiver to be valid, the waiver must be knowing

and intelligent. On these facts, Patterson's (D) waiver satisfied those requirements. Twice the State (P) informed Patterson (D) of his right to counsel. Moreover, the forms also informed him that his statements could be used against him. Patterson (D) has also not identified any additional information that the police should have provided to him. Lastly, we hold that the *Miranda* warnings that suffice at the arrest stage also suffice for the interrogations at the postindictment phase. The value of counsel at this questioning phase is of minimal value, as opposed to the right to counsel at the trial stage. Therefore, defendant may validly waive his Sixth Amendment right to counsel at the postindictment phase. Affirmed.

DISSENT: (Blackmun, J.) The Sixth Amendment mandates that the defendant should not be subject to interrogation postindictment. However, I would allow for an exception where the accused further initiates the contact with the police.

DISSENT: (Stevens, J.) This Court should make a bright-line rule that once a jury indicts a defendant, the prosecutor who will try the case against the defendant should not be able to question the defendant without the presence of counsel. In civil litigation, once a complaint is filed, it is unethical to contact an opposing party without the presence of the party's attorney. The same rule should apply, with even more force, on the criminal side. The defendant's adversary, the prosecutor, cannot adequately provide the defendant with the advice that he can remain silent if he chooses. After jury empanelment at the trial stage, this Court would no doubt disallow contact between the prosecutor and the defendant. The same should hold true for contacts after the criminal complaint is filed.

▶ ANALYSIS

Note that Justice Blackmun's dissent actually appears to agree with the majority's view that postindictment interrogations are not completely barred. However, in an effort to limit the majority's holding, Justice Blackmun emphasized that he would only allow postindictment interrogations when the accused initiates the further contact. Several state courts have disagreed with this decision on state constitutional grounds.

■=■

Continued on next page.

Quicknotes

BRIGHT-LINE RULE A legal rule of decision to help resolve ambiguous issues simply and in a straight-forward manner, sometimes sacrificing equity for certainty.

INDICTMENT A formal written accusation made by a prosecutor and issued by a grand jury, charging an individual with a criminal offense.

SIXTH AMENDMENT Provides the right to a speedy and public trial by impartial jury, the right to be informed of the accusation, the right to confront witnesses, and the right to have the assistance of counsel in all criminal prosecutions.

WAIVER The intentional or voluntary forfeiture of a recognized right.

McNeil v. Wisconsin

Multiple-crime suspect (D) v. State (P)

501 U.S. 171 (1991).

NATURE OF CASE: Appeal from convictions for murder and armed robbery.

FACT SUMMARY: McNeil (D) contended that his courtroom appearance with an attorney for the West Allis crime constituted an invocation of his *Miranda* right to counsel and that his subsequent waiver during police-initiated questioning regarding the Caledonia crime was invalid.

🏛 RULE OF LAW
An accused's invocation of his Sixth Amendment right to counsel during a judicial proceeding does not constitute an invocation of his *Miranda* right to counsel.

FACTS: McNeil (D) was represented by counsel at his arraignment for an armed robbery committed in West Allis. Later that evening Sheriff Butts questioned McNeil (D) about a murder committed in Caledonia. Butts later questioned McNeil (D) on three other occasions, each time administering *Miranda* warnings to McNeil (D). On every occasion, McNeil (D) signed the *Miranda* waiver form. After confessing to the Caledonia crime, McNeil (D) was charged with and convicted of the Caledonia murder and the West Allis armed robbery. He moved unsuccessfully to suppress the incriminating statements he made during the sheriff's questions, claiming his invocation of his Sixth Amendment right to counsel at his West Allis arraignment also invoked his *Miranda* right to counsel for purposes of the Caledonia murder questioning. The motion was denied. McNeil (D) appealed.

ISSUE: Does an accused's invocation of his Sixth Amendment right to counsel during a judicial proceeding constitute an invocation of his *Miranda* right to counsel?

HOLDING AND DECISION: (Scalia, J.) No. An accused's invocation of his Sixth Amendment right to counsel during a judicial proceeding does not constitute an invocation of his *Miranda* right to counsel. The Sixth Amendment right to counsel is offense-specific. It cannot be invoked once for all future prosecutions; it does not attach until a prosecution is commenced. Because McNeil (D) provided the statements at issue here before his Sixth Amendment right to counsel with respect to the Caledonia offense had been (or even could have been) invoked, that right poses no bar to the admission of the statements in this case. McNeil (D) relies, however, upon a different right to counsel, using a combination of the Fifth Amendment guarantee that no person shall be compelled in any criminal case to be a witness against himself and the Sixth Amendment right to counsel. If McNeil's (D) rule were adopted, most persons in pretrial custody for serious offenses would be unapproachable by police officers suspecting them of involvement in other crimes, even though they never expressed any unwillingness to be questioned. Since the ready ability to obtain uncoerced confessions is not an evil but an unmitigated good, society would be the loser if such a rule was adopted. Affirmed.

DISSENT: (Stevens, J.) In this case, the Court undermines the significance of an accused's right to counsel. Although the opinion will doubtless have only a small effect on existing custodial interrogation procedures, as a theoretical matter, the Court's novel creation of an "offense-specific" limitation on the scope of the attorney-client relationship can only create confusion in the law and undermine the protections that underscore the adversarial system of justice.

▶ ANALYSIS

In response to a comment in the dissent that they prefer an inquisitorial system of justice, the majority pointed out that what makes a system adversarial rather than inquisitorial is not the presence of counsel but, rather, the presence of a judge who does not (as an inquisitor does) conduct the factual and legal investigation himself but instead decides on the basis of facts and arguments pro and con adduced by the parties. The majority also stressed that the U.S. system of justice is, and has always been, an inquisitorial one at the investigatory stage, and no other disposition is conceivable.

Quicknotes

ARRAIGNMENT The formal charging of an individual with a criminal offense.

CUSTODIAL INTERROGATION The questioning of a suspect by police while in custody.

RIGHT TO COUNSEL Right conferred by the Sixth Amendment that the accused shall be provided effective legal assistance in a criminal proceeding.

SIXTH AMENDMENT Provides the right to a speedy and public trial by impartial jury, the right to be informed of the accusation, the right to confront witnesses, and the right to have the assistance of counsel in all criminal prosecutions.

Kansas v. Ventris

State (P) v. Individual (D)

556 U.S. ___, 129 S.Ct. 1841 (2009).

NATURE OF CASE: Appeal from state high court decision in favor of defendant.

FACT SUMMARY: While awaiting trial for murder, Ventris (D) made statements in his jail cell to an informant that he committed the murder. Ventris (D) blamed the murder on another person at trial, and the State (P) attempted to impeach him with his statements to the informant.

🏛 RULE OF LAW
Evidence obtained in violation of the Sixth Amendment right to counsel may still be used for impeachment purposes, but not in the prosecution's case in chief.

FACTS: Ventris (D) was in jail awaiting trial for robbery and murder. Prior to the trial, the police planted an informant in Ventris's (D) cell. Ventris (D) stated to the informant that he committed the murder. At trial, Ventris (D) blamed the murder on another person. In response, the State (P) called the informant to testify as to Ventris's (D) statements that Ventris (D) committed the murder. The trial court allowed the testimony of the informant. The jury found Ventris (D) guilty only of robbery, but not murder. Ventris (D) appealed on the grounds the statement to the informant should not have been allowed for any reason, including impeachment. The Kansas Supreme Court agreed and reversed the conviction. The State (P) appeals.

ISSUE: May evidence obtained in violation of the Sixth Amendment right to counsel still be used for impeachment purposes, but not in the prosecution's case in chief?

HOLDING AND DECISION: (Scalia, J.) Yes. Evidence obtained in violation of the Sixth Amendment right to counsel may still be used for impeachment purposes, but not in the prosecution's case in chief. The right to counsel is a trial right, but that right also includes the right to counsel at the interrogation phases of the criminal case. In this case, the issue is not the prevention of a constitutional violation, but the remedy for one. The State (P) concedes the elicitation of Ventris's (D) statement via a jail cell informant is a likely violation of the Sixth Amendment right to counsel. The State (P) also concedes it could not use the informant's testimony during its case in chief. Here, exclusion of the tainted evidence via impeachment is outweighed by the need to prevent perjury and safeguard the trial process. Once the defendant testified inconsistently with prior statements, the State (P) should be allowed to test the veracity of his trial testimony via impeachment.

Barring the use of the statements for impeachment purposes would not add to law enforcement's deterrent level. Law enforcement already has the incentive to follow constitutional guidelines in order to have statements introduced for all purposes, not just impeachment. We have held in many prior cases that tainted evidence, while not proper for a case-in-chief, may be used for impeachment purposes if the defendant testifies inconsistently during his portion of the case. Reversed and remanded.

DISSENT: (Stevens, J.) The Sixth Amendment's right to counsel is violated when the tainted evidence is admitted during the prosecution's case-in-chief or via impeachment. The pretrial phases of a criminal case are often the most significant. It is during these times that the defendant requires the experienced guidance of a criminal defense attorney. The use of the evidence, even for impeachment purposes, damages the adversarial process.

▶ ANALYSIS

In this seven to two decision, years of case law and criminal procedure would have been altered had the court decided differently. Evidence not proper for a case-in-chief can be allowed in to impeach a defendant who makes contradictory statements while on the stand. In this matter, the trial court allowed the testimony, but also cautioned the jury to "consider with caution" testimony given by the informant in exchange for promises from the state. As it turned out, the jury did not convict Ventris (D) of murder.

■▬■

Quicknotes

CASE-IN-CHIEF The portion of a proceeding where the party with the burden of proof presents evidence to support its case.

IMPEACHMENT The discrediting of a witness by offering evidence to show that the witness lacks credibility.

SIXTH AMENDMENT Provides the right to a speedy and public trial by impartial jury, the right to be informed of the accusation, the right to confront witnesses, and the right to have the assistance of counsel in all criminal prosecutions.

■▬■

Entrapment

Quick Reference Rules of Law

Sherman v. United States

Convicted drug dealer (D) v. Federal government (P)

356 U.S. 369 (1958).

NATURE OF CASE: On certiorari from appellate court judgment upholding narcotics conviction.

FACT SUMMARY: Sherman (D), upon the repeated entreaties of a government informer, supplied the informer with narcotics.

🏛 RULE OF LAW
The government may not originate a criminal design and implant it in the mind of an innocent person so that the government may prosecute that person.

FACTS: Sherman (D) met another man at a doctor's office where apparently both were seeking treatment of a narcotics addiction. Sherman's (D) acquaintance informed him that he was not responding to treatment and that he was suffering greatly, and asked Sherman (D) if he knew a source of narcotics. Sherman (D) tried to avoid the issue, but the acquaintance repeatedly prevailed on Sherman's (D) sympathy. Sherman (D) finally obtained a quantity of narcotics, which he shared with his acquaintance. The acquaintance, who turned out to be a government informant, then advised police that Sherman (D) had sold him drugs.

ISSUE: May the government originate a criminal design and implant it in the mind of an innocent person so that the government may prosecute that person?

HOLDING AND DECISION: (Warren, C.J.) No. The government may not originate a criminal design and implant it in the mind of an innocent person so that the government may prosecute them. In considering whether entrapment has occurred, we look not only to the conduct of government agents, but to the subjective willingness of the defendant to commit the crime. If a person is predisposed to commit an offense, and the government merely affords him an opportunity to do that wrong which he was ready and willing to do, then the conduct of the government does not constitute entrapment. However, in this case, the testimony of the prosecution's witnesses indicate that Sherman (D) was anything but ready and willing, and that only repeated entreaties by the informer, who claimed to be in great suffering, caused Sherman (D) to supply him with narcotics. On that basis, we find that Sherman (D) was entrapped as a matter of law, and order the indictment against him dismissed.

CONCURRENCE: (Frankfurter, J.) Conduct is not less criminal because it is the result of temptation. The better test for entrapment would focus solely on the conduct of the police. As Justice Holmes wrote, "[F]or my part I think it a less evil that some criminals should escape than that the government should play an ignoble part."

▶ ANALYSIS

In addition to disagreeing with the majority over whether the predisposition of the defendant should be considered in evaluating an entrapment defense, Justice Frankfurter argued that entrapment should be a question of law for the judge, not a jury issue. "It is the province of the court and the court alone," he wrote, "to protect itself and the government from such prostitution of the criminal law."

■▬■

Quicknotes

CERTIORARI A discretionary writ issued by a superior court to an inferior court in order to review the lower court's decisions; the Supreme Court's writ ordering such review.

ENTRAPMENT An act by public officers that induces a defendant into committing a criminal act.

QUESTION OF LAW An issue regarding the legal significance of a particular act or event, which is usually left to the judge to ascertain.

■▬■

Jacobson v. United States

Convicted purchaser of child pornography (D) v. Federal government (P)

503 U.S. 540 (1992).

NATURE OF CASE: On certiorari from appellate court judgment affirming conviction for purchase of child pornography.

FACT SUMMARY: Jacobson (D) was arrested for purchasing materials in violation of child pornography laws, following a lengthy sting operation.

🏛 RULE OF LAW
Proof that a defendant possesses certain generalized personal inclinations is not sufficient evidence to prove beyond a reasonable doubt that he would have been predisposed to commit the crime independent of the government's coaxing.

FACTS: Jacobson (D) ordered magazines depicting nude male minors. He later claimed that he was expecting magazines with pictures of young men eighteen or older; however, his receipt of the magazines was lawful at the time. Shortly thereafter, the child pornography laws changed. Jacobson (D) was contacted by numerous government agencies, pretending to be organizations promoting freedom of expression and sexual freedom, and encouraged him to purchase child pornography. After nearly three years of such efforts, Jacobson (D) ordered a magazine called Boys Who Love Boys. It was delivered, and he was arrested.

ISSUE: Is proof that a defendant possesses certain generalized personal inclinations sufficient evidence to prove beyond a reasonable doubt that he would have been predisposed to commit the crime independent of the government's (P) coaxing?

HOLDING AND DECISION: (White, J.) No. Proof that a defendant possesses certain generalized personal inclinations is not sufficient evidence to prove beyond a reasonable doubt that he would have been predisposed to commit the crime independent of the government's (P) coaxing. The evidence that Jacobson (D) was ready and willing to commit the offense came only after the government (P) had devoted two and a half years to convincing him that he had or should have had the right to engage in the very behavior proscribed by law. Rational jurors could not say beyond a reasonable doubt that Jacobson (D) possessed the requisite predisposition prior to the government's (P) investigation. The conviction is reversed.

DISSENT: (O'Connor, J.) The enthusiasm with which Jacobson (D) responded to the opportunity to commit the instant crime is sufficient for a reasonable jury to conclude that his predisposition to commit the crime charged since the jury is charged with deciding whether predisposition exists. Here, a jury could reasonably have concluded that Jacobson (D) was not entrapped by the government.

▶ ANALYSIS

The dissent also claimed that the majority was significantly redefining the understanding of predisposition. Justice O'Connor argued that the Court's opinion could be read as holding that government investigators must have a reasonable suspicion of criminal activity before it begins an investigation. Such a requirement, O'Connor said, would prevent the government from advertising the seductions of criminal activity, an essential part of such a sting operation.

■=■

Quicknotes

CERTIORARI A discretionary writ issued by a superior court to an inferior court in order to review the lower court's decisions; the Supreme Court's writ ordering such review.

ENTRAPMENT An act by public officers that induces a defendant into committing a criminal act.

STING OPERATION A method by which police apprehend offenders by posing as criminals.

■=■

Eyewitness Identification Procedures

Quick Reference Rules of Law

United States v. Wade

Federal government (P) v. Bank robber (D)

388 U.S. 218 (1967).

NATURE OF CASE: Appeal from conviction for robbery and conspiracy to commit robbery.

FACT SUMMARY: The police arranged a lineup where two witnesses recognized Wade (D) as the robber. Wade's (D) appointed counsel was not present at the lineup.

RULE OF LAW
Once the accused is formally charged in an indictment, information, preliminary hearing, or arraignment, the accused is entitled to have counsel present at a lineup where witnesses seek to identify the perpetrator of a crime.

FACTS: Wade (D) and an accomplice were charged in an indictment with robbing a federally insured bank. Two witnesses told police that a man with a small strip of tape on each side of his face entered the bank and ordered at gunpoint that the witnesses fill a pillowcase with money. The perpetrator drove away with an accomplice who was waiting in a stolen car. Pursuant to the indictment, Wade (D) was arrested on April 2, and counsel was appointed to represent him on April 26. Fifteen days after counsel was appointed, the FBI arranged to have the two witnesses observe a lineup made up of Wade (D) and five or six other prisoners which was conducted in a courtroom of the local county courthouse. Each participant wore tape and said, "Put the money in the bag." Both witnesses identified Wade (D) as the robber. Wade's (D) appointed counsel was not notified of the lineup, nor was he present at the lineup. At the trial, the witnesses identified Wade (D), and on cross-examination the prior lineup was exposed. Wade (D) moved for an acquittal, or alternatively, to strike the witness's identification, on the grounds that the lineup without presence of counsel violated Wade's (D) Fifth Amendment privilege against self-incrimination and his Sixth Amendment right to counsel. The motions were denied and Wade (D) was convicted. The court of appeals reversed the conviction and ordered a new trial at which the in-court identification evidence was to be excluded on Sixth Amendment grounds.

ISSUE: Is a post-indictment lineup a critical stage of criminal proceedings so as to require the presence of counsel?

HOLDING AND DECISION: (Brennan, J.) Yes. Once the accused is formally charged in an indictment, information, preliminary hearing, or arraignment, the accused is entitled to have counsel present at a lineup where witnesses seek to identify the perpetrator of a crime. The

confrontation of the accused with witnesses in order to elicit identification evidence is particularly susceptible to innumerable dangers that might deny the accused a fair trial. The lineup is therefore a critical stage of the criminal proceedings. The right of the accused to a meaningful cross-examination is indispensable to a fair trial. There can be a high degree of suggestion inherent in the manner in which the accused is presented to the witnesses and it would be difficult for the defense to reconstruct the way in which the lineup was conducted. Thus, the issue of identification may be permanently settled at the lineup. As a result, there may be a denial of the right to cross-examination because the conviction may rest on a courtroom identification that is in fact the fruit of a suspect pretrial identification that the accused is helpless to subject to effective scrutiny at trial. As a result, the lineup is a critical stage of the criminal proceedings because of the prejudice that may not be capable of reconstruction at trial, and because counsel's presence can often avert prejudice and assure a meaningful confrontation. Because the accused and his counsel should have been notified and because counsel's presence is a prerequisite to the conduct of the lineup absent intelligent waiver, the conviction is vacated and the case remanded to the district court to determine whether the in-court identifications had an independent source or whether the identifications were harmless error. The Court rejects any assertion of a Fifth Amendment violation. Self-incrimination applies only against being compelled to testify against himself or otherwise provide the state with testimonial or communicative evidence. The lineup does not force the accused to be a source of real or physical evidence. Vacated and remanded.

DISSENT: (White, J.) The Court is mistakenly propounding a per se rule based on assumptions of improper police practices and pressures that have a derogatory impact on the right to a fair trial. There is no basis for these assumptions. The mistakes that have occurred in criminal trials are as much the consequence of eyewitness testimony problems as police misconduct. The states should not be impaired in their conduct of the criminal process by per se constitutional rules.

ANALYSIS

Under *Wade*, a post-indictment lineup requires notice both to the defendant and his counsel, and lineup cannot be held until counsel is present. The rationale for this decision is the defendant's right of confrontation; by being present at the lineup, counsel will be aware of any prejudicial

Continued on next page.

factors at the lineup and will be able to more effectively attack the credibility of later courtroom identification. The Court also expressly holds that a lineup, and requiring a defendant to speak or wear certain items, is not a denial of the Fifth Amendment privileges against self-incrimination. Although the opinion does not address itself to the issue, a later case held that the *Wade* protection extends only to post-indictment lineups, and the accused does not have a right to counsel at lineups held before he is arrested or charged with a crime.

Quicknotes

ACQUITTAL The discharge of an accused individual from suspicion of guilt for a particular crime and from further prosecution for that offense.

PER SE By itself; not requiring additional evidence for proof.

PRETRIAL LINEUP Procedure whereby police officers place an alleged perpetrator of a crime in a line with several other persons for purposes of identification by a witness or victim.

SIXTH AMENDMENT Provides the right to a speedy trial by impartial jury, the right to be informed of the accusation, to confront witnesses and to have the assistance of counsel in all criminal prosecutions.

Stovall v. Denno

Convicted murderer (P) v. Warden (D)

388 U.S. 293 (1967).

NATURE OF CASE: On certiorari from court of appeals judgment affirming dismissal of petition for habeas corpus following murder conviction.

FACT SUMMARY: Stovall (P) was convicted of murder after a witness identified him from her hospital bed.

🏛 RULE OF LAW
A witness identification arranged by police that focuses the witness's attention on a single suspect must be evaluated for due process purposes in light of the totality of the circumstances.

FACTS: Dr. Paul Behrendt was stabbed to death in his kitchen. His wife had followed him and jumped at the assailant, who knocked her down and stabbed her eleven times. Police found a shirt and keys on the kitchen floor which they traced to Stovall (P). Without allowing Stovall (P) time to obtain counsel, they brought him to Mrs. Behrendt's hospital room, where she was undergoing major surgery to save her life. Stovall (P) was the only Negro in the room. Mrs. Behrendt identified Stovall (P) as the assailant from her bed, and also identified his voice. Stovall (P) was convicted of murder. He petitioned unsuccessfully for habeas corpus review.

ISSUE: Is a witness-suspect confrontation arranged by police for identification purposes impermissibly suggestive and a violation of due process if it focuses attention on a single suspect?

HOLDING AND DECISION: (Brennan, J.) No. A witness identification arranged by police that focuses the witness's attention on a single suspect must be evaluated for due process purposes in light of the totality of the circumstances. The practice of showing suspects to persons for the purpose of identification singly rather than as part of a lineup has been widely condemned. However, the circumstances in the present case indicates that showing Stovall (P) to Mrs. Behrendt was imperative, as no one knew how long she might live. Under these circumstances, as the court of appeals noted, the usual police station lineup was out of the question. The conviction is affirmed.

CONCURRENCE: (Douglas, J.) Right to counsel in the context of this case should be given retroactive effect.

DISSENT: (Fortas, J.) The prosecutor's reference during trial to the unconstitutional hospital identification violated Fourteenth Amendment rights, constituting reversible prejudice.

▶ ANALYSIS

The same day as *Stovall* was decided, the Court decided *United States v. Wade*, 388 U.S. 218 (1967) and *Gilbert v. California*, 388 U.S. 263 (1967), two cases in which the right to counsel at witness identification procedures was considered. Because Stovall (P) was brought to Mrs. Behrendt's hospital room before being given an opportunity to obtain counsel, Justice Douglas argued in dissent that the holdings of *Wade* and *Gilbert* required the conclusion that Stovall (P) was unlawfully deprived of his right to counsel. However, the majority of the Court's members ruled that *Wade* and *Gilbert* were not to be given retroactive effect, and would only be applied to cases decided after the day of their decision.

■=■

Quicknotes

CERTIORARI A discretionary writ issued by a superior court to an inferior court in order to review the lower court's decisions; the Supreme Court's writ ordering such review.

HABEAS CORPUS A proceeding in which a defendant brings a writ to compel a judicial determination of whether he is lawfully being held in custody.

PRETRIAL LINEUP Procedure whereby police officers place an alleged perpetrator of a crime in a line with several other persons for purposes of identification by a witness or victim.

■=■

Manson v. Brathwaite

Prosecution (P) v. Heroin dealer (D)

432 U.S. 98 (1977).

NATURE OF CASE: Appeal from the reversal of a conviction for the sale of narcotics.

FACT SUMMARY: Glover, a police officer, after describing the man who had sold him heroin, was given a photograph of the suspect for identification purposes.

🏛 RULE OF LAW
If an identification is independently reliable, it will not be excluded solely because police identification techniques were suggestive.

FACTS: Glover, an undercover policeman, purchased heroin from Brathwaite (D). During the purchase, which took several minutes, Glover was no more than two or three feet from him. Glover returned to headquarters and described the individual whom he had seen in great detail. From the description another officer pulled a picture of Brathwaite (D) from their files. Glover saw the photograph two days later and promptly identified Brathwaite (D) as the seller. The photograph and identification were subsequently admitted at trial without objection. Brathwaite (D) was found guilty and was sentenced to prison. Fourteen months later, Brathwaite (D) challenged the photographic identification on the grounds that it was too suggestive thereby rendering the identification itself per se excludable. The court of appeals reversed the conviction on this basis holding that independent indicia of reliability could not overcome the suggestibility of the identification technique.

ISSUE: Will independent indicia of reliability allow admissibility of a witness whose original police identification was based on suggestive identification techniques?

HOLDING AND DECISION: (Blackmun, J.) Yes. Independent indicia of reliability may allow admissibility of a witness whose original police identification was based on suggestive identification techniques. The circuits have split over whether or not a per se rule should apply to excluding identification based on suggestive identification procedures. Some favor per se exclusion. Others take each case separately in order to determine if the identification would be otherwise reliable, and if so allowing it in evidence. We think the latter theory is correct. To hold otherwise would exclude relevant information from the jury merely because of improper police procedure. The case-by-case approach will be a deterrent to the police and will prevent the guilty from being freed. The linchpin in this area is the independent reliability of the identification. Here, we have a trained police officer who viewed Brathwaite (D) closely for two to three minutes from a short distance. Glover then described Brathwaite (D) in

detail shortly thereafter. The pictorial identification was two days later. All of this indicates independent reliability based on a trained observer, a prompt identification, and a reasonable opportunity to view the suspect. Independently reliable identifications need not be excluded to satisfy due process requirements. Reversed.

CONCURRENCE: (Stevens, J.) While this case is extremely close, the Court's opinion properly relies upon appropriate indicia of the reliability of the identification itself.

DISSENT: (Marshall, J.) Only through an application of the per se rule can police abuses be effectively curbed. The interests in protecting the innocent far outweigh the danger of allowing the guilty to occasionally escape conviction. Suggestive identification techniques are too fraught with the potential to injure the innocent.

▶ ANALYSIS

The per se rule is used to discourage police abuses. The majority appears to indicate that non-police witnesses will be less likely to survive an ad hoc, case-by-case approach because they are more prone to misidentification since they are not trained observers. The stress on them is also deemed greater which may cause faulty identifications. No hard and fast rules can be developed in this area, but the Court apparently focuses on: (1) the length of time in which the accused was viewed; (2) the nature of the witness; (3) the circumstances; (4) the length of time between the incident and the identification; and (5) the ability to give an initial description of the accused.

■■■

Quicknotes

AD HOC For a specific purpose.

DUE PROCESS The constitutional mandate requiring the courts to protect and enforce individuals' rights and liberties consistent with prevailing principles of fairness and justice and prohibiting the federal and state governments from such activities that deprive its citizens of life, liberty, or property interest.

PER SE By itself; not requiring additional evidence for proof.

■■■

Pretrial Release

Quick Reference Rules of Law

Stack v. Boyle

Twelve defendants indicted for conspiracy (D) v. Government official (P)

342 U.S. 1 (1951).

NATURE OF CASE: Motion to reduce bail as excessive under the Eighth Amendment.

FACT SUMMARY: Petitioners (D) were charged with conspiring to overthrow the federal government by violence or destruction.

🏛 RULE OF LAW
Bail must be set as to each individual defendant in an amount reasonably calculated to ensure the presence of the accused at trial.

FACTS: Petitioners, members of the Communist Party U.S.A. (D), were charged with conspiring to overthrow the federal government by violence or destruction in violation of the Smith Act. Upon arrest, bail was set as to each petitioner (D) in widely varying amounts. On the motion of the government, bail was fixed in the uniform amount of $50,000 for each petitioner (D). The only evidence offered by the government was a record showing that four persons, apparently unconnected to petitioners (D), had forfeited bail after being convicted under the Smith Act.

ISSUE: Must bail be set as to each individual defendant in an amount reasonably calculated to ensure the presence of the accused at trial?

HOLDING AND DECISION: (Vinson, C.J.) Yes. Bail must be set as to each individual defendant in an amount reasonably calculated to ensure the presence of the accused at trial. Unless the right to bail is preserved, the presumption of innocence loses its meaning. The standards used in fixing bail are to be applied in each case to each defendant. If there is a need for bail greater than that normally necessary to ensure the presence of any of the petitioners (D) given their circumstances and the seriousness of the charges, the petitioners (D) are constitutionally entitled to a hearing. Petitioners (D) may move for a reduction of bail so that a hearing may be held for the purpose of fixing reasonable bail for each petitioner (D).

CONCURRENCE: (Jackson, J.) Every accused person is entitled to the benefits of their own record. Defendants do not lose their separateness or identity even when charged with conspiracy.

▶ ANALYSIS

Chief Justice Vinson noted the irony in the district court's readiness to deprive petitioners (D) of their freedom before trial. This arbitrary act, Vinson wrote, "would inject into our own system of government the very principles of totalitarianism that Congress was seeking to guard against in passing the statute under which petitioners (D) have been indicted."

■=■

Quicknotes

CONSPIRACY Concerted action by two or more persons to accomplish some unlawful purpose.

EIGHTH AMENDMENT The Eighth Amendment to the federal Constitution prohibiting the imposition of excessive bail, fines, and cruel and unusual punishment.

SMITH ACT Federal law prohibiting the violent overthrow of government.

■=■

United States v. Salerno

Federal government (P) v. Mob leaders (D)

481 U.S. 739 (1987).

NATURE OF CASE: Appeal of reversal of denial of bail.

FACT SUMMARY: Salerno (D) and Cafaro (D) were denied bail on the grounds that they were dangers to the community.

RULE OF LAW
The Bail Reform Act of 1984, which allows a federal court to detain an arrestee without bail before trial if the court finds the arrestee dangerous to any other person and the community, is not unconstitutional.

FACTS: Salerno (D) and Cafaro (D), alleged organized-crime leaders, were indicted on a number of serious charges, including conspiracy to commit murder. On a Government (P) motion based on the Bail Reform Act of 1984, the district court held a fully adversarial hearing to determine whether they would be held without bail pending trial. The court denied bail, finding that the Government (P) had established by clear and convincing evidence that no condition of release could secure the safety of the community, since Salerno (D) and Cafaro (D) would likely continue their violent, organized-crime activities if released while awaiting trial. They appealed, arguing that the Act was unconstitutional on its face as a violation of the Due Process Clause of the Fifth Amendment and the Eighth Amendment prohibition against excessive bail. The court of appeals struck down the Act on due process grounds, and the Government (P) appealed.

ISSUE: Is the Bail Reform Act of 1984 unconstitutional on the grounds it allows a federal court to detain an arrestee without bail before trial if the court finds the arrestee dangerous to any other person and the community?

HOLDING AND DECISION: (Rehnquist, C.J.) No. The Bail Reform Act of 1984, which allows a federal court to detain an arrestee without bail before trial if the court finds the arrestee dangerous to any other person and the community, is not unconstitutional. Punishment without trial would violate substantive due process. However, this Act is regulatory, not punitive, since Congress rationally intended regulatory detention to achieve the legitimate goal of protecting the community from dangerous individuals, and the incidents of pretrial detention are not excessive in relation to that goal. Where the arrestee presents a demonstrable, serious danger to the community, the Government's (P) compelling regulatory interest in safety may outweigh the arrestee's right to liberty. The Act also complies with procedural due process requirements

by providing for a full-blown adversarial hearing on the issue of detention without ban. Finally, the Eighth Amendment does not require release on bail where Congress has mandated detention on the basis of a compelling interest other than flight; it simply requires that if bail is set that it not be excessive in light of the perceived evil. Reversed.

DISSENT: (Marshall, J.) First, the majority allows the Due Process Clause to be violated by simply redefining punishment as regulation." Second, a refusal to set bail does implicate the Eighth Amendment prohibition against excessive bail, since there is no difference between the consequences of setting outrageously high bail and setting no bail at all. Third, the Act is an unconstitutional limitation on the presumption of innocence, since it allows individuals under indictment for one crime to be imprisoned by the government for crimes not yet committed. If these same individuals had not been indicted, or had been indicted and acquitted, any imprisonment on the grounds that they were "dangerous" would surely be found unconstitutional. Clearly, then, the majority's decision allows an indictment to be used as evidence of criminal activity and as a justification for imprisonment.

DISSENT: (Stevens, J.) There are some circumstances where an individual's dangerousness may justify a brief detention, but in such cases the danger should be serious enough to warrant detention regardless of whether the person has been indicted, convicted, or acquitted of some other offense. Where, as here, an indictment becomes the prerequisite to emergency detention, the detention unconstitutionally infringes upon the presumption of innocence and the prohibition against excessive bail as explained by Justice Marshall.

▶ ANALYSIS

In finding pretrial detention under the Bail Reform Act not excessive, Chief Justice Rehnquist states that the Speedy Trial Act limits the length of pretrial detention. Some courts have required release on bail where pretrial detention has become too lengthy. Other courts have found the length of pretrial detention of up to ten months irrelevant under the Bail Reform Act.

■=■

Quicknotes

CONSPIRACY Concerted action by two or more persons to accomplish some unlawful purpose.

Continued on next page.

DUE PROCESS CLAUSE Clauses found in the Fifth and Fourteenth Amendments to the United States Constitution providing that no person shall be deprived of "life, liberty, or property, without due process of law."

EIGHTH AMENDMENT The Eighth Amendment to the federal Constitution prohibiting the imposition of excessive bail, fines, and cruel and unusual punishment.

INDICTMENT A formal written accusation made by a prosecutor and issued by a grand jury, charging an individual with a criminal offense.

Case Screening

Quick Reference Rules of Law

United States v. Armstrong

Federal government (P) v. Drug and firearms violator (D)

517 U.S. 456 (1996).

NATURE OF CASE: Review of dismissal of an indictment for possession of crack cocaine and federal firearms offenses.

FACT SUMMARY: After charges were brought against him for violating federal drug laws, Armstrong (D), alleging that he was selected for prosecution because he was black, brought a motion for discovery in support of his selective-prosecution claim or for dismissal of the indictment.

🏛 RULE OF LAW
A criminal defendant bringing a selective-prosecution claim must make a credible showing of different treatment of similarly situated persons in order to obtain discovery in support of the claim.

FACTS: Armstrong (D) was arrested for violation of federal drug and firearms laws. Armstrong (D) alleged that he had been selected for prosecution because he was black, and filed a motion for dismissal of the charges or for discovery of Government (P) documents regarding their prosecution of similar defendants. The district court granted the discovery motion and dismissed the indictment when the Government (P) would not comply with discovery. The court of appeals reversed but then, upon hearing the case en banc, affirmed the district court's order of dismissal. The U.S. Supreme Court granted certiorari.

ISSUE: Must a criminal defendant bringing a selective-prosecution claim make a credible showing of different treatment of similarly situated persons in order to obtain discovery in support of the claim?

HOLDING AND DECISION: (Rehnquist, C.J.) Yes. A criminal defendant bringing a selective-prosecution claim must make a credible showing of different treatment of similarly situated persons in order to obtain discovery in support of the claim. Under Federal Rule of Civil Procedure 16, which controls discovery in a criminal case, a defendant must show some evidence of disparate treatment—similar to the requirement under equal protection claims. Here, Armstrong (D) did not make such a showing. Thus, the district court's dismissal of the case was improper. Reversed and remanded.

DISSENT: (Stevens, J.) While the defendant did not make a strong enough showing to merit discovery, the district court did not abuse its discretion in requiring some response from the United States Attorney's Office (P).

▶ ANALYSIS

The Court notes that the test for obtaining discovery for a selective-prosecution claim should be similar to that of an equal protection claim. Recall that to successfully pursue an equal protection claim, the claimant must show both a discriminatory effect and a discriminatory purpose. In order to show a discriminatory effect, the claimant must also show that similarly situated persons (but of a different race or religion) were not prosecuted. From this equal protection language, the Court developed the test in this case.

Quicknotes

CERTIORARI A discretionary writ issued by a superior court to an inferior court in order to review the lower court's decisions; the Supreme Court's writ ordering such review.

DISCOVERY Pretrial procedure during which one party makes certain information available to the other.

EN BANC The hearing of a matter by all the judges of the court, rather than only the necessary quorum.

EQUAL PROTECTION A constitutional guarantee that no person shall be denied the same protection of the laws enjoyed by other persons in like circumstances.

Blackledge v. Perry

State (P) v. Convicted armed assailant (D)

417 U.S. 21 (1974).

NATURE OF CASE: On certiorari from conviction for assault with a deadly weapon with intent to kill or inflict serious bodily injury.

FACT SUMMARY: Perry (D) pled guilty to a felony charge of assault with intent to kill after appealing his misdemeanor assault conviction.

🏛 RULE OF LAW

When a defendant invokes a statutory right to a new trial, the prosecution may not bring a more serious charge against him prior to the trial de novo.

FACTS: While imprisoned, Perry (D) became involved in a fight with another inmate. He was convicted of assault with a deadly weapon, a misdemeanor. He then appealed his conviction, exercising a right to trial de novo under North Carolina law. After the filing of appeal but before the trial de novo, the prosecutor charged Perry (D) with the felony of assault with a deadly weapon with intent to kill and inflict serious bodily injury.

ISSUE: When a defendant invokes a statutory right to a new trial, may the prosecution bring a more serious charge against him prior to the trial de novo?

HOLDING AND DECISION: (Stewart, J.) No. When a defendant invokes a statutory right to a new trial, the prosecution may not bring a more serious charge against him prior to the trial de novo. The Due Process Clause is not offended by all possibilities of increased punishment upon retrial, but only by those that pose a realistic likelihood of prosecutorial vindictiveness. There was no evidence in this case that the prosecutor acted maliciously or in bad faith. However, since the fear of such vindictiveness might discourage defendants from exercising their right to appeal, we hold that no retaliatory motivation need be shown. It is not constitutionally permissible to respond to a defendant who has exercised his statutory right to appeal by bringing more serious charges. The conviction is reversed.

DISSENT: (Rehnquist, J.) The Court's conclusion that the respondent may allege the *Pearce* claim (*North Carolina v. Pearce*, 395, U.S. 711 (1969)), in this federal habeas action even though he pled guilty after his petition of a trial de novo means an unnecessary desertion from the principles we have recently stated.

▶ *ANALYSIS*

On appeal, Perry (D) pled guilty to the felony charges, and was sentenced to a term concurrent to the term of imprisonment he was then serving. In dissent, Justice Rehnquist

argued that the guilty plea waived Perry's (D) right to contest the felony indictment. However, the majority concluded that a guilty plea did not affect Perry's (D) right to challenge the fundamental corruption of the process by which he was brought into court.

∎══∎

Quicknotes

CERTIORARI A discretionary writ issued by a superior court to an inferior court in order to review the lower court's decisions; the Supreme Court's writ ordering such review.

DUE PROCESS CLAUSE Clauses found in the Fifth and Fourteenth Amendments to the United States Constitution providing that no person shall be deprived of "life, liberty, or property, without due process of law."

TRIAL DE NOVO A new trial of a case as if there had not previously been a trial.

∎══∎

Coleman v. Alabama

Criminal convict (D) v. State (P)

399 U.S. 1 (1970).

NATURE OF CASE: Appeal from a criminal conviction.

FACT SUMMARY: Coleman (D) appealed his conviction, arguing that Alabama's (P) failure to provide him with counsel at the preliminary hearing denied him the Sixth Amendment right to counsel at a critical stage of the prosecution.

🏛 RULE OF LAW
A preliminary hearing is a critical stage of a criminal prosecution where counsel's absence might derogate from the accused's right to a fair trial.

FACTS: Following his conviction, Coleman (D) appealed, arguing that Alabama's (P) failure to provide him with counsel at the preliminary hearing denied him the Sixth Amendment right to counsel at a critical stage of the prosecution. The Alabama courts denied that claim because the accused is not required to advance any defenses at the preliminary hearing, and failure to do so does not preclude the accused from every defense he may have at trial. Also, the admission of testimony given at a pretrial proceeding where the accused did not have the benefit of cross-examination by counsel is barred. Coleman (D) appealed.

ISSUE: Is a preliminary hearing a critical stage of a prosecution at which an indigent accused must be provided with counsel?

HOLDING AND DECISION: (Brennan, J.) Yes. A preliminary hearing is such a critical stage of prosecution, the "guiding hand" of counsel is needed to protect the indigent against improper prosecution. Skilled cross-examination can expose fatal weaknesses in the state's case, can fashion a vital impeachment tool for use at trial, or preserve testimony of witnesses who do not appear at trial. Counsel can better discover the case and prepare for trial. Counsel can be influential in arguing on such matters as the necessity for early psychiatric examination or bail. Thus, the conviction is vacated and the case remanded for determination of whether the failure to appoint counsel for the preliminary hearing was harmless error. If not, the conviction should be reinstated; if so, a new trial should be ordered.

CONCURRENCE: (Black, J.) An accused has the constitutional right to the assistance of counsel at a preliminary hearing since a preliminary hearing is a definite stage of a criminal prosecution. Moreover, adequate representation requires that counsel be present at the preliminary hearing to protect the interests of the client.

DISSENT: (Stewart, J.) The majority at least refrains from turning back the clock by ordering a new preliminary hearing to determine all over again whether there is sufficient evidence against the accused to present the case to the grand jury. Instead, the Court has set aside the convictions and remanded the case for determination whether the convictions should be reinstated or a new trial ordered. This action seems "quixotic."

▶ ANALYSIS

Due process and equal protection taken together are one source of the right to counsel. That right is unqualified at trial. Generally, where there is a proceeding where there is a possibility of adverse findings or consequences to a person, he has a right to counsel. These are "critical stages" of prosecution that include custodial police interrogation, non-custodial interrogations after the accused has been formally charged, a postindictment lineup, any appearance at which a plea or any defense must be made, a preliminary hearing, and sentencing.

━■━

Quicknotes

CRITICAL STAGE OF PROCEEDINGS That stage in criminal proceedings, when an accused's right to counsel arises, at which some action may be taken that will prejudice later proceedings.

CROSS-EXAMINATION The interrogation of a witness by an adverse party either to further inquire as to the subject matter of the direct examination or to call into question the witness's credibility.

INDIGENT A person who is poor and thus is unable to obtain counsel to defend himself in a criminal proceeding and for whom counsel must be appointed.

PRELIMINARY HEARING A hearing to determine whether there is sufficient evidence to require the detention of, and requirement of bail for, an individual accused of committing a criminal offense.

SIXTH AMENDMENT Provides the right to a speedy and public trial by impartial jury, the right to be informed of the accusation, the right to confront witnesses, and the right to have the assistance of counsel in all criminal prosecutions.

━■━

United States v. Williams

Federal government (P) v. Grand jury indictee (D)

504 U.S. 36 (1992).

NATURE OF CASE: Appeal from dismissal of grand jury indictment.

FACT SUMMARY: When Williams (D) argued that imposition of the disclosure rule applied to the Government (P) prosecutor's failure to disclose substantial exculpatory evidence in his possession to the grand jury, the lower courts agreed with Williams (D) and dismissed the indictment.

🏛 RULE OF LAW
A district court may not dismiss an otherwise valid indictment because the government failed to disclose to the grand jury substantial exculpatory evidence in its possession.

FACTS: Williams (D) was indicted by a grand jury. The Government (P) did not reveal to the grand jury that it possessed substantial exculpatory evidence in Williams's (D) favor. Williams (D), in seeking dismissal of the indictment, did not contend that the Fifth Amendment obliged the prosecutor to disclose substantial exculpatory evidence in his possession to the grand jury but argued instead that imposition of the disclosure rule was supported by the courts' "supervisory power." That power has been applied not only to improve the truth-finding process of the trial, but also to prevent parties from reaping benefit or incurring harm from violations of substantive or procedural rules governing matters apart from the trial itself. The lower courts agreed with Williams (D) and dismissed the indictment. This appeal to the U.S. Supreme Court followed.

ISSUE: May a district court dismiss an otherwise valid indictment because the government failed to disclose to the grand jury substantial exculpatory evidence in its possession?

HOLDING AND DECISION: (Scalia, J.) No. A district court may not dismiss an otherwise valid indictment because the government failed to disclose to the grand jury substantial exculpatory evidence in its possession. While courts' supervisory power may be used as a means of establishing standards of prosecutorial conduct before the courts themselves, it cannot be used as a means of prescribing standards of prosecutorial conduct before the grand jury. Because the grand jury is an institution separate from the courts, over whose functioning the courts do not preside, it is clear that as a general matter no such "supervisory" judicial authority exists. It is axiomatic that the grand jury sits not to determine guilt or innocence, but to assess whether there is adequate basis for bringing a criminal charge. To make the assessment, it has always been thought sufficient to hear only the prosecutor's side. As a consequence, neither in this country nor in England has the suspect under investigation by the grand jury ever been thought to have a right to testify or to have exculpatory evidence presented. It would make little sense to abstain from reviewing the evidentiary support for the grand jury's judgment while scrutinizing the sufficiency of the prosecutor's presentation. Review of facially valid indictments on such grounds would run counter to the whole history of the grand jury institution, and neither justice nor the concept of a fair trial requires it. Reversed and remanded.

DISSENT: (Stevens, J.) The grand jury is not merely an investigatory body, but also serves as a protector of citizens against arbitrary and oppressive governmental action. It blinks reality to say that the grand jury can adequately perform this important historic role if it is intentionally misled by the prosecutor, on whose knowledge of the law and facts of the underlying criminal investigation the jurors will, of necessity, rely. Unrestrained prosecutorial misconduct in grand jury proceedings is inconsistent with the administration of justice in the federal courts and should be redressed in appropriate cases by the dismissal of indictments obtained by improper methods.

▶ ANALYSIS

As the dissent points out to support its position, the majority cites a number of cases in which it declined to impose categorical restraints on the grand jury. The majority does state, however, that one of its prior decisions makes it clear that the supervisory power can be used to dismiss an indictment because of misconduct before the grand jury, at least where that misconduct amounts to a violation of one of those "few, clear rules which were carefully drafted and approved by this Court and by Congress to ensure the integrity of the grand jury's functions." Since the role of the prosecutor in representing the people is to discover the truth, the withholding of substantial exculpatory evidence from the grand jury does not serve to fulfill that function: an indicted defendant who at trial is not found guilty still suffers severe damage for reputation and incurs significant expense in presenting a defense.

■=■

Quicknotes

EXCULPATORY CLAUSE A clause in a contract relieving one party from liability for certain unlawful conduct.

GRAND JURY A group summoned to investigate, inform, and accuse persons of crimes when sufficient evidence exists to do so.

INDICTMENT A formal written accusation made by a prosecutor and issued by a grand jury, charging an individual with a criminal offense.

■=■

CHAPTER 13

Preparing for Adjudication

Quick Reference Rules of Law

Hoffman v. United States

Individual held in criminal contempt (D) v. Federal government (P)

341 U.S. 479 (1951).

NATURE OF CASE: Appeal from a finding of criminal contempt.

FACT SUMMARY: Hoffman (D) asserted the Fifth Amendment in refusing to answer questions before a federal grand jury and was taken before a federal district court where he was held in criminal contempt and sentenced to five months imprisonment. The court of appeals affirmed, and Hoffman (D) appealed to the U.S. Supreme Court.

🏛 RULE OF LAW

The Fifth Amendment privilege against self-incrimination embraces questions that it can reasonably be said furnish a link in the chain of evidence needed to prosecute for a federal crime.

FACTS: When called before a special federal grand jury convened to investigate a wide variety of federal crimes, Hoffman (D) was asked questions, some of which he answered but several of which he refused to answer, asserting the Fifth Amendment on the grounds that, while standing alone, the answers might not have incriminated him of a federal offense, his answers might reasonably have furnished a link that could have led prosecutors to evidence he had committed one or more crimes. The district court rejected Hoffman's (D) argument and ordered him to answer the questions under penalty of criminal perjury. The court of appeals affirmed, and he appealed to the U.S. Supreme Court.

ISSUE: Does the Fifth Amendment privilege against self-incrimination embrace questions that it can reasonably be said furnish a link in the chain of evidence needed to prosecute for a federal crime?

HOLDING AND DECISION: (Clark, J.) Yes. The Fifth Amendment privilege against self-incrimination embraces questions that it can reasonably be said furnish a link in the chain of evidence needed to prosecute for a federal crime. Such protection, however, must be confined to instances where the witness, as here, has reasonable cause to apprehend danger from a direct answer. The lower court should have considered, in connection with several of the questions, that the chief occupation of some of persons about whom Hoffman (D) was asked, involved evasion of a variety of federal criminal laws. The questions asked could easily have required answers that would "forge links in a chain of facts" imperiling Hoffman (D) with conviction of a federal crime. Three of the questions, if answered affirmatively, would establish contacts between Hoffman (D) and another person at a time when such other person was eluding the grand jury. Hoffman (D) could reasonably have sensed the peril of prosecution for federal offenses ranging from obstruction of justice to conspiracy. The judge who ruled on the privilege had himself impaneled the special grand jury. Reversed.

▶ ANALYSIS

In *Hoffman,* the Supreme Court is clear to express its viewpoint that the immediate and potential evils of compulsory self-disclosure transcend any difficulties that the exercise of the privilege may impose on society in the detection and prosecution of crime.

∎≡∎

Quicknotes

GRAND JURY A group summoned to investigate, inform, and accuse persons of crimes when sufficient evidence exists to do so.

PRIVILEGE AGAINST SELF-INCRIMINATION A privilege guaranteed by the Fifth Amendment to the federal Constitution in a criminal proceeding for communications made by an accused and protecting an accused or witness from having to give testimony that may incriminate himself.

∎≡∎

People v. Vilardi

State (P) v. Arsonist (D)

N.Y. Ct. App., 76 N.Y.2d 67, 555 N.E.2d 915 (1990).

NATURE OF CASE: Appeal from an arson conviction.

FACT SUMMARY: Vilardi (D) argued that the prosecutor's failure to comply with his pretrial discovery request violated his constitutional right to be informed of exculpatory information known to the state.

🏛 RULE OF LAW
Where there is a reasonable possibility that failure to disclose specifically requested pretrial material contributes to a verdict, failure to supply such material constitutes error.

FACTS: Vilardi (D) was convicted of first degree arson and of having conspired with Ronnie and William Bernacet, Ephraim Flores, and Gino Romano to plant and set off a pipe bomb at a pizzeria. The Bernacet brothers were tried first on the same charges. Among the prosecution witnesses in that trial was Officer Kiely of the Bomb Squad who had inspected the scene. In that first trial, the defense counsel argued there was insufficient proof of the explosion element for a first degree arson conviction, and the Bernacet brothers were acquitted by the jury. Before Vilardi's (D) instant trial, defense counsel made a pretrial request for all reports by experts, including specifically explosives experts concerning the explosion. The prosecutor (not the same prosecutor who tried the Bernacets) sent 12 reports but failed to include Officer Kiely's first report. When preparing the instant appeal, appellate counsel reviewed the Bernacet trial record, discovered the undisclosed explosives report, and moved to vacate the present judgment for failure of the requested disclosure. The intermediate appellate court ordered a new trial, and the state appealed to New York's highest court.

ISSUE: Where there is a reasonable possibility that failure to disclose specifically requested pretrial material contributes to a verdict, does the failure to supply such material constitute error?

HOLDING AND DECISION: (Kaye, J.) Yes. Where there is a reasonable possibility that failure to disclose specifically requested pretrial material contributes to a verdict, failure to supply such material constitutes error. Failure to disclose in the face of a specific request, as here, is serious in its potential to undermine fairness of a trial. Where the defense itself has provided specific notice of its interest in particular material, heightened rather than lessened prosecutorial care is called for. The "reasonable possibility" standard, which is essentially a reformulation of the "seldom if ever excusable" rule, is a clear rule that properly encourages compliance with discovery obligations. On the other hand, a "reasonable probability" standard would remit the impact of the exculpatory evidence to appellate hindsight, thus significantly diminishing the vital interest of the court in a decision rendered by a jury whose ability to render that decision is unimpaired by failure to disclose important evidence. Here, there was at least a reasonable possibility that Vilardi (D) would not have been convicted in the first degree arson charge had the exculpatory report been available to him at trial. Affirmed.

▶ ANALYSIS

In *Vilardi*, the Court takes the position that a "backward-looking" and "outcome-oriented" standard of review which gives dispositive weight to the strength of the state's case clearly provides less reason for a prosecutor, in responding to discovery requests, carefully to review the files for exculpatory material or to err on the side of disclosure where exculpatory value is unsettled.

■=■

Quicknotes

DISCOVERY Pretrial procedure during which one party makes certain information available to the other.

EXCULPATORY EVIDENCE A statement or other evidence that tends to excuse, justify, or absolve the defendant from alleged fault or guilt.

■=■

Arizona v. Youngblood

State (P) v. Kidnapping suspect (D)

488 U.S. 51 (1988).

NATURE OF CASE: Review of reversal of conviction for kidnap and sexual assault.

FACT SUMMARY: Certain fluid samples removed from a sexual assault victim were improperly stored by the police and could not be examined on behalf of Youngblood (D).

🏛 RULE OF LAW
Absent bad faith, failure by the police to preserve potentially exculpatory evidence does not violate due process.

FACTS: A minor was kidnapped and repeatedly assaulted sexually, before being released by the perpetrator. His mother then took him to a hospital. A physician diagnosed sexual assault, and then took certain evidence in the form of residual body fluids. The evidence was put into storage. Police tests proved inconclusive. Meanwhile, the victim picked out Youngblood's (D) photo from a photo lineup, and he was arrested. Upon being informed of the fluid samples, Youngblood's (D) counsel requested specimens for testing. It turned out that the remaining samples had been improperly stored and could not be used. Youngblood (D) was convicted. The state court of appeals reversed, holding the loss of the evidence to have constituted a due process violation. The U.S. Supreme Court granted review.

ISSUE: Will a good faith failure by the police to preserve potentially exculpatory evidence violate due process?

HOLDING AND DECISION: (Rehnquist, C.J.) No. A good faith failure by the police to preserve potentially exculpatory evidence does not violate due process. In the case of evidence that is only potentially exculpatory, courts have the difficult task of divining the import of materials whose significance is unknown and often disputed. To impose a duty on police to preserve all potential evidence creates too great a burden on law enforcement. The better rule is that only intentional, bad-faith destruction of evidence should constitute reversible error. Here, the loss of evidence was at worst negligent, so the court of appeals erred. Reversed and remanded.

CONCURRENCE: (Stevens, J.) There may well be cases in which the defendant is unable to prove that the state acted in bad faith but in which the loss or destruction of evidence is nonetheless so critical to the defense as to make a criminal trial fundamentally unfair. This, however, is not such a case.

DISSENT: (Blackmun, J.) The Constitution requires that a criminal defendant receive a fair trial, not a "good faith" try at a fair trial. When evidence is lost due to police activity, due process has been violated.

▶ ANALYSIS

The tests done by the police department did not include a certain "state of the art" test. Youngblood (D) contended that failure to use this most reliable test was improper. The Court disagreed, noting that a defendant did not have a constitutional right to any particular type of test.

■■■

Quicknotes

DUE PROCESS The constitutional mandate requiring the courts to protect and enforce individuals' rights and liberties consistent with prevailing principles of fairness and justice and prohibiting the federal and state governments from such activities that deprive its citizens of life, liberty, or property interest.

EXCULPATORY EVIDENCE A statement or other evidence that tends to excuse, justify, or absolve the defendant from alleged fault or guilt.

■■■

Williams v. Florida

Alibi user (D) v. State (P)

399 U.S. 78 (1970).

NATURE OF CASE: Appeal from conviction of robbery.

FACT SUMMARY: Florida law requires that a defendant submit to a limited form of pretrial discovery by the state whenever he intends to rely at trial on the defense of alibi.

🏛 RULE OF LAW
The constitutional privilege against self-incrimination is not violated by a requirement that the defendant give notice of an alibi defense and disclose his alibi witnesses.

FACTS: Williams (D) was charged with robbery. Prior to his trial, Williams (D) sought a protective order to be excused from complying with a Florida law that requires a defendant, on written demand of the prosecution, to give notice in advance of trial if the defendant intends to claim an alibi, and to furnish the prosecution with information as to the place he claims to have been and with the names and addresses of the alibi witnesses he intends to use. Williams (D) wanted to declare his intent to use an alibi, but objected to further disclosure on the ground that the notice-of-alibi rule would compel him to be a witness against himself in violation of the Fifth and Fourteenth Amendments. The rule also obligated the state to notify a defendant of any rebuttal witnesses to the alibi defense the state will call. Failure to comply, by either side, results in the exclusion of the defendant's alibi evidence or the state's rebuttal evidence. When Williams's (D) motion for the protective order was denied, he complied with the rule. On the morning of his trial, the state interviewed a Mrs. Scotty, Williams's (D) chief alibi witness. At trial, Mrs. Scotty gave testimony that contradicted her pretrial statements. The state also furnished a rebuttal witness. Williams (D) was convicted.

ISSUE: Is a notice-of-alibi rule violative of the Fifth and Fourteenth Amendments by compelling a defendant to be a witness against himself?

HOLDING AND DECISION: (White, J.) No. The notice-of-alibi rule is not violative of the Fifth and Fourteenth Amendments by compelling a defendant to be a witness against himself. The rule is fair to both the defendant and state in permitting liberal discovery. The state has a legitimate interest in protecting itself against eleventh hour defenses: although based on an adversary system, a trial is not yet a poker game in which players may conceal their cards at will. No pretrial statements of Mrs. Scotty were introduced at trial; her pretrial testimony was only used to find rebuttal witnesses. A defendant is always in a dilemma whether to remain silent or present a defense that may prove disastrous. Nothing in the rule obligates the defendant to rely on an alibi or prevents him from abandoning it as a defense. The rule only requires that a defendant accelerate the timing of his disclosure of information he would have revealed at trial anyway. A defendant is not entitled to await the end of the prosecution's case against him before announcing the nature of his defense anymore than he can await the jury's verdict on the state's case before deciding to take the stand himself. Absent the rule, the prosecution would be entitled to a continuance at trial on the grounds of surprise; the rule thus serves to prevent a disrupted trial.

CONCURRENCE AND DISSENT: (Black, J.) Before trial, defense counsel can only guess at what the state's case might be. The notice-of-alibi rule thus compels defendants with any thoughts at all of pleading alibi to be forced to disclose their intentions so as to preserve the possibility of later raising the defense—the decision goes to more than just "timing." Pretrial disclosure will adversely affect the defendant who then decides to forego raising an alibi defense. His alibi witnesses will still help the prosecution to new leads or evidence. The rule is a clear violation of the Fifth Amendment because it requires a defendant to give information to the state that may destroy him. The entire burden of proving criminal activity rests on the state: no constitutional provision is designed to make conviction easier. The defendant need not do anything to defend or convict himself. While a criminal trial is in part a search for truth, it also is designed to protect "freedom" by insuring that the state carries its burden. Efficiency is not a consideration. The majority's decision opens the way to compel complete pretrial discovery of a defendant's case, and any defenses he might raise.

▶ ANALYSIS

At the time *Williams* was decided, 15 states other than Florida had notice-of-alibi requirements of varying kinds. One such rule, in *Wardins v. Oregon,* 412 U.S. 470 (1973), was struck down because it failed to provide reciprocal discovery rights to the defendant. The Court found this omission violative of the Due Process Clause of the Fourteenth Amendment. Because exclusion of the testimony of alibi witnesses is a drastic sanction for failure on the defendant's part to comply with the rule's disclosure requirements, other sanctions have been suggested. These include: (1) granting a continuance to the prosecution; (2) allowing the prosecution or court to comment on the defendant's failure to the jury; (3) placing the defense counsel in contempt when the failure was not in "good faith."

■=■

Continued on next page.

Quicknotes

ALIBI Provable documentation of an individual's activities at the time a criminal offense was committed, thereby relieving him of possible guilt.

CONTINUANCE The postponement of a case to a later date.

DUE PROCESS CLAUSE Clause found in the Fifth and Fourteenth Amendments to the United States Constitution providing that no person shall be deprived of "life, liberty, or property, without due process of law."

PRIVILEGE AGAINST SELF-INCRIMINATION A privilege guaranteed by the Fifth Amendment to the federal Constitution in a criminal proceeding for communications made by an accused and protecting an accused or witness from having to give testimony that may incriminate himself.

State v. Reldan

State (P) v. Accused murderer (D)

N.J. Super. Ct., 167 N.J. Super. 595, 401 A.2d 563 (1979).

NATURE OF CASE: Motion to sever trial upon indictment of Reldan (D) for two murders.

FACT SUMMARY: Reldan (D) was charged with the murder of two women and sought separate trials, claiming that the jury would be prejudiced by a joint trial.

🏛 RULE OF LAW
More than a mere allegation of prejudice must be offered to warrant an order for separate trials of properly joined offenses.

FACTS: Within two days, two women in their twenties were found strangled to death in New York, in different locations, but within the same county. They were both nude and had both died by the unusual method of a fractured hyoid bone. Reldan (D) was charged with both murders in a single indictment, and moved for separate trials, alleging prejudice.

ISSUE: Is more than a mere allegation of prejudice necessary to warrant an order for separate trials of properly joined offenses?

HOLDING AND DECISION: (Madden, J.) Yes. More than a mere allegation of prejudice must be offered to warrant an order for separate trials of properly joined offenses. Reldan (D) did not proffer that he wished to testify as to one count only; if he made such a proffer at trial, I would then be empowered to decide whether to grant a severance. As to the evidence of one crime being used to infer guilt as to the other, even if the trials were severed, the prosecution would still be able to offer evidence of one crime at the trial for the other to show motive, intent, common scheme, knowledge, absence of mistake, or identity. The evidence here is not so prejudicial as to outweigh its probative value; and the defendant has not made an adequate showing that a jury would be unable to fairly hear the two counts of murder in the same trial. The motion is denied.

▶ ANALYSIS

Judge Madden distinguished a case in which the only evidence against the defendant was the testimony of his two victims, and severance was ordered. Madden observed that a joinder in that case would have given the prosecution two witnesses instead of one to overcome the denial of either offense.

Quicknotes

JOINDER The joining of claims or parties in one lawsuit.

PROBATIVE Tending to establish proof.

SEVERANCE Dividing or separating.

Barker v. Wingo

Murder suspects (D) v. State (P)

407 U.S. 514 (1972).

NATURE OF CASE: Petition for certiorari of a murder conviction.

FACT SUMMARY: Although Barker (D) made no objections during the first four years of a five-year delay between his arrest and conviction for murder, he subsequently claimed that his right to a speedy trial had been violated.

🏛 RULE OF LAW
The determination of whether a defendant has been deprived of his Sixth Amendment right to a speedy trial must be made on a case-by-case basis by balancing the following four factors: (1) length of delay, (2) reason for delay, (3) the defendant's assertion of his right, and (4) prejudice to the defendant.

FACTS: On July 20, 1958, an elderly couple was murdered. Shortly afterwards, Silas Manning and Willie Barker (D) were arrested as suspects. On September 15 they were indicted, counsel was appointed on September 17, and Barker's (D) trial was set for October 21. However, Barker (D) was not brought to trial for more than five years after his arrest due to numerous continuances by the prosecution. Initially the continuances were for the purpose of first convicting Manning, against whom the Commonwealth had a stronger case, to assure his testimony at Barker's (D) trial (i.e., to eliminate problems of self-incrimination). However, Manning was not convicted until 1962. Afterwards, Barker's (D) trial was delayed another seven months due to the illness of the chief investigating officer in the case. During these continuances, Barker (D) was free for all but ten months in jail, and he made no objections during the first four years of delay. However, Barker (D) objected to the last few continuances, and, at his trial, he moved for dismissal on the basis that his Sixth Amendment right to a speedy trial had been violated. This motion was denied and Barker (D) was convicted of murder. Upon appeal to the Kentucky court of appeals, the conviction was affirmed. Barker (D) then petitioned for habeas corpus in the U.S. district court. Upon denial of that petition he appealed to the Sixth Circuit Court of Appeals. Upon affirmance of his conviction, Barker (D) brought a petition for certiorari.

ISSUE: Is a delay of five years between the arrest and trial of a defendant a violation per se of his Sixth Amendment right to a speedy trial?

HOLDING AND DECISION: (Powell, J.) No. The determination of whether a defendant has been deprived of his Sixth Amendment right to a speedy trial must be made on a case-by-case basis by balancing the following four factors: (1) length of delay, (2) reason for delay,

(3) the defendant's assertion of his right, and (4) prejudice to the defendant. Since the deprivation of the right to a speedy trial does not per se prejudice the ability of an accused to defend himself, it is impossible to state "with precision" when the right has been denied. Each factor, therefore, must be separately analyzed. First, it is true that a long delay before trial is more likely to be justified for a serious, complex crime (e.g., murder) than for a simple one. Here, however, the delay of over five years was extreme by any standard. Second, it is true that a delay in bringing an accused to trial may be justified by a showing of some strong reason for it. Here, however, there was a strong reason for delay (i.e., illness of the chief investigator) for only seven months of the five-year delay. Although some additional delay might also have been necessary to acquire Manning as a witness, over four years was clearly unreasonable. Third, it is true that failure to assert the right to a speedy trial will not constitute a waiver of that right, unless it is found to be an "intentional relinquishment or abandonment of a known right." Here, however, it is obvious that Barker (D) did not want a trial at all, hoping, rather, that the delays would ultimately result in dismissal of the charges against him. Fourth, it is true that the prejudice that results from a delay of a defendant's trial must be evaluated in light of those interests that a speedy trial was designed to protect (i.e., prevention of "oppressive pretrial incarceration," minimization of anxiety and concern of the accused, and limitation on the possibility that the defense will be "impaired"). Here, however, prejudice was minimal. Although Barker (D) was prejudiced to some extent by spending some time in jail and by living for years under "a cloud of suspicion," none of his witnesses died or became unavailable. In conclusion, the facts that Barker (D) did not want a trial and was not prejudiced by the delay outweigh the unjustified length of delay. Judgment affirmed.

CONCURRENCE: (White, J.) The concurrence emphasizes that a delay, whether the defendant is free or not, may "disrupt his employment, drain his financial resources, curtail his associations, subject him to public obloquy and create anxiety in him." For these reasons, any defendant who "desires" a speedy trial should have it within a "reasonable" time, regardless of whether or not delay would prejudice his defense at trial, unless there are "special considerations."

▌ ANALYSIS

This case illustrates the discretion available (through the balancing test) to the courts in determining when the right

Continued on next page.

to a speedy trial has been violated, and the emphasis on the desire of an accused to have a speedy trial. Note that an accused "waives" the right to a speedy trial if he flees the state after arraignment or requests postponement of his trial. Note, also, that the right to a speedy trial attaches only after a person is accused (i.e., indicted or arrested), so that it is not violated by police delay in filing charges. However, if such a delay was purposeful, due process requires dismissal of the charges.

■═■

Quicknotes

CERTIORARI   A discretionary writ issued by a superior court to an inferior court in order to review the lower court's decisions; the Supreme Court's writ ordering such review.

CONTINUANCE   The postponement of a case to a later date.

SIXTH AMENDMENT   Provides the right to a speedy trial by impartial jury, the right to be informed of the accusation, to confront witnesses and to have the assistance of counsel in all criminal prosecutions.

WRIT OF HABEAS CORPUS   A proceeding in which a defendant brings a writ to compel a judicial determination of whether he is lawfully being held in custody.

■═■

The Role of Defense Counsel

Quick Reference Rules of Law

Nix v. Whiteside

Prosecution on appeal (P) v. Murder convict (D)

475 U.S. 157 (1986).

NATURE OF CASE: Appeal from a reversal of denial of habeas corpus following conviction for murder.

FACT SUMMARY: Whiteside (D), who was dissuaded by his attorney from committing perjury, sought habeas corpus relief for ineffective assistance of counsel.

RULE OF LAW
A defendant is not denied effective assistance of counsel if his attorney dissuades him from committing perjury.

FACTS: Whiteside (D) stabbed and killed Love. Prior to the trial, Whiteside (D) told his attorney that he was going to testify that he saw Love holding a gun, something he had earlier stated was not the case. Whiteside's (D) attorney said that he would inform the court of Whiteside's (D) perjury if Whiteside (D) did this, so Whiteside (D) did not make the assertion. Whiteside (D) was convicted, and the conviction was affirmed. A district court denied habeas corpus, but the Eighth Circuit Court of Appeals reversed, holding that Whiteside (D) had been denied effective assistance of counsel.

ISSUE: Is a defendant denied effective assistance of counsel if his attorney dissuades him from committing perjury?

HOLDING AND DECISION: (Burger, C.J.) No. A defendant is not denied effective assistance of counsel if his attorney dissuades him from committing perjury. A defendant is denied effective counsel only if counsel's errors are so serious as to amount to not functioning as counsel. An attorney is under an ethical duty to prevent perjury, and counsel's efforts to dissuade were perfectly in keeping with this duty. A defendant does not have a right to testify falsely, and that is the only "right" that Whiteside (D) could possibly have been denied. Therefore, Whiteside's (D) counsel's acts were perfectly proper. Reversed.

CONCURRENCE: (Brennan, J.) The Court has no authority to establish rules of ethical conduct for lawyers practicing in state courts.

CONCURRENCE: (Stevens, J.) In this case, Whiteside (D) intended to commit perjury, his lawyer knew it, and the lawyer had a duty to take extreme measures to prevent the perjury from occurring. In this task, the lawyer was successful, and it is clear that his client, Whiteside (D), suffered no legally cognizable prejudice.

▶ ANALYSIS

The duty of an attorney not to tolerate perjury from his client is time-honored. Written guidelines go as far back as 1908, but the tradition goes much further than that. This principle is embodied today in MR 3.3(a)(3) of the Model Rules of Professional Conduct.

Quicknotes

HABEAS CORPUS A proceeding in which a defendant brings a writ to compel a judicial determination of whether he is lawfully being held in custody.

INEFFECTIVE ASSISTANCE OF COUNSEL Whether an attorney's representation so undermined the adjudicatory process that the result cannot be determined to be just.

PERJURY The unlawful communication of a false statement knowingly and under oath.

Gideon v. Wainwright

Indigent suspect (D) v. State (P)

372 U.S. 335 (1963).

NATURE OF CASE: Felony prosecution.

FACT SUMMARY: Gideon (D) was charged with a felony in a state prosecution. He requested court-appointed counsel, but was refused on the basis state law only required appointment of counsel in capital cases.

🏛 RULE OF LAW
The right of an indigent to appointed counsel is a right fundamental and essential to a fair trial.

FACTS: Gideon (D) was charged with felony breaking and entering, a violation of state law. He was without funds and requested the court appoint an attorney for him at trial. The request was refused since Florida state law did not require appointment of counsel for indigents except in capital offense cases. Gideon (D) then conducted his own defense and was convicted and sentenced to five years. He filed a writ of habeas corpus based on the denial of counsel at trial.

ISSUE: Is the right to the assistance of counsel at trial a fundamental and essential right required to insure a fair trial?

HOLDING AND DECISION: (Black, J.) Yes. This Court first expressed the view that the right to counsel at trial was a fundamental right essential to a fair trial in *Powell v. Alabama,* 287 U.S. 45 (1932). That decision was limited to its facts, however. In *Betts v. Brady,* 316 U.S. 455 (1942), the right to counsel was predicated on a case-by-case examination of the special circumstances of each case to determine if denial of counsel was a denial of a fair trial. But it is evident that every defendant who can afford a lawyer will have one at his criminal trial. It does not appear to be a luxury but is viewed as a necessity. This Court is of the opinion, now, that *Powell v. Alabama* was right in holding that the right to counsel is fundamental to a fair trial and that *Betts v. Brady* was wrong in limiting that right to special circumstances. The Court holds that the right to counsel is a fundamental right for all criminal defendants at trial.

CONCURRENCE: (Harlan, J.) For capital cases, the special circumstances rule has been formally abandoned. It is now time when such rule similarly should be abandoned also in noncapital cases, at least in situations in which a substantial prison sentence is a possibility.

▶ ANALYSIS

Upon retrial, with the assistance of appointed counsel, Gideon (D) was acquitted. The *Gideon* decision was read to require counsel in only non-petty (i.e., six months or more imprisonment) cases. However, in a subsequent case, *Argersinger v. Hamlin*, 497 U.S. 25 (1972), the right to appointed counsel was extended to any case where the possibility of imprisonment existed. There was no minimum time specified and so if the judge wishes to imprison the defendant, if convicted, he must have appointed counsel, if indigent. The denial of counsel at trial where imprisonment results is error per se and is not subject to the harmless error rule.

■══■

Quicknotes

HARMLESS ERROR An error taking place during trial that does not require the reviewing court to overturn or modify the trial court's judgment in that it did not affect the appellant's substantial rights or the disposition of the action.

INDIGENT A person who is poor and thus is unable to obtain counsel to defend himself in a criminal proceeding and for whom counsel must be appointed.

WRIT OF HABEAS CORPUS A proceeding in which a defendant brings a writ to compel a judicial determination of whether he is lawfully being held in custody.

■══■

Scott v. Illinois

Petty offender (D) v. State (P)

440 U.S. 367 (1979).

NATURE OF CASE: Appeal of theft conviction.

FACT SUMMARY: Without assistance of counsel, Scott (D) was convicted of misdemeanor theft, a crime carrying a possibility of one year of imprisonment, for which Scott (D) was fined $50.

🏛 RULE OF LAW
The Constitution does not guarantee a right to counsel to a person charged in state court with a misdemeanor punishable by imprisonment, unless a prison term actually is imposed.

FACTS: Scott (D) was charged with misdemeanor theft, for which an Illinois statute set the penalty at up to a $500 fine and one year in prison. The trial court refused to appoint counsel to represent him. Scott (D) was convicted and fined $50 but received no prison term. Scott (D) appealed to the Illinois Supreme Court, claiming the Sixth and Fourteenth Amendments require appointment of counsel whenever imprisonment is an authorized penalty. (In *Argersinger v. Hamlin*, 407 U.S. 25 (1972), the Court held that a defendant charged with a "petty" offense has a right to counsel if he is sentenced to a term of imprisonment.) Scott's (D) conviction was upheld. Scott (D) appealed to the U.S. Supreme Court.

ISSUE: Does the Constitution guarantee a right to counsel to a person charged in state court with a misdemeanor punishable by imprisonment, where no prison term actually is imposed?

HOLDING AND DECISION: (Rehnquist, J.) No. The Constitution does not guarantee a right to counsel to a person charged in state court with a misdemeanor punishable by imprisonment, unless a prison term actually is imposed. The premise of *Argersinger* was that actual imprisonment is a more severe penalty than a fine or the mere threat of imprisonment, justifying actual imprisonment as the line defining right to counsel. This line has proven workable, whereas extension of right to counsel would create confusion and impose substantial costs on the states. Affirmed.

CONCURRENCE: (Powell, J.) The right to counsel should not be dependent on whether there is imprisonment. Drawing the line at imprisonment can have the practical effect of precluding the right to counsel in nonimprisonment cases where conviction can have more serious consequences. Moreover, a state trial judge must decide before trial, before hearing evidence, whether to appoint counsel or to forgo his discretion to impose imprisonment and abandon his legislatively imposed duty to consider the full range of possible punishments.

DISSENT: (Brennan, J.) *Argersinger* held that the right to counsel extends to "petty" offenses where actual imprisonment is imposed. The assumption in *Argersinger* was that the right to counsel also applies to all "nonpetty" offenses, i.e., offenses punishable by more than six months' imprisonment. This "authorized imprisonment" standard is a better predictor of whether the consequences of conviction are so serious that the Sixth Amendment requires appointment of counsel. An authorized imprisonment test also avoids forcing state judges to make pretrial choices between appointing counsel or forgoing the option of imposing imprisonment. The Court's concern that an authorized imprisonment rule would place a serious economic burden on the states should not serve to deny constitutional rights. The Court's concern also is questionable in light of the proven economic feasibility of public defender systems and the fact that most states' laws currently mandate some form of an authorized imprisonment rule. The offense with which Scott (D) was charged, "theft," is certainly a "nonpetty" offense, carrying with it the moral stigma attached to common law crimes, as well as a possible one-year jail term. Scott (D) should have a right to counsel.

DISSENT: (Blackmun, J.) The Sixth and Fourteenth Amendments' right to counsel should be held to extend at least as far as the right to jury trial. Defendants, prosecutors, and courts deserve such a "bright line."

▶ ANALYSIS

The Court's opinion "adopt(s) actual imprisonment as the line defining the constitutional right to appointment of counsel." Scott (D) committed a misdemeanor, but neither the express words nor the logic of the opinion limit the holding to misdemeanors. Thus, it could be argued that after *Scott* indigents charged in state court with any crime, felony, or misdemeanor are not entitled to appointed counsel unless a prison term actually is imposed. However, the dominant interpretation is that *Scott* left the rule of *Gideon* intact: all felony defendants are entitled to appointed counsel.

Quicknotes

COMMON LAW CRIME An activity that has been defined as a crime not by legislative enactment but by the courts through case law.

FOURTEENTH AMENDMENT Declares that no state shall make or enforce any law that shall abridge the privileges and immunities of citizens of the United States. No state

Continued on next page.

shall deny to any person within its jurisdiction the equal protection of the laws.

MISDEMEANOR Any offense that does not constitute a felony, which is generally less severe and for which a lesser punishment is imposed.

SIXTH AMENDMENT Provides the right to a speedy and public trial by impartial jury, the right to be informed of the accusation, the right to confront witnesses, and the right to have the assistance of counsel in all criminal prosecutions.

■══■

Douglas v. California

Indigent convict (D) v. State (P)

372 U.S. 353 (1963).

NATURE OF CASE: Appeal from criminal conviction.

FACT SUMMARY: After his conviction, Douglas (D) was denied appointed counsel for assistance in pursuing his right of first appeal. The denial came after the appellate court had reviewed the transcript of his trial and, pursuant to state law, had determined that counsel would not be of help to the defendant.

RULE OF LAW
An indigent is entitled to appointed counsel to prepare an appellate brief where the appeal pursued is granted as a matter of right to all defendants.

FACTS: Douglas (D) was convicted in a state proceeding and was sentenced. He served notice that he wished to appeal his conviction and that he was in need of appointed counsel due to indigency. The first appeal after a trial conviction is granted as a matter of right in California (P). However, Douglas (D) was denied the appointment of counsel to prosecute the appeal. The denial came after the appellate court had reviewed the transcript and determined that appointed counsel would not be of help to either Douglas (D) or the court. The decision was in line with a state rule providing for this procedure.

ISSUE: Is an indigent entitled to appointed counsel to assist in preparation of an appeal from a state criminal conviction where the appeal is granted to all defendants as a manner of right?

HOLDING AND DECISION: (Douglas, J.) Yes. In spite of California's (P) otherwise forward-looking favorable treatment of indigents, the problem presented by this case is the same as that presented by *Griffin v. Illinois,* 351 U.S. 12 (1956) (i.e., discrimination against the indigent). By the system employed, only a defendant affluent enough to retain counsel will obtain a full judicial review of his conviction. The indigent is entitled to no more than a review of the bare transcript by the appellate court. Not all appealable issues will appear on the face of a transcript. While the Fourteenth Amendment does not demand absolute equality, due process cannot be denied by "invidious discrimination." While the rich man can employ counsel to focus on appealable issues and to raise hidden objections to the conduct of the trial, the indigent is denied this same right. Our decision is not directed toward discretionary appeals, but toward appeals granted as a matter of right to all defendants. In such an instance, the indigent is entitled to appointed counsel.

DISSENT: (Harlan, J.) The majority appears to rely on both the Equal Protection Clause and the Due Process Clause of the Fourteenth Amendment. I do not think the former

is applicable or the latter violated in this case. The Equal Protection Clause prohibits discrimination between rich and poor "as such." The California (P) procedure affords everyone the right to appeal and to transcript of the trial. The difference comes in determining whether appointed counsel is necessary. California (P) has determined appointed counsel is not necessary in nonmeritorious cases. To compel counsel in all cases is to say that the State is obligated to provide absolute equality of all services which is both an impossibility and not mandated by the Equal Protection Clause. In *Griffin v. Illinois,* this Court, while finding that a transcript must be furnished to the indigent appellant, also said that the State could find other means of affording adequate and effective appellate review to indigent defendants. This is what California (P) has done and yet the majority strikes down the procedure California (P) has apparently gone beyond what this Court has recently required for indigents in federal courts, yet it has been found insufficient. A state can legitimately advance its own economic interests in the face of needless expense. That is what California (P) has done. The indigent is not denied appellate review or counsel in a meritorious case, but the State need not fund frivolous appeals.

▶ ANALYSIS

Some commentators have viewed the *Douglas* decision as a precursor to a requirement for appointed counsel whenever retained counsel is permitted. In fact, some lower courts (not a majority) have held that the difference between appeals of right and discretionary appeals is not a barrier to the right to appointive counsel. However, the weight of the commentaries appears to favor viewing the *Douglas-Griffin* decisions as interposing the right to counsel only where the lack of such counsel, in relation to retained counsel cases, works an inequality so significant as to amount to fundamental unfairness. On that basis, the right to counsel on a discretionary appeal is not found since such appeals rarely delve into new ground not covered in the first appeal and involve broad policy decisions fully developed in the first appeal.

Quicknotes

EQUAL PROTECTION CLAUSE A constitutional provision that each person be guaranteed the same protection of the laws enjoyed by other persons in like circumstances.

INDIGENT A person who is poor and thus is unable to obtain counsel to defend himself in a criminal proceeding and for whom counsel must be appointed.

INVIDIOUS DISCRIMINATION Unequal treatment of a class of persons that is particularly malicious or hostile.

Ross v. Moffitt

Forgery convict (P) v. Court (D)

417 U.S. 600 (1974).

NATURE OF CASE: Appeal of decision granting a writ of habeas corpus.

FACT SUMMARY: Ross (P) wanted the state to provide him an attorney to appeal his convictions to the state supreme court and the United States Supreme Court.

🏛 RULE OF LAW
The states do not have to provide attorneys to indigent defendants for appeals beyond the appeal granted as a matter of right.

FACTS: Ross (P) was convicted of forgery in both Mecklenberg County and in Guilford County, North Carolina. He wanted the state to provide him with an attorney to assist him in seeking discretionary review in the state supreme court of the Mecklenberg County conviction and he also wanted court-appointed counsel to prepare a writ of certiorari to the U.S. Supreme Court for the Guilford County conviction. Ross (P) was represented by the public defender in the state supreme court in his appeal of the Guilford County conviction. When the state refused to honor his request, he sought a writ of habeas corpus in federal court, claiming the right to have counsel provided for him by the state. North Carolina authorizes appointment of counsel for a convicted defendant appealing to the intermediate court of appeals, but not for a defendant who seeks either discretionary review in the state supreme court or a writ of certiorari in the U.S. Supreme Court. The U.S. court of appeals ruled that under the rationale of *Douglas v. California*, 372 U.S. 353 (1963), the state was required to provide counsel for Ross (P) in both cases.

ISSUE: Are states required to provide indigent convicted defendants with counsel in making discretionary appeals to state and federal appellate courts?

HOLDING AND DECISION: (Rehnquist, J.) No. The Court held that the Due Process and Equal Protection Clauses do not require that the state provide a convicted indigent defendant with counsel for appeals beyond the one granted as a matter of right by the states. There is no question that under the Due Process Clause the states must provide an indigent defendant with counsel at his trial, but the nature of appellate review is materially different from the trial court. The convicted defendant is no longer trying to protect himself from having the state prove him guilty of some crime, but is trying, instead, to overturn a finding of guilt made by a judge or jury. Just because the state has provided appellate courts doesn't mean that a state must provide counsel to indigent defendants at every stage of appellate review. The Court stated that the fact that some people have enough money to obtain counsel in making

discretionary appeals doesn't mean that the Equal Protection Clause requires that all defendants be provided with the same opportunity. The fact that a particular service might be a benefit to an indigent defendant does not mean that the service is constitutionally required. Ross (P) had counsel in making his appeal to the intermediate court of appeals in the state and the state is not required to provide counsel for any further appeals. The decision of the court of appeals was, therefore, reversed.

DISSENT: (Douglas, J.) The right to seek discretionary review is a substantial right grounded upon concepts of fairness and equality. In discretionary review, an attorney can be of significant assistance to an accused who is indigent.

▶ ANALYSIS

The Supreme Court has refused to appoint counsel for persons seeking to file petitions for certiorari with that court and, as pointed out in this case, has refused to require the states to provide counsel for indigents appealing to the Supreme Court. Up until this case was decided it wasn't clear how far the Supreme Court was willing to extend the ruling in the *Douglas* case. Many commentators have felt that under the Equal Protection Clause the state was required to provide counsel for indigents in all cases where more affluent defendants had a right to be represented by counsel. This case clearly points out that equal protection doesn't require that poor defendants be treated just like rich defendants in all instances.

■■■

Quicknotes

CERTIORARI A discretionary writ issued by a superior court to an inferior court in order to review the lower court's decisions; the Supreme Court's writ ordering such review.

EQUAL PROTECTION CLAUSE A constitutional provision that each person be guaranteed the same protection of the laws enjoyed by other persons in like circumstances.

INDIGENT A person who is poor and thus is unable to obtain counsel to defend himself in a criminal proceeding and for whom counsel must be appointed.

RIGHT TO COUNSEL Right conferred by the Sixth Amendment that the accused shall be provided effective legal assistance in a criminal proceeding.

WRIT OF HABEAS CORPUS A proceeding in which a defendant brings a writ to compel a judicial determination of whether he is lawfully being held in custody.

■■■

Faretta v. California

Grand theft suspect (D) v. State (P)

422 U.S. 806 (1975).

NATURE OF CASE: Appeal of a conviction for grand theft.

FACT SUMMARY: Faretta (D) was charged with grand theft. Before and during trial, he moved to represent himself. The trial judge refused, and he was convicted.

> ## 🏛 RULE OF LAW
> A state may not constitutionally impose a lawyer on a defendant who wishes to represent himself, so long as the defendant has made a knowing and intelligent waiver of his right to a lawyer.

FACTS: Faretta (D) was charged with grand theft. Several weeks before the date of his trial, Faretta (D) requested that he be permitted to defend himself. The trial judge, in a preliminary ruling, accepted Faretta's (D) waiver of counsel. Several weeks later, but still before trial, the judge held a sua sponte hearing to determine Faretta's (D) ability to conduct his own defense, and decided on the basis of Faretta's (D) answers to questions on state law that Faretta (D) had not made a knowing and intelligent waiver of his right to assistance of counsel. The trial judge ruled that Faretta (D) had no constitutional right to conduct his own defense and appointed a public defender to represent him. Faretta (D) was convicted and sentenced to prison. This decision was affirmed by the court of appeals, and the state supreme court refused to hear the case. The U.S. Supreme Court granted certiorari.

ISSUE: Can a state constitutionally impose a lawyer on a defendant who wishes to represent himself, if the defendant has made a knowing and intelligent waiver of his right to a lawyer?

HOLDING AND DECISION: (Stewart, J.) No. A state may not constitutionally impose a lawyer on a defendant who wishes to represent himself so long as the defendant has made a knowing and intelligent waiver of his right to a lawyer. The rationale for this rule lies within the structure of the Sixth Amendment in that it is consistent with the Sixth Amendment's right to make a personal defense. Here, Faretta (D) was literate and competent, and knowingly exercised his free will to make a choice to represent himself. His level of legal knowledge was not relevant to an assessment of his knowing exercise of the right to defend himself. Vacated.

DISSENT: (Burger, C.J.) Society has an interest in ensuring that trials are fair, and permitting an ill-advised defendant to represent himself undercuts that interest. Moreover, the "right" recognized here is found nowhere in the Constitution.

DISSENT: (Blackmun, J.) The questions raised today by this Court's opinion as to the standards of waiver by a pro se defendant will haunt the trial of every defendant who seeks to assert the right of self-representation.

▶ ANALYSIS

The right of an accused to proceed pro se is a constitutional right. Moreover, on the federal level, it is a statutory right as well. However, this right is qualified by the requirement that a waiver of counsel is, taking into account all of the circumstances, knowingly and intelligently made. The trial judge should himself ask the accused about the circumstances of the waiver. If a defendant has successfully waived his right to counsel, a written memorial of this should be made. (Wright, Fed. Prac. & Proc., Vol. 3, at 213–216.)

■=■

Quicknotes

CERTIORARI A discretionary writ issued by a superior court to an inferior court in order to review the lower court's decisions; the Supreme Court's writ ordering such review.

KNOWING AND INTELLIGENT WAIVER The intentional or voluntary forfeiture of a recognized right.

PRO SE An individual appearing on his own behalf.

SIXTH AMENDMENT Provides the right to a speedy trial by impartial jury, the right to be informed of the accusation, to confront witnesses and to have the assistance of counsel in all criminal prosecutions.

■=■

Strickland v. Washington

Defense attorney (D) v. Criminal defendant (P)

466 U.S. 668 (1984).

NATURE OF CASE: Review of order granting writ of habeas corpus.

FACT SUMMARY: Washington (P), in a federal habeas proceeding, contended that, in a capital sentence hearing, he had been denied effective assistance of counsel.

🏛 RULE OF LAW
At a capital sentence hearing, a Sixth Amendment violation occurs only if counsel's performance was deficient and such deficiency resulted in actual prejudice.

FACTS: Washington (P) went on a crime spree that resulted in three deaths. He was charged with numerous offenses, including burglary, kidnapping, and murder. Against his attorney's wishes, he confessed. Also against his attorney's advice, he waived a jury. Finally, he pleaded guilty on all counts, again against his attorney's advice. At the sentence hearing, his attorney stressed Washington's (P) absence of a prior criminal record, his generally good character, and alleged mental disturbance due to poor economic circumstances. He did not introduce character witnesses. He also did not introduce psychiatric testimony, as he had not been able to find a mental health professional who would testify that Washington (P) was mentally disturbed. The judge, citing numerous aggravating circumstances due to the gruesome nature of the murders, imposed the death sentence. The Florida Supreme Court affirmed. Washington (P) petitioned for a writ of habeas corpus. The district court denied relief, but the Eleventh Circuit reversed. The U.S. Supreme Court granted review.

ISSUE: At a capital sentence hearing, will a Sixth Amendment violation occur only if counsel's performance was deficient and such deficiency resulted in actual prejudice?

HOLDING AND DECISION: (O'Connor, J.) Yes. At a capital sentence hearing, a Sixth Amendment violation occurs only if counsel's performance was deficient and such deficiency resulted in actual prejudice. The Sixth Amendment's right to counsel envisions effective assistance of counsel; ineffective assistance is tantamount to no assistance. The purpose of assistance of counsel is to ensure a fair trial. Consequently, ineffectiveness of counsel is that type of ineffectiveness that renders a trial unfair. The proper standard for evaluating effectiveness is that counsel will be considered ineffective if counsel's performance is so deficient that counsel was not functioning as counsel. Further, such deficiency must result in prejudice, as an absence of prejudice removes concerns of trial fairness. Exactly what constitutes a deficient performance by counsel cannot be set out in specific guidelines; rather, counsel's performance must be viewed against

professional standards, taking into account the facts reasonably available to counsel at the time of his tactical decisions. It must be emphasized that counsel's competence is to be presumed, and counsel's performance should not be second-guessed with the benefit of hindsight not available to counsel at the time of his decisions. With respect to prejudice, prejudice will not be presumed in other than a narrow set of circumstances, such as corruption or conflict of interest. Applying the foregoing standards to the present case, it is clear that Washington's (P) counsel's performance was far from ineffective. Operating under severe disadvantages, not the least being Washington's (P) habitual rejection of his advice, counsel made certain tactical decisions with respect to evidence and argument that were quite reasonable. Beyond this, the circumstances were so aggravating that it is unlikely that prejudice could have resulted from ineffectiveness even had it occurred. Therefore, no Sixth Amendment violation occurred in this case. Reversed.

CONCURRENCE AND DISSENT: (Brennan, J.) The death penalty is in all circumstances cruel and unusual punishment forbidden by the Eighth and Fourteenth Amendments. Thus, the death sentence here should be vacated and the case remanded for further proceedings. The standards set forth by the Court in this decision, however, do provide helpful guidance when considering claims of ineffectiveness of counsel, the standard being "that of reasonably effective assistance."

DISSENT: (Marshall, J.) The majority opinion is excessively deferential to counsel in several respects. The standard for competency is too lenient and the level of prejudice that needs to be shown for a Sixth Amendment violation to occur excessive. Finally, the Court errs in applying the same standard to capital cases as less crucial cases.

▶ ANALYSIS

Prior to the present opinion, lower courts had grappled with the same issue, reaching widely varied results. Both objective and subjective standards of competence had been applied. With respect to prejudice, some courts had employed the "outcome-determinative" test the Court used. Others had held prejudice to be presumed.

■=■

Quicknotes

EIGHTH AMENDMENT The Eighth Amendment to the federal Constitution prohibits the imposition of excessive bail, fines, and cruel and unusual punishment.

Continued on next page.

FOURTEENTH AMENDMENT Declares that no state shall make or enforce any law that shall abridge the privileges and immunities of citizens of the United States. No state shall deny to any person within its jurisdiction the equal protection of the laws.

INEFFECTIVE ASSISTANCE OF COUNSEL Whether an attorney's representation so undermined the adjudicatory process that the result cannot be determined to be just.

SIXTH AMENDMENT Provides the right to a speedy and public trial by impartial jury, the right to be informed of the accusation, the right to confront witnesses, and the right to have the assistance of counsel in all criminal prosecutions.

WRIT OF HABEAS CORPUS A proceeding in which a defendant brings a writ to compel a judicial determination of whether he is lawfully being held in custody.

■══■

Plea Bargaining and Guilty Pleas

Quick Reference Rules of Law

Brady v. United States

Kidnapping suspect (D) v. Federal government (P)

397 U.S. 742 (1970).

NATURE OF CASE: Petition for collateral relief attacking conviction of kidnapping.

FACT SUMMARY: Brady (D) claimed that rather than risk trial, and a possible death sentence, he pled guilty.

🏛 RULE OF LAW
Although a federal penal statute that permits imposition of the death sentence only upon a jury's recommendation is unconstitutional because it makes the risk of death the price of a jury trial, not every guilty plea entered under the act is invalidated simply upon an assertion that the defendant pled guilty from a fear of death.

FACTS: In 1959, Brady (D) was charged with kidnapping in violation of 18 U.S.C. § 1201(a). The section provided for a maximum penalty of death upon conviction if the jury should so recommend. At first, Brady (D) elected to plead not guilty and made no serious attempt to waive a jury trial. Upon learning that a codefendant would be available to testify against him, Brady (D) changed his plea to guilty. His plea was accepted after the trial judge questioned Brady (D) as to its voluntariness. In 1967, Brady (D) petitioned for collateral post-conviction relief, claiming that § 1201(a) operated to coerce his confession. In 1968, the U.S. Supreme Court, in *United States v. Jackson*, 390 U.S. 570 (1968), held that § 1201(a) was unconstitutional in that it "needlessly penalize(d)" the assertion of the Sixth Amendment right to jury trial and the Fifth Amendment right not to plead guilty.

ISSUE: Does the decision in *United States v. Jackson* require the invalidation of every plea of guilty entered under 18 U.S.C. § 1201(a), at least when the fear of death is shown to have been a factor in the plea?

HOLDING AND DECISION: (White, J.) No. Although *Jackson* prohibited the imposition of death under 18 U.S.C. § 1201(a), it did not fashion a new standard to supplant the test that guilty pleas are valid if both "voluntary" and "intelligent." Even assuming that Brady (D) would not have pled guilty but for the death penalty provision, this does not prove that the entering of the plea was an involuntary act. There is no claim here that Brady's (D) plea was induced by actual or threatened physical harm or by mental coercion or that he did not rationally weigh the advantages of not going to trial. There is nothing here to differentiate Brady (D) from the defendant who is advised to plead guilty out of a desire to get more lenient treatment from the judge or to get favorable plea bargaining. Such plea inducements conform with accepted notions of conserving judicial time and resources and with commencing with the rehabilitative goals of the criminal justice system. A contrary holding would require government to forbid guilty pleas altogether. Brady's (D) plea was also intelligently made. Although § 1201(a) was later invalidated, a defendant is not entitled to withdraw his plea because he discovers the statute is unconstitutional long after his plea has been accepted simply because he miscalculated. The truth or reliability of Brady's (D) plea is not impugned by *Jackson*. A word of caution: not all forms of plea negotiation will be upheld.

▶ ANALYSIS

While the Court was not inclined to expand the scope of the voluntariness standard, it indicated, in *Boykin v. Alabama*, 395 U.S. 238 (1969), a willingness to provide for more controls over the acceptance, by the trial court, of a "voluntary" plea. The Court held that a guilty plea is not presumed voluntary where the judge does not question the defendant concerning his plea and the defendant does not address the court, and the trial judge must employ great care in canvassing the plea with the accused to make sure he completely understands what the plea connotes and its consequences.

■■■

Quicknotes

18 U.S.C. § 1201(a) Provides that discretion for assigning the death penalty rest with the jury; later, this section was invalidated.

COERCED CONFESSION A statement made by a person charged with the commission of a criminal offense, acknowledging his guilt in respect to the charged offense, that was made when the confessor's free will was overcome as a result of threats, promises, or undue influence, and that is inadmissible at trial.

■■■

North Carolina v. Alford

State (P) v. Plea-bargaining murder suspect (D)

400 U.S. 25 (1970).

NATURE OF CASE: Appeal from a conviction for second-degree murder.

FACT SUMMARY: Alford (D), although still claiming his innocence, pleaded guilty and was convicted of second-degree murder.

🏛 RULE OF LAW
An assertion of innocence by a defendant does not, of itself, render a plea of guilty invalid.

FACTS: Faced with strong evidence of guilt and no substantial evidentiary support for the claim of innocence, Alford's (D) attorney recommended that he plead guilty. The prosecutor agreed to accept a plea of guilty to a charge of second-degree murder, and Alford (D) pleaded guilty to the reduced charge. Alford (D), however, maintained that he had not committed the murder but that he was pleading guilty because he faced the threat of the death penalty if he did not do so. The court sentenced Alford (D) to the maximum penalty allowed, and Alford (D) sought post-conviction relief in state court, which was refused. After two unsuccessful petitions for a writ of habeas corpus, the court of appeals reversed the conviction on the ground that Alford's (D) guilty plea was made involuntarily, and the state appealed.

ISSUE: Does a defendant's assertion of innocence negate any admission of guilt and render his guilty plea invalid?

HOLDING AND DECISION: (White, J.) No. The Constitution does not bar imposition of a prison sentence upon an accused who is unwilling expressly to admit his guilt but who, faced with grim alternatives, is willing to waive his trial and accept the sentence. The standard remains whether the plea represents a voluntary and intelligent choice among the alternative courses of action open to the defendant. Here, confronted with the choice between a trial for first-degree murder, on the one hand, and a plea of guilty to second-degree murder, on the other, Alford (D) quite reasonably chose the latter and thereby limited the maximum penalty to a 30-year term. That he would not have pleaded except for the opportunity to limit the possible penalty does not necessarily demonstrate that the plea of guilty was not the product of a free and rational choice, especially where the defendant was represented by competent counsel whose advice was that the plea would be to the defendant's advantage. Vacated.

▶ ANALYSIS

The problem with Alford's (D) assertion of innocence here is that it was not in accord with his actions. According to confirmed testimony, Alford (D) left his home with his gun stating his intention to kill and he later declared that he had carried out his intention.

■■■■

Quicknotes

SECOND-DEGREE MURDER The unlawful killing of another person, without premeditation, and characterized by either an intent to kill or by a reckless disregard for human life.

WRIT OF HABEAS CORPUS A proceeding in which a defendant brings a writ to compel a judicial determination of whether he is lawfully being held in custody.

■■■■

Bordenkircher v. Hayes

State (P) v. Forgery convict (D)

434 U.S. 357 (1978).

NATURE OF CASE: Appeal from a criminal conviction and penalty enhancement.

FACT SUMMARY: The prosecutor informed Hayes (D) that he would seek an indictment under the Kentucky Habitual Criminal Act if he did not plead guilty to the charge of uttering a forged instrument; Hayes (D) pled innocent, a jury convicted him, and his sentence was enhanced when the prosecutor initiated the Habitual Criminal indictment.

🏛 RULE OF LAW
A prosecutor can attempt to gain a defendant's assent to a plea bargain by informing the defendant that more severe charges will be brought if no bargain is struck.

FACTS: Hayes (D), who was charged with uttering a forged instrument (for $88.30), faced a sentence of two to ten years if convicted. The prosecutor offered a five-year sentence in return for a guilty plea and told Hayes (D) that refusal to take the "bargain" would result in his seeking an additional indictment under the Kentucky Habitual Criminal Act, which makes a life sentence mandatory if there are two prior felony convictions. When Hayes (D) declined the plea bargain, he was subjected to the additional indictment and sentenced to life imprisonment under the Habitual Criminal Act, after having been found guilty of the uttering charge. The two previous felonies in which Hayes (D) was involved had never resulted in his imprisonment; one was a rape charge reduced to a plea of detaining a female, and the other was a robbery conviction resulting in five years in a reformatory. Finding the prosecutor to have acted vindictively in securing the second indictment, the cour of appeals reversed Hayes's (D) conviction for violation of due process of law.

ISSUE: Is it constitutionally permissible for a prosecutor to try to influence a defendant to accept a plea bargain by informing him that more severe charges will be brought if it is refused?

HOLDING AND DECISION: (Stewart, J.) Yes. It is constitutionally permissible for a prosecutor to try to influence a defendant to accept a plea bargain by informing him that more severe charges will be brought if it is refused. As the constitutionality and utility of plea bargaining have been recognized, there is no bar to the prosecutor's use of the possibility of more severe charges being brought for purposes of persuading a defendant to accept a plea bargain. As long as the defendant is advised that the bringing of additional charges will accompany his refusal to bargain, the situation becomes similar to that where the prosecutor offers to drop a charge as part of the plea bargain. If plea bargaining is a recognized process, neither can be forbidden simply because the charging decision is influenced by what a prosecutor hopes to gain in plea bargaining negotiations. In accepting plea bargaining, it is implicit that there is acceptance of the notion that the prosecutor's interest is to persuade the defendant not to exercise his right to plead not guilty. As long as the prosecutor has probable cause to believe the accused committed the offense, and he properly exercises his discretion, decisions not being influenced by standards of race, religion, etc., there is no due process violation. Reversed.

DISSENT: (Blackmun, J.) Past cases indicate that prosecutorial vindictiveness resulting from a defendant's exercise of his rights is a constitutionally impermissible basis for discretionary actions. Here, it is admitted that such vindictiveness was the sole reason for the new indictment.

DISSENT: (Powell, J.) Discretion used to deter the exercise of constitutional rights is not constitutionally exercised. The prosecutor's initial failure to charge indicates his own appreciation of the unreasonableness of placing Hayes (D) in jeopardy of life imprisonment when many murderers and rapists face lighter sentences.

▶ ANALYSIS

The case in which the Court first recognized plea bargaining as a legitimate practice was *Brady v. United States*, 397 U.S. 742 (1969). While the majority here suggests that such an acceptance implies sanctioning of prosecutorial use of charging powers to influence a defendant to plead guilty, the *Brady* decision specifically states that it makes no reference to such use by the prosecutor or a similar use by the judge of his sentencing power.

▬▬

Quicknotes

INDICTMENT A formal written accusation made by the prosecution to the grand jury under oath, charging an individual with a criminal offense.

PLEA BARGAIN An agreement between a criminal defendant and a prosecutor, which is submitted to the court for approval, generally involving the defendant's pleading guilty to a lesser charge or count in exchange for a more lenient sentence.

▬▬

Santobello v. New York

Plea-negotiating convict (D) v. State (P)

404 U.S. 257 (1971).

NATURE OF CASE: Appeal from a felony conviction and one-year prison sentence.

FACT SUMMARY: Santobello (D) challenged his conviction and sentence, based on the breach of a commitment by the prosecutor made in the course of plea bargaining.

🏛 RULE OF LAW
Where the state fails to keep a commitment concerning the sentence recommendation on a guilty plea, a new trial is required.

FACTS: Indicted on two felony counts, Santobello (D) negotiated with the assistant district attorney and agreed to plead guilty to a lesser included offense, provided the prosecutor agreed to make no recommendation as to the sentence. Following procedural delays between Santobello's (D) conviction and the imposition of sentence, during which time both defense counsel and prosecutor were replaced, the new prosecutor at the sentence hearing requested the maximum sentence of one year. The trial judge imposed the maximum sentence and Santobello (D) appealed.

ISSUE: Does the state's failure to keep a commitment concerning the sentence recommended on a guilty plea require a new trial?

HOLDING AND DECISION: (Burger, C.J.) Yes. The state's failure to keep a commitment concerning the sentence recommended on a guilty plea requires a new trial. The disposition of criminal charges by agreement between the prosecutor and the accused, sometimes loosely called "plea bargaining," is an essential component of the administration of justice. Properly administered, it is to be encouraged. It leads to prompt and largely final disposition of most criminal cases. However, these considerations presuppose fairness in securing agreement between an accused and a prosecutor. When a plea rests in any significant degree on a promise or agreement of the prosecutor, so that it can be said to be part of the inducement or consideration, such promise must be fulfilled. Here, on the record Santobello (D) "bargained" and negotiated for a particular plea in order to secure dismissal of more serious charges, but also on condition that no sentence recommendation would be made by the prosecutor. That a breach of agreement was inadvertent does not lessen its impact. We conclude that the interests of justice and appropriate recognition of the duties of the prosecution in relation to promises made in the negotiation of pleas of guilty will be best served by remanding the case to the state courts for further consideration. Judgment vacated and case remanded for reconsideration.

CONCURRENCE: (Douglas, J.) A sentence must be vacated when a prosecutor fails to honor a "plea bargain." Upon such failure, it is then for the state court to determine in view of the facts of each case whether due process requires that there be specific performance of the plea bargain or that the defendant be provided with the option to go to trial on the original charges.

CONCURRENCE AND DISSENT: (Marshall, J.) When a prosecutor breaks a plea bargain, they weaken the basis for the waiver of constitutional rights that is implicit in the plea. This provides sufficient reason to rescind the plea.

▌ ANALYSIS

The Court here, in not only the majority but also the concurring and dissenting opinions, affirmed both the constitutionality and viability of modern plea bargaining. What is noteworthy here is that the Court, per Justice Douglas, applied the common law principles of contract law, rather than criminal law, in fashioning the "remedies" available to the defendant when the prosecutor "breaches" his commitment (i.e., specific performance of the bargain, or rescission of the entire agreement, including the guilty plea).

■=■

Quicknotes

PLEA BARGAIN An agreement between a criminal defendant and a prosecutor, which is submitted to the court for approval, generally involving the defendant's pleading guilty to a lesser charge or count in exchange for a more lenient sentence.

■=■

United States v. Brechner

Federal government (P) v. Accused tax evader (D)

99 F.3d 96 (2d Cir. 1996).

NATURE OF CASE: Appeal from finding that the Government (P) was required to move for downward departure at sentencing.

FACT SUMMARY: Brechner (D) negotiated for a downward departure in sentencing, conditional on his complete cooperation with law enforcement authorities.

🏛 RULE OF LAW
A slight breach in an agreement to cooperate may be material if it undermines the credibility of the defendant as a potential government witness.

FACTS: Brechner (D), a manufacturer of stuffed toy animals, was investigated by tax officials and agreed to plead guilty to income tax evasion. Through counsel, Brechner (D) contacted the prosecution and offered to provide information about bribes paid to a corrupt bank officer. The Government (P) agreed to move for a downward departure at sentencing if it determined that Brechner (D) had provided complete, accurate, and truthful information. At a debriefing, Brechner (D) denied receiving kickbacks. His lawyer then asked to speak with him in private. After a break, Brechner (D) acknowledged receiving the payments, and provided details. At sentencing, the Government (P) refused to move for a downward departure; but the court determined that the alleged breach of the cooperation agreement was not material.

ISSUE: May a slight breach in an agreement to cooperate be material if it undermines the credibility of the defendant as a potential government witness?

HOLDING AND DECISION: (Leval, J.) Yes. A slight breach in an agreement to cooperate may be material if it undermines the credibility of the defendant as a potential Government (P) witness. By lying to the Government (P) during the period of his cooperation, Brechner (D) made it impossible for the prosecution to argue at a future trial that he had turned over a new leaf and that his testimony was believable. The disclosure of his lies to the bank officer's counsel would have invited the powerful argument that Brechner (D) was no more trustworthy as a witness than as a crook. The reversal of his lie was obviously not due to honesty but to his attorney's warning about his own self-interest. Brechner's (D) conduct provided a good-faith basis for the Government's (P) refusal to move for a downward departure. The sentence of the district court is vacated and the matter remanded for resentencing.

▶ ANALYSIS

Although the agreement between Brechner (D) and the prosecution expressly provided that the Assistant U.S. Attorney prosecuting the case retained discretion to determine if Brechner (D) had fully cooperated, the district court judge found that his "substantial assistance to the investigation" was sufficient to require a motion for downward departure. The court of appeals emphasized the significance of the damage Brechner's (D) lies had done to his credibility, noting that he was the Government's (P) sole witness in the contemplated prosecution of the bank officer.

■═■

Quicknotes

MATERIAL BREACH Breach of a contract's terms by one party that is so substantial as to relieve the other party from its obligations pursuant thereto.

■═■

McMann v. Richardson

State (P) v. Coerced confessor (D)

397 U.S. 759 (1970).

NATURE OF CASE: Petition for writ of habeas corpus in federal court collaterally attacking state court conviction.

FACT SUMMARY: In his petition, Richardson (D) alleged that he would not have pled guilty at his trial but for fear that a coerced confession would be introduced into evidence.

🏛 RULE OF LAW
A defendant, who in a habeas corpus petition alleges that he pled guilty because of a prior coerced confession, is not, without more, entitled to a hearing on his petition for habeas corpus.

FACTS: Prior to *Jackson v. Denno*, 378 U.S. 368 (1964) (which held unconstitutional a New York procedure that required the trial judge, when a confession was offered and a prima facie case of voluntariness established, to submit the issue of voluntariness of confession to the jury without himself finally resolving disputed issues of fact and determining whether or not the confession was voluntary), Richardson (D), on advice of counsel, entered a plea of guilty in a New York court. After conviction, Richardson (D) filed a petition for a writ of habeas corpus in which he alleged that he had pled guilty because he was afraid that a coerced confession he had made would be introduced at trial against him. The Second Circuit Court of Appeals held that he was entitled to a hearing on his petition because of *Jackson v. Denno*.

ISSUE: After conviction on a plea of guilty, is a defendant entitled to a hearing and to relief if his factual claims are accepted, when his petition for habeas corpus alleges that his confession was, in fact, coerced and that it motivated his plea?

HOLDING AND DECISION: (White, J.) No. After conviction on a plea of guilty, a defendant is not entitled to a hearing and to relief if his factual claims are accepted, when his petition for habeas corpus alleges that his confession was, in fact, coerced and that it motivated his plea. If a defendant thinks his confession to be involuntary, and hence inadmissible against him at trial, he should not enter a guilty plea. Here, Richardson (D) is attempting to accept the benefits of a guilty plea in state court, and also to pursue his coerced confession claim in federal court. All that Richardson (D) is raising here is an assertion that his counsel mistakenly assessed the admissibility of Richardson's (D) confession under the then-applicable law. The question is whether Richardson's (D) counsel gave Richardson (D) competent advice; uncertainty is always inherent in predicting court decisions. The decision to plead guilty before all the evidence is in involves the making of a difficult judgment

and one that the appellate court should not lightly second-guess. Whether or not the guilty plea was entered before or after *Jackson v. Denno*, 378 U.S. 368 (1964), the question of the validity of the plea still remains: was it a voluntary and intelligent act of the defendant? Richardson (D) cannot allege gross error on the part of his counsel for, prior to *Jackson v. Denno*, the law was settled adversely against Richardson (D); the decision in *Jackson v. Denno* could not be readily anticipated. Because Richardson (D) pled guilty, his prior confession is not the basis for the judgment. Reversed.

▶ *ANALYSIS*

The Court, in *Tollett v. Henderson*, 411 U.S. 258 (1973), reiterated its decision in *McMann* by holding that where a defendant pled guilty on advice of counsel, he is not entitled to collateral relief in federal court simply because, unknown to himself or his counsel, the indicting grand jury was unconstitutionally selected. The Court stated that a guilty plea may not be vacated merely because the trial judge failed to advise the defendant of "every conceivable constitutional plea in abatement he might have to the charge, no matter how peripheral such a plea might be to the normal focus of counsel's inquiry [here, a factual one]. . . . Often the interests of the accused are not advanced by challenges that would only delay the inevitable date of prosecution or by contesting all guilt. . . . "

Quicknotes

COERCED CONFESSION A statement made by a person charged with the commission of a criminal offense, acknowledging his guilt in respect to the charged offense, that was made when the confessor's free will was overcome as a result of threats, promises, or undue influence, and that is inadmissible at trial.

PRIMA FACIE CASE An action where the plaintiff introduces sufficient evidence to submit the issue to the judge or jury for determination.

WRIT OF HABEAS CORPUS A proceeding in which a defendant brings a writ to compel a judicial determination of whether he is lawfully being held in custody.

The Trial Process

Quick Reference Rules of Law

Duncan v. Louisiana

Simple battery convict (D) v. State (P)

391 U.S. 145 (1968).

NATURE OF CASE: Appeal from conviction for simple battery.

FACT SUMMARY: Duncan (D) was convicted without the right to a jury trial of simple battery, a crime punishable by two years imprisonment and a $300 fine.

🏛 RULE OF LAW
Fourteenth Amendment due process guarantees a right of jury trial in all state criminal cases "which, were they to be tried in federal court, would come within the Sixth Amendment's guarantee."

FACTS: Duncan (D), a black youth, was convicted in Louisiana of simple battery and sentenced to 60 days imprisonment and to pay a fine of $150. Before his trial, Duncan (D) requested a jury trial but his request was denied. Under Louisiana law, a jury trial is guaranteed only in cases where capital punishment or imprisonment at hard labor may be imposed. Simple battery, however, is a misdemeanor punishable only with up to two years imprisonment and a $300 fine. After his conviction, Duncan (D) appealed on the basis that denial of a jury trial violated his Sixth and Fourteenth Amendment rights. After the Louisiana Supreme Court upheld his conviction, Duncan (D) appealed to the U.S. Supreme Court.

ISSUE: Does the Constitution impose a duty upon the state to give a jury trial in any criminal case, regardless of the seriousness of the crime or the punishment that may be imposed?

HOLDING AND DECISION: (White, J.) Yes. Fourteenth Amendment due process guarantees a right of jury trial in all state criminal cases "which, were they to be tried in a federal court, would come within the Sixth Amendment's guarantee." Furthermore, any "serious" crime tried in a federal court comes within the Sixth Amendment's guarantee of a jury trial. Trial by jury in such "serious" criminal cases is so "fundamental to the American scheme of justice" (i.e., as a defense against "arbitrary law enforcement") that it cannot be denied by state courts either. Of course, the possible penalty for a particular crime is of major importance in determining if it is "serious." Here, however, the Court does not need to settle the "exact location" of the line between petty offenses and serious crimes. "It is sufficient for our purposes to hold that a crime punishable by two years in prison (as here) is, based on past and contemporary standards in this country, a serious crime and not a petty offense." As such, Duncan (D) should have received a jury trial. Reversed.

DISSENT: (Harlan, J.) "Due process of law" requires nothing more than that a criminal trial be fundamentally fair. Trial by jury is not the only fair means of resolving issues of fact. Even if a jury trial were a fundamental right in some criminal cases, there is no fundamental rule saying that a simple battery is within the category of "jury crimes" rather than "petty crimes."

▶ ANALYSIS

This case illustrates the doctrine of "selective incorporation" of the Bill of Rights into the Fourteenth Amendment Due Process Clause. Under this doctrine, the Bill of Rights is incorporated by the Due Process Clause only to the extent that the Court decides that the protections and rights therein are "so essential to fundamental principles of due process of law, as to be preserved against both federal and state action" (*Bloom v. Illinois,* 391 U.S. 194 (1968)). A minority of the justices of the Supreme Court (especially Black and Douglas), though, have argued for "total incorporation." Note that the Court has only specifically found two of the guarantees of the Bill of Rights to be nonfundamental. The first is the Fifth Amendment right to indictment by grand jury (some states permit criminal prosecutions to proceed upon the filing of an information only). The second is the Eighth Amendment's guarantees regarding bail and fines.

━━━

Quicknotes

DUE PROCESS CLAUSE Clause found in the Fifth and Fourteenth Amendments to the United States Constitution providing that no person shall be deprived of "life, liberty, or property, without due process of law."

MISDEMEANOR Any offense that does not constitute a felony, which is generally less severe and for which a lesser punishment is imposed.

RIGHT TO JURY TRIAL The right guaranteed by the Sixth Amendment to the federal Constitution that in all criminal prosecutions the accused has a right to a trial by an impartial jury of the state and district in which the crime was allegedly committed.

━━━

Taylor v. Louisiana

Kidnapping convict (P) v. State (D)

419 U.S. 522 (1975).

NATURE OF CASE: Appeal from conviction for aggravated kidnapping.

FACT SUMMARY: Taylor (D), a male who was convicted of aggravated kidnapping, challenged the jury that convicted him on the ground that 53% of the eligible jurors in the community were women, but that 90% of those in the actual jury pool were men.

🏛 RULE OF LAW
Women as a class may not be excluded or given automatic exemptions from jury duty based solely on sex if the consequence is that criminal jury venires are almost totally male.

FACTS: Under Louisiana (P) law women were not selected for jury duty unless they had previously filed a written declaration of desire to serve. Taylor (D), a male, was charged with aggravated kidnapping and moved in the trial court to quash the petit jury venire on the ground that women were systematically excluded from the venire and that this deprived him of his constitutional right to a fair trial by a jury of a representative segment of the community. His motion was denied, and Taylor (D) was subsequently convicted and sentenced to death. The Louisiana Supreme Court affirmed. Taylor (D) appealed arguing that 53% of the eligible jurors in the community were women, but that 90% of those in the actual jury pool were men.

ISSUE: May women as a class be excluded or given automatic exemptions from jury duty based solely on sex if the consequence is that criminal jury venires are almost totally male?

HOLDING AND DECISION: (White, J.) No. Women as a class may not be excluded or given automatic exemptions from jury duty based solely on sex if the consequence is that criminal jury venires are almost totally male. While the Louisiana (P) jury system did not disqualify women from jury service, in operation its conceded effect was that only a very few women, greatly disproportionate to the number of eligible women, were called for jury service. While Taylor (D) was not a member of the excluded class, he had standing to raise the issue because his claim went to the community makeup of the jury and not just the exclusion of women. The American concept of the jury trial contemplates a jury drawn from a fair cross section of the community. To exclude a class of persons from the cross section of the community to create a fair jury requires more than just rational grounds; it cannot be argued that it would be too great a hardship on every woman to perform jury service. While petit juries must be drawn from a source fairly representative of the community, petit juries actually chosen need

not mirror the community or reflect the various distinctive groups in the population. All that is required is that the jury pool does not systematically exclude distinctive groups in the community so as to be unrepresentative. Reversed.

DISSENT: (Rehnquist, J.) It is not conceivable that the majority's decision is necessary to guard against oppressive or arbitrary law enforcement, or to prevent miscarriages of justice and to assure fair trials, especially when the criminal defendant makes no claims of prejudice or bias. The Court in its decision fails to provide any satisfactory explanation of the mechanism by which the Louisiana system undermines the prophylactic role of the jury, either in general or in this case. The Court's decision "smacks more of mysticism than of law."

▶ ANALYSIS

J. Marshall wrote: "A state cannot, consistent with due process, subject a defendant to indictment or trial by a jury that has been selected in an arbitrary and discriminatory manner, in violation of the Constitution and the laws of the United States. Illegal and unconstitutional jury selection procedures cast doubt on the integrity of the whole judicial process. They create the appearance of bias. . . . But the exclusion from jury service of a substantial and identifiable class of citizens has a potential impact that is too subtle and too pervasive to admit of confinement to particular issues or particular cases." *Peters v. Kiff,* 407 U.S. 493 (1972).

Quicknotes

RIGHT TO JURY TRIAL The right guaranteed by the Sixth Amendment to the federal Constitution that in all criminal prosecutions the accused has a right to a trial by an impartial jury of the state and district in which the crime was allegedly committed.

VENIRE A list of jurors called to serve for a particular term.

Ham v. South Carolina

Drug possession convict (D) v. State (P)

409 U.S. 524 (1973).

NATURE OF CASE: Appeal from a conviction for marijuana possession.

FACT SUMMARY: Ham (D) was convicted of marijuana possession but contended that the trial judge's refusal to examine jurors on voir dire as to possible prejudice against blacks violated Ham's (D) federal constitutional rights.

🏛 RULE OF LAW
Where the state creates a framework for the examination of jurors, the Due Process Clause of the Fourteenth Amendment requires that a defendant be permitted to have the jurors interrogated on the issue of racial bias.

FACTS: Ham (D) was convicted of marijuana possession and sentenced to 18 months' confinement. Prior to the trial judge's voir dire examination of prospective jurors, Ham's (D) lawyer requested that the judge ask the jurors four questions—two concerning racial prejudice, one relating to prejudice against beards, and one relating to pretrial publicity. The trial judge refused and, instead, posed questions required by the South Carolina code. These were general questions as to bias, prejudice, and partiality. A divided South Carolina Supreme Court affirmed, and the U.S. Supreme Court granted certiorari limited to the question of prejudice on voir dire.

ISSUE: Does the Due Process Clause of the Fourteenth Amendment require that a defendant be permitted to have the jurors interrogated on the issue of racial bias where the state has created a framework for the examination of jurors?

HOLDING AND DECISION: (Rehnquist, J.) Yes. Where the state has created a framework for the examination of jurors, the Due Process Clause of the Fourteenth Amendment requires that a defendant be permitted to have the jurors interrogated on the issue of racial bias. A major purpose in adopting the Fourteenth Amendment was to prevent the states from invidiously discriminating on the basis of race. The Due Process Clause is designed to ensure essential fairness. Therefore, Ham (D) had the right to have the jurors interrogated on the issue of racial bias. However, the Due Process Clause permits a wide discretion as to the form and number of questions, and, thus, Ham's (D) particular questions did not have to be adopted. An inquiry into racial prejudice need not be in any particular form. Ham's (D) request to have a question put forth concerning prejudice against beards fails because it is not a constitutional violation. Reversed.

CONCURRENCE AND DISSENT: (Douglas, J.) The trial judge was constitutionally compelled to inquire into the possibility of racial prejudice on voir dire. In denying the defendant to probe the prejudices of prospective jurors concerning hair growth, the trial court judge denied the defendant his most effective means of voir dire examination.

▶ ANALYSIS

The Court, in recent years, has cast a stern eye on racial matters in jury selection. Peremptory challenges in particular have been closely scrutinized. The use of peremptories to exclude members of a certain race is, for the most part, not allowed.

■═■

Quicknotes

DUE PROCESS CLAUSE Clause found in the Fifth and Fourteenth Amendments to the United States Constitution providing that no person shall be deprived of "life, liberty, or property, without due process of law."

INVIDIOUS DISCRIMINATION Unequal treatment of a class of persons that is particularly malicious or hostile.

PEREMPTORY CHALLENGE The exclusion by a party to a lawsuit of a prospective juror without the need to specify a particular reason.

VOIR DIRE Examination of potential jurors on a case.

■═■

People v. Newton

State (P) v. Member of Black Panther Party (D)

Cal. Ct. of App., 8 Cal. App. 3d 359 (1970).

NATURE OF CASE: Preliminary jury selection for a trial on a charge of murder.

FACT SUMMARY: Excerpts from a transcript of the voir dire proceedings prior to the trial of murder suspect Newton (D), on the examination of a potential juror by the trial judge as well as the parties.

🏛 RULE OF LAW
Although a trial judge possesses the authority to conduct voir dire, the defense or prosecution may be permitted to participate prior to determining whether to challenge a juror for cause or exercise a peremptory challenge in cases where the possibility of pretrial impressions in prospective jurors is strong.

FACTS: Newton (D), a member of the Black Panther Party, was charged with murdering a white police officer, wounding another officer, and kidnapping a bystander. He testified that the first officer shot him in the stomach and that he did not recall anything after that. Due to the controversial nature and notoriety of the Black Panther Party as well as the extensive pretrial publicity that followed, the defense was concerned as to whether it could secure an impartial jury. During the course of the voir dire proceedings, the trial judge permitted defense counsel and the prosecution to alternatively question a potential juror regarding his pretrial biases of the defendant's culpability. As the result of his responses, the juror was dismissed by defense counsel on a challenge for cause.

ISSUE: Should the defense or prosecution be permitted to participate in voir dire proceedings prior to determining whether to challenge a juror for cause or exercise a peremptory challenge in cases where the possibility of pretrial impressions in prospective jurors is strong?

HOLDING AND DECISION: [Judge not stated in casebook excerpt.] Yes. Although a trial judge possesses the authority to conduct voir dire, the defense or prosecution may be permitted to participate prior to determining whether to challenge a juror for cause or exercise a peremptory challenge in cases where the possibility of pretrial impressions in prospective jurors is strong. The juror in question, Mr. Strauss, had a strong belief that Newton (D) was guilty, despite being informed by the trial judge at several points during the proceedings that the system of criminal justice in the United States provides a presumption of innocence until proven guilty. Upon questioning by defense counsel, the juror verbally retracted his statements and was further bolstered by additional inquiry from the prosecution into characterizing his opinions as neutral, permitting him to evade a challenge for cause from the defense.

However, the defense persisted and Strauss's biases were made clear, permitting the court to recognize the defense's challenge and dismiss him as a potential juror due to the fact that Strauss clearly believed that Newton (D) was guilty prior to the presentation of evidence in support of such an assertion. Conviction reversed on other grounds.

▎ ANALYSIS

A challenge for cause and peremptory challenges are used during jury selection to dismiss jurors; however, it is favorable for a party to dismiss a juror based on a challenge for cause as opposed to a peremptory challenge because the latter are limited in number. The primary benefit of a peremptory challenge is that the party making the challenge need not provide a rationale for dismissal, while a challenge for cause, to be granted, requires a satisfactory rationale as to the nature of the challenge. Note that since a reason is required, challenges for cause may be exercised whenever the rationale arises.

■══■

Quicknotes

CHALLENGE FOR CAUSE The right to refuse a jury seat to a prospective juror where that person possesses bias or other knowledge of the case that would impair the ability to render a fair verdict, predicated upon the showing by counsel of a compelling reason as to why that juror should be dismissed.

PEREMPTORY CHALLENGE A challenge issued by counsel during voir dire proceedings to refuse a jury seat to a prospective juror, for which no reason need be advanced other than the preference of counsel advocating exclusion.

VOIR DIRE A preliminary examination conducted by the court for the purpose of selecting prospective jurors to serve at trial.

■══■

United States v. Salamone

Federal government (P) v. Convicted violator of gun registration laws (D)

800 F.2d 1216 (3d Cir. 1986).

NATURE OF CASE: Appeal from conviction on charges of illegal gun possession and failure to register firearms.

FACT SUMMARY: The court granted the Government's (P) motion to dismiss a potential juror for cause on the basis of his former membership in the National Rifle Association (NRA).

🏛 RULE OF LAW
A potential juror may not be disqualified for cause based on his membership in an organization without an individualized determination by the court as to the potential juror's ability to faithfully and impartially apply the law.

FACTS: During voir dire in Salamone's (D) trial on various charges, including the possession of and failure to register an illegally made machine gun, the court inquired as to each juror's membership in the National Rifle Association (NRA). One potential juror stated that he was a former member of the NRA and supported its principles; and another stated that her husband belonged to it and that she supported its principles. On the motion of the prosecution, the court found that the former member of the NRA was unfit to serve on the jury because of his support of the organization, which has a record of opposition to gun control. The court did not inquire as to whether that potential juror felt he would be able to impartially apply the law to the facts of the case. The other juror who had indicated her support of the NRA was dismissed by a peremptory challenge.

ISSUE: May a potential juror be disqualified for cause based on his membership in an organization without an individualized determination by the court as to the potential juror's ability to faithfully and impartially apply the law?

HOLDING AND DECISION: (Higginbotham, J.) No. A potential juror may not be disqualified for cause based on his membership in an organization without an individualized determination by the court as to the potential juror's ability to faithfully and impartially apply the law. To allow judges to determine juror eligibility based solely on their perceptions of the external associations of a juror threatens the right of the accused to a fair trial by an impartial jury. Juror bias need not be established with "unmistakable clarity." However, at no time were the excluded jurors questioned about their ability to faithfully and impartially apply the law. Jury competence is an individual rather than a class matter, and such presumed bias is impermissible. The judgment of the district court is reversed.

▶ ANALYSIS

Although Circuit Judge Higginbotham states that no individualized inquiry was made as to the excluded jurors' ability to fairly hear the case, it seems incorrect to say that no individualized inquiry was made. The trial court judge did not merely ask the potential jurors about their membership or former membership in the NRA, but further asked whether they, personally, supported the principles and policies of the organization. The jurors' positive response was thus in some sense an indication of individual bias, though evidently not sufficient to satisfy the court of appeals.

Quicknotes

CHALLENGE FOR CAUSE The right to refuse a jury seat to a prospective juror where that person possesses bias or other knowledge of the case that would impair the ability to render a fair verdict, predicated upon the showing by counsel of a compelling reason as to why that juror should be dismissed.

PEREMPTORY CHALLENGE A challenge issued by counsel during voir dire proceedings to refuse a jury seat to a prospective juror, for which no reason need be advanced other than the preference of counsel advocating exclusion.

Batson v. Kentucky

Burglary suspect (D) v. State (P)

476 U.S. 79 (1986).

NATURE OF CASE: Appeal of conviction for burglary and receiving stolen goods.

FACT SUMMARY: After the Kentucky (P) prosecutor used peremptory challenges to strike all African-American jurors, Batson (D), an African-American, unsuccessfully moved to dismiss the jury on grounds he was denied equal protection.

🏛 RULE OF LAW

To establish an equal protection violation for a state's use of peremptory challenges to exclude members of his race from a petit jury, a defendant must make out a prima facie case by showing: (1) he is a member of a cognizable racial group and (2) either that members of his race have not been summoned for jury duty in that jurisdiction for an extended period of time, or that the circumstances of his case raise an inference of purposeful discrimination.

FACTS: At Batson's (D) trial for burglary and receiving stolen goods, the Kentucky (P) prosecutor used peremptory challenges to remove all four African-Americans from the jury. Batson (D), an African-American, moved to dismiss the jury before it was sworn in, arguing that the State's (P) use of its peremptory challenges violated Batson's (D) Sixth Amendment right to a jury drawn from a fair cross section of the community and his Fourteenth Amendment right to equal protection. The trial judge denied the motion, stating that peremptory challenges could be used to strike anyone. Batson (D) was convicted, and he appealed.

ISSUE: To establish an equal protection violation for a state's use of peremptory challenges to exclude members of his race from a petit jury, must a defendant make out a prima facie case by showing: (1) he is a member of a cognizable racial group and (2) either that members of his race have not been summoned for jury duty in that jurisdiction for an extended period of time, or that the circumstances of his case raise an inference of purposeful discrimination?

HOLDING AND DECISION: (Powell, J.) Yes. To establish an equal protection violation for a state's use of peremptory challenges to exclude members of his race from a petit jury, a defendant must make out a prima facie case by showing: (1) he is a member of a cognizable racial group and (2) either that members of his race have not been summoned for jury duty in that jurisdiction for an extended period of time, or that the circumstances of his case raise an inference of purposeful discrimination. Once a prima facie case has been established, the State must provide a neutral explanation for the exercise of its peremptory challenges or else the defendant's conviction will be overturned. Whether a defendant has made out a prima facie showing based solely on evidence from his own case involves consideration of all relevant circumstances, for example, any "pattern" of strikes against jurors of the defendant's race and any questions and statements made by the prosecutor during voir dire. Once the burden shifts to the state to rebut a prima facie case, the prosecutor's explanation need not rise to the level of justifying a challenge for cause, but a statement that jurors will be partial to members of their own race or a simple denial of discriminatory intent will not suffice. African-Americans have an equal right to participation on juries, and their discriminatory exclusion impedes the pursuit of equal justice for defendants, excluded jurors, and the entire community. Thus, the Equal Protection Clause extends beyond selection of the jury venire to the petit jury and to the prosecutor's peremptory challenges. While peremptory challenges are important in our judicial system, they are often used to discriminate against African-Americans, and so a requirement that trial judges be sensitive to the discriminatory use of peremptory challenges strikes a balance between the continued use of peremptory challenges and equal protection. Remanded for further proceedings. If the trial court decides that the facts establish, prima facie, purposeful discrimination and the prosecutor does not come forward with a neutral explanation for his action, our precedents require that petitioner's conviction be reversed.

CONCURRENCE: (Marshall, J.) Peremptory challenges should be completely eliminated because their use cannot be reconciled with the requirements of equal protection. The discriminatory use of peremptory challenges will not be ended by this decision. Defendants cannot attack challenges unless their use is so flagrant as to establish a prima facie case. Even if a prima facie case can be made out, a prosecutor may easily fabricate non-discriminatory motives, or his "neutral" determination that a juror is, for example, "sullen" or "distant" may be based on unconscious racism. The trial judge will have a difficult time determining the prosecutor's motives, and the judge's decision may be based on his own conscious or unconscious racism.

DISSENT: (Rehnquist, J.) The use of peremptory challenges to strike minorities from juries does not violate equal protection so long as challenges are also used to exclude whites in cases involving white defendants.

▶ ANALYSIS

Justice Powell's opinion explicitly left open the issue of whether a criminal defendant can use race-based peremptory challenges. In *Edmonson v. Leesville Concrete Co.,* 500 U.S.

Continued on next page.

614 (1991), the Supreme Court extended the bar against discriminatory peremptory challenges to civil cases involving private litigants. The Court found state action in the discrimination, a prerequisite for Equal Protection Clause analysis, since it is the state that empowers the jury and discharges a juror upon the use of a peremptory challenge. This reasoning would seem to extend to the use of peremptory challenges by criminal defendants.

■═■

Quicknotes

EQUAL PROTECTION CLAUSE   A constitutional provision that each person be guaranteed the same protection of the laws enjoyed by other persons in like circumstances.

PEREMPTORY CHALLENGE   A challenge issued by counsel during voir dire proceedings to refuse a jury seat to a prospective juror, for which no reason need be advanced other than the preference of counsel advocating exclusion.

PETIT JURY   A trial jury as distinguished from the grand jury.

PRIMA FACIE CASE   An action where the plaintiff introduces sufficient evidence to submit the issue to the judge or jury for determination.

VOIR DIRE   Examination of potential jurors on a case.

■═■

United States v. Thomas

Federal government (P) v. Convicted drug dealer (D)

116 F.3d 606 (2d Cir. 1997).

NATURE OF CASE: Appeal from conviction under federal narcotics laws.

FACT SUMMARY: After retiring to deliberate, numerous jurors complained about the conduct of one of their number; that juror was dismissed and a verdict returned.

🏛 RULE OF LAW
If there is any indication that the request to discharge a juror is based on that juror's view of the sufficiency of the evidence, the request must be denied.

FACTS: In a trial where all the defendants were black, a jury was selected with one black member, identified as Juror No. 5. The prosecution attempted to remove Juror No. 5 by means of a peremptory challenge, but the challenge was denied. During the defense summation, several jurors complained that Juror No. 5 was showing agreement with defense counsel. However, in interviews with each juror, including Juror No. 5, the jurors indicated they would be able to apply the law to the facts as sworn. After the jurors retired to deliberate, several jurors complained again about Juror No. 5, informing the court that he was unyieldingly in favor of acquittal. Several jurors cited various reasons for Juror No. 5's apparent behavior, such as his statements that the defendants were "his people" or were "good people." Other jurors recalled him discussing his opposition to conviction in terms of the evidence, and challenging the sufficiency or reliability of the prosecution's witnesses. Juror No. 5 himself, in an interview with the court, said nothing to indicate that he was not making a good-faith effort to apply the law to the facts of the case. Finally, the court dismissed Juror No. 5, and the remaining eleven jurors returned a verdict.

ISSUE: If there is any indication that the request to discharge a juror is based on that juror's view of the sufficiency of the evidence, must the request be denied?

HOLDING AND DECISION: (Cabranes, J.) Yes. If there is any indication that the request to discharge a juror is based on that juror's view of the sufficiency of the evidence, the request must be denied. If a juror is ignoring the law, the court has the authority to remove that juror. Jurors do not have a right to engage in the practice described as nullification. However, that power must be exercised with great caution. A court may not delve deeply into a juror's motivations because it may not intrude on the secrecy of deliberations. Because there was some evidence here—his own statements, as well as the statements of other jurors—that Juror No. 5 was weighing the evidence and was

unconvinced by the government's case, it was inappropriate to dismiss him. Reversed.

▶ ANALYSIS

Judge Cabranes discusses at some length the double-edged sword of jury nullification. On the one hand, he recalls the case of John Peter Zenger, acquitted of criminal libel in 1735; and the acquittals in prosecutions under the fugitive slave laws in the nineteenth century. However, he also notes cases—more numerous and more recent—such as the two hung juries in the prosecution of Byron De La Beckwith for the murder of NAACP secretary Medgar Evers.

■▬■

Quicknotes

JURY NULLIFICATION The inherent power of a jury to ignore the strength of evidence and override the decision-making authority of the forum, to render a binding verdict acquitting the defendant according to its own impulses.

■▬■

Olden v. Kentucky

Convicted sodomist (D) v. Commonwealth (P)

488 U.S. 227 (1988).

NATURE OF CASE: On certiorari from appellate judgment upholding sodomy conviction.

FACT SUMMARY: Olden (D), a black man was convicted of forcibly sodomizing a white woman he met in a bar.

🏛 RULE OF LAW
Speculation as to the effect of jurors' racial biases cannot justify exclusion of cross-examination that may seriously compromise the prosecution's case.

FACTS: Olden (D) and his co-defendant, another black man, met a married white woman in a bar. The three left and engaged in sexual activities that may have involved other men; Olden (D) and the co-defendant then dropped the woman near the home of a black man with whom she was having an extramarital affair. The woman subsequently accused Olden (D) and the other men allegedly involved in the incident of kidnapping, rape, and forcible sodomy. The defense argued that the sex was consensual. Olden (D) sought to introduce evidence of her extramarital affair, arguing that she claimed she was raped to protect her relationship with her lover, who saw her getting out of the defendants' car and would otherwise have been suspicious. The prosecution successfully moved to exclude evidence of the woman's current living arrangements, arguing that if the jury knew that she, a white woman, had separated from her spouse and moved in with a black man, the prosecution would be prejudiced to an extent that would outweigh the probative value of such testimony. The evidence was excluded and the defense was not permitted to raise the issue on cross-examination.

ISSUE: Can speculation as to the effect of jurors' racial biases justify exclusion of cross-examination that may seriously compromise the prosecution's case?

HOLDING AND DECISION: (Per curiam) No. Speculation as to the effect of jurors' racial biases cannot justify exclusion of cross-examination that may seriously compromise the prosecution's case. The Sixth Amendment includes the right to reasonable cross-examination. The impeachment evidence sought to be introduced was highly relevant. The alleged victim's testimony was crucial to the prosecution's case, and was only corroborated by the testimony of her lover. The State's (P) case against Olden (D) was far from overwhelming, and the witness made inconsistent and contradictory statements regarding the incident. The judgment of the court of appeals is therefore reversed and the case remanded.

▶ ANALYSIS

The Court applied harmless-error analysis to the *Olden* case, a standard that allows a conviction to stand if, after considering "a host of factors" specific to the case, the reviewing court determines beyond a reasonable doubt that the jury would have reached the same result in the absence of the error. The Court, noting that the jury convicted Olden (D) of forcible sodomy but acquitted him on kidnapping and rape charges, concluded that denial of Olden's (D) right to impeach his alleged victim was not harmless beyond a reasonable doubt.

■≡∎

Quicknotes

IMPEACHMENT The introduction of evidence to show that a witness is not credible.

IN LIMINE Motion by one party brought prior to trial to exclude the potential introduction of highly prejudicial evidence.

PER CURIAM Denotes a decision that represents the opinion of the entire court.

SIXTH AMENDMENT Provides the right to a speedy trial by impartial jury, the right to be informed of the accusation, to confront witnesses and to have the assistance of counsel in all criminal prosecutions.

■≡∎

Maryland v. Craig

State (P) v. Accused child abuser (D)

497 U.S. 836 (1990).

NATURE OF CASE: On certiorari from appellate court judgment overturning conviction.

FACT SUMMARY: Four children were permitted to testify via a one-way closed-circuit television procedure designed to keep the witness from having to look at the defendant.

🏛 RULE OF LAW

A state's interest in the physical and psychological well-being of child witnesses may outweigh the right of a defendant to confront his accusers face-to-face.

FACTS: Craig (D) was accused of sexually abusing young children, and expert testimony suggested that the children alleged to have been abused would be unable to testify if required to do so in front of Craig (D). A Maryland statutory procedure was invoked, permitting the child witness and the prosecuting and defense attorneys to retire to a separate room, while the judge, defendant, and jury remained in the courtroom. The defendant remained in communication with counsel by electronic means, and those in the courtroom were able to observe the witness via a one-way, closed-circuit television hookup. The witnesses testified by this means and Craig (D) was convicted; however, the court of appeals concluded that the State (P) had not made a sufficient showing of the necessity to prevent a face-to-face confrontation, and reversed.

ISSUE: May a state's interest in the physical and psychological well-being of child witnesses outweigh the right of a defendant to confront his accusers face-to-face?

HOLDING AND DECISION: (O'Connor, J.) Yes. A state's interest in the physical and psychological well-being of child witnesses may outweigh the right of a defendant to confront his accusers face-to-face. The clear preference of the Confrontation Clause of the Sixth Amendment is for a face-to-face meeting between the defendant and the witnesses testifying against him. We have never held, however, that the right to such a face-to-face confrontation is absolute. The Confrontation Clause serves several purposes: to ensure that a witness's statements are given under oath; to permit cross-examination; and to permit the jury to observe the demeanor of the witness. Maryland's procedure permits all these purposes. To insist upon face-to-face confrontation in every instance would not only make examination of child witnesses in cases such as these difficult; it would virtually abrogate every exception to the hearsay rule. The purpose of the Confrontation Clause is to promote the seeking of truth, and we determine that where a procedure such as this is used to protect a young child from trauma, the truth-seeking function of the clause is furthered rather than hindered. The judgment of the court of appeals is reversed and the case is remanded for a determination of whether the procedure was necessary in this case under our holding today.

DISSENT: (Scalia, J.) Constitutional requirements may not be subordinated to currently favored public policy. We are not free to conduct a cost-benefit analysis of clear and explicit constitutional guarantees. The Maryland procedure may be virtually constitutional, but it is not actually constitutional.

▌ ANALYSIS

Justice Scalia, in dissent, states that the defendant's "right, 'to be confronted with the witnesses against him' means always and everywhere, at least what it explicitly says: the 'right to meet face to face all those who appear and give evidence at trial.'" His reading of the phrase "to be confronted," while reasonable, seems interpretive rather than literal; the Constitution simply does not refer anywhere to a "face-to-face" confrontation. Yet the majority opinion did not take issue with Scalia's claim that the text permitted only one "literal reading"; instead, it justified the Maryland procedure wholly on policy grounds.

■■■

Quicknotes

ABROGATE Annul; cancel; void.

CONFRONTATION CLAUSE A provision in the Sixth Amendment to the United States Constitution that an accused in a criminal action has the right to confront the witnesses against him, including the right to attend the trial and to cross-examine witnesses called on behalf of the prosecution.

HEARSAY An out-of-court statement made by a person other than the witness testifying at trial that is offered in order to prove the truth of the matter asserted.

SIXTH AMENDMENT Provides the right to a speedy trial by impartial jury, the right to be informed of the accusation, to confront witnesses and to have the assistance of counsel in all criminal prosecutions.

■■■

Crawford v. Washington

Attempted murder convict (D) v. State (P)

541 U.S. 36 (2004).

NATURE OF CASE: Appeal from an attempted murder conviction.

FACT SUMMARY: When at Michael Crawford's (D) trial, the prosecutor played for the jury a witness's prior out-of-court tape-recorded statement to the police, thus providing Crawford (D) with no opportunity for cross-examination, Crawford (D) argued deprivation of his constitutional rights on the grounds that the Sixth Amendment Confrontation Clause applies not only to in-court testimony.

RULE OF LAW
The Sixth Amendment Confrontation Clause applies not only to in-court testimony.

FACTS: Michael Crawford (D) stabbed a man who allegedly tried to rape his wife, Sylvia. At his trial, the prosecutor played for the jury Sylvia's tape-recorded statement to the police describing the stabbing, even though Crawford (D) had no opportunity for cross-examination. Crawford (D) claimed self-defense. Sylvia did not testify at trial because of the state's marital privilege; in Washington, this privilege does not extend to a spouse's out-of-court statements admissible under a hearsay exception. The Washington Supreme Court upheld Crawford's (D) attempted murder conviction after determining that Sylvia's statement was reliable. Crawford (D) appealed to the U.S. Supreme Court on Confrontation Clause grounds.

ISSUE: Does the Sixth Amendment Confrontation Clause apply only to in-court testimony?

HOLDING AND DECISION: (Scalia, J.) No. The Sixth Amendment Confrontation Clause applies not only to in-court testimony. The history of the Confrontation Clause supports two inferences about its meaning. First, the principal evil at which it was directed was the civil-law mode of criminal procedure, particularly its use of ex parte examinations as evidence against the accused. The Sixth Amendment must be interpreted with this focus in mind. Leaving the regulation of out-of-court statements to the law of evidence would render the Clause powerless to prevent even the most flagrant inquisitorial practices. This focus also suggests that not all hearsay implicates the Sixth Amendment's core concerns. An off-hand, overheard remark, for example, might be unreliable evidence and thus a good candidate for exclusion under hearsay rules, but it bears little resemblance to the civil-law abuses the Clause targeted. On the other hand, ex parte examinations might sometimes be admissible under modern hearsay rules, but the Framers certainly would not have condoned them. Statements taken by police officers in the course of investigations,

as here, are testimonial evidence under even a narrow standard. Police interrogations bear a striking resemblance to examinations by justices of the police in England; the statements are not sworn testimony, but the absence of oath was not dispositive. In sum, police interrogations fall squarely within the class of statements to which the right of confrontation is historically required. Secondly, the Framers would not have allowed admission of testimonial statements of a witness who did not appear at trial unless unavailable and the defendant had had a prior opportunity for cross-examination. The text of the Sixth Amendment "does not suggest any open-ended exceptions from the confrontation requirement to be developed by the courts." Dispensing with confrontation because testimony is "obviously reliable" is akin to dispensing with jury trial because a defendant is "obviously guilty." Reversed and remanded for further proceedings not inconsistent with this decision.

CONCURRENCE: (Rehnquist, C.J.) Although the wife's statement should have been excluded, adoption of a new approach in this area is not backed by sufficiently persuasive reasoning to overrule long-established precedent.

► ANALYSIS

In *Crawford*, the Supreme Court makes clear that where testimonial evidence is involved, the Framers did not intend to leave the Sixth Amendment's protections "to the vagaries of the rules of evidence, much less to amorphous notions of 'reliability.'" Admitting statements deemed reliable by a judge is fundamentally at odds with the right of confrontation. The Confrontation Clause commands, not that evidence be reliable, but that reliability be assessed in a particular manner: by testing in the crucible of cross-examination.

Quicknotes

CONFRONTATION CLAUSE A provision in the Sixth Amendment to the United States Constitution that an accused in a criminal action has the right to confront the witnesses against him, including the right to attend the trial and to cross-examine witnesses called on behalf of the prosecution.

HEARSAY EXCEPTION Out-of-court statement made by a person other than the witness testifying at trial that is offered in order to prove the truth of the matter asserted, and is admissible at trial notwithstanding the fact that it is hearsay.

Cruz v. New York

Convicted murderer (D) v. State (P)

481 U.S. 186 (1987).

NATURE OF CASE: On certiorari from appellate court judgment affirming murder conviction.

FACT SUMMARY: Testimony concerning Cruz's (D) confession to the murder of a gas station attendant was admitted; his co-defendant's confession was likewise admitted with a limiting instruction.

RULE OF LAW

The Confrontation Clause bars the admission of a nontestifying co-defendant's confession incriminating the defendant at their joint trial, even if the defendant's confession is admitted.

FACTS: Cruz (D), his brother, and two other men robbed a gas station; in the course of the robbery, Cruz's (D) brother shot and killed the gas station attendant. Cruz (D) and his brother were indicted and tried jointly for felony murder. The prosecution called a witness who testified that Cruz (D) had confessed to his participation in the incident. Cruz's (D) brother had confessed in detail to the assistant district attorney, and identified Cruz (D) as one of the participants in the robbery-murder. The court, instructing the jury not to consider Cruz's (D) brother's confession against Cruz (D), admitted the brother's confession.

ISSUE: Does the Confrontation Clause bar the admission of a nontestifying co-defendant's confession incriminating the defendant at their joint trial, even if the defendant's confession is admitted?

HOLDING AND DECISION: (Scalia, J.) Yes. The Confrontation Clause bars the admission of a nontestifying co-defendant's confession incriminating the defendant at their joint trial, even if the defendant's confession is admitted. We have previously held that a nontestifying co-defendant's confession may not be admitted where the defendant seeking to bar admission has not himself confessed. Even a limiting instruction will not cure the Confrontation Clause violation in such an instance. Regardless of such an instruction, the chance that a jury will be unable to ignore the incriminating effect of one co-defendant's statements concerning another is too great, and the stakes too high. Cruz's (D) own confession may have increased the reliability of his brother's confession, but it operated to increase the very risk sought to be avoided by our prior decisions. It seems more likely, once Cruz's (D) confession is admitted, that his brother's confession would be considered by the jury in evaluating Cruz's (D) guilt regardless of any limiting instruction. Reversed and remanded for further proceedings not inconsistent with this opinion.

DISSENT: (White, J.) It is not even remotely possible that in all cases admission of a defendant's interlocking confession will have devastating effects.

ANALYSIS

Justice White, claiming "common sense" on his side, argued that "interlocking confessions" were more reliable than the confession of a single defendant who might be determined to take his co-defendants down with him. Justice Scalia noted that the dissent missed the point; the nontestifying co-defendant's confession was inadmissible because it was apparently extremely reliable. In fact, Scalia wrote, it might seem so reliable that a jury would be unable to ignore a limiting instruction.

Quicknotes

CONFRONTATION CLAUSE A provision in the Sixth Amendment to the United States Constitution that an accused in a criminal action has the right to confront the witnesses against him, including the right to attend the trial and to cross-examine witnesses called on behalf of the prosecution.

LIMITING INSTRUCTION Directions given to a judge or jury prior to deliberation.

Gray v. Maryland

Convicted murderer (D) v. State (P)

523 U.S. 185 (1998).

NATURE OF CASE:
Appeal from murder conviction.

FACT SUMMARY:
Defendant was convicted of beating a victim to death; he was tried jointly with another alleged participant in the beating.

🏛 RULE OF LAW
The prosecution may not introduce the confession of a nontestifying co-defendant where the confession implicates another defendant in their joint trial, even if a blank space or the word "deleted" is inserted wherever the implicated defendant is identified in the confession.

FACTS:
Stacy Williams was beaten to death. Anthony Bell confessed to police, and named Gray (D) and another man as participants in the beating. The other man subsequently died, but Bell and Gray (D) were jointly tried for murder. Bell's confession was redacted to put the word "deleted" wherever the name of Gray (D) appeared, and the jury was instructed that it was not to consider the confession as evidence against Gray (D). Both Bell and Gray (D) were convicted.

ISSUE:
May the prosecution introduce the confession of a nontestifying co-defendant where the confession implicates another defendant in their joint trial, if a blank space or the word "deleted" is inserted wherever the implicated defendant is identified in the confession?

HOLDING AND DECISION:
(Breyer, J.) No. The prosecution may not introduce the confession of a nontestifying co-defendant where the confession implicates another defendant in their joint trial, even if a blank space or the word "deleted" is inserted wherever the implicated defendant is identified in the confession. We have held that such confessions, where one defendant is named in the confession of another who does not testify in their joint trial, is so prejudicial that even a limiting instruction to the jury to consider the statement as evidence against only the confessing defendant will not overcome the prejudice thus created. We hold today that confessions redacted in a manner indicating that other participants were involved in the crime, where the alleged co-participants are being jointly tried, are still highly prejudicial and inadmissible. As Judge Learned Hand wrote in a similar case, "[T]here could not have been the slightest doubt as to whose names had been blacked out," but "even if there had been, that blacking out would have not only laid the doubt, but underscored the answer." The conviction is reversed.

DISSENT:
(Scalia, J.) We have held that the rule against admitting incriminating confessions of non-testifying jointly tried defendants does not extend to statements that incriminate only by inference from other evidence. The Court concedes that "the jury must use inference to connect the statement in this redacted confession with the defendant." Though the jury may speculate, the statement expressly implicates no one but the speaker.

▶ ANALYSIS
The majority suggested that a confession might be acceptably redacted by eliminating all references to co-participants in the crime. Scalia argued that such redactions would misrepresent the confessing defendant's statement; moreover, he said, a defendant who replied "Me" to the question "Who agreed to beat the victim?" would have an insanity defense.

■■■

Quicknotes

LIMITING INSTRUCTION Directions given to a judge or jury prior to deliberation.

■■■

United States v. Burr

Federal government (P) v. Criminal defendant (D)

25 Fed.Cas. 30 (No. 14,692D) (D. Va. 1807).

NATURE OF CASE: Defense motion in a criminal proceeding for a subpoena duces tecum.

FACT SUMMARY: Defense counsel moved for a subpoena duces tecum against the President of the United States to obtain letters relevant to the defense of a criminal prosecution.

🏛 RULE OF LAW
In a criminal case, a subpoena duces tecum may be directed to the President of the United States.

FACTS: In the prosecution of Burr (D), defense counsel moved for a subpoena duces tecum to obtain an original letter from General Wilkinson to the President of the United States in relation to Burr (D), together with the President's answer to that letter, as material to the defense.

ISSUE: In a criminal case, may a subpoena duces tecum may be directed to the President of the United States?

HOLDING AND DECISION: (Marshall, C.J.) Yes. In a criminal case, a subpoena duces tecum may be directed to the President of the United States. The Sixth Amendment right must be deemed sacred by the courts and must be so construed as to be something more than a dead letter. In the provision of the Constitution that gives to the accused a right to the compulsory process of the court, there is no exception whatsoever. This Court would be very unwilling to say that upon fair construction, the constitutional and legal right to obtain its processes to compel the attendance of witnesses does not extend to their bringing with them such papers as may be material in the defense. Motion granted.

▶ ANALYSIS

In the *Burr* case, Chief Justice Marshall expressed the viewpoint that where documents may be important to the defense of a criminal action, "it would be a blot in the page which records the judicial proceedings of this country," if in such a serious case as the present one, the accused were denied the use of a subpoena duces tecum.

■=■

Quicknotes

SIXTH AMENDMENT Provides the right to a speedy and public trial by impartial jury, the right to be informed of the accusation, the right to confront witnesses, and the right to have the assistance of counsel in all criminal prosecutions.

SUBPOENA A command issued by court to compel a witness to appear at trial.

■=■

Taylor v. Illinois

Criminal defendant (D) v. State (P)

484 U.S. 400 (1988).

NATURE OF CASE: Appeal of criminal conviction.

FACT SUMMARY: Illinois (P) requires pretrial disclosure of all defense witnesses, but Taylor (D), who claimed that an exculpatory witness was not on the list because he could not be located before trial, was not allowed by the trial judge to call the witness to testify.

🏛 RULE OF LAW
Where the defense intentionally omits a witness from a required pretrial witness list to gain a tactical advantage, the trial judge may refuse to let the witness testify.

FACTS: Illinois (P) law requires the defense to provide a pretrial list of all witnesses it intends to call. During his trial, Taylor's (D) defense counsel wished to call a witness who was not on the pretrial list. Taylor (D) claimed that the witness could not be located before trial, but the witness admitted at a hearing that defense counsel had visited him the week before trial. The trial judge, concluding that the witness was not credible and that the evidence might be manufactured, did not allow the witness to testify. Taylor (D) appealed, arguing that the Sixth Amendment Compulsory Process Clause bars a judge from precluding the testimony of a surprise witness.

ISSUE: Where the defense intentionally omits a witness from a required pretrial witness list to gain a tactical advantage, may the trial judge refuse to let the witness testify?

HOLDING AND DECISION: (Stevens, J.) Yes. Where the defense intentionally omits a witness from a required pretrial witness list to gain a tactical advantage, the trial judge may refuse to let the witness testify. The Compulsory Process Clause mandates not only that a defendant may compel the presence of a witness, but also that the trier of fact must hear the witness. However, where the defendant fails to comply with discovery rules, the defendant's rights must be weighed against the public interest in excluding unreliable or perjured testimony, in avoiding prejudice to the prosecution, and in enforcing rules for the fair and efficient functioning of the adversary process. While there are less drastic sanctions available (granting a continuance or mistrial or disciplining the defendant or defense counsel, for example), in the event a discovery violation is willful only the severest sanction—witness preclusion—may be strong enough to combat the defendant's powerful incentive to present perjured testimony. Finally, unless defense counsel is constitutionally ineffective, the adversary process requires a client to be held responsible for the actions of his attorney. Accordingly, there was no error committed by not allowing Taylor's (D) omitted witness to testify at trial. Affirmed.

DISSENT: (Brennan, J.) Where the defendant is not personally responsible for the discovery violation, alternative sanctions are adequate and avoid the arbitrary and disproportionate sanction of witness preclusion. Unless the defendant is responsible, the Compulsory Process Clause should require a per se rule against discovery sanctions that exclude criminal defense evidence.

▶ ANALYSIS

Under *Wardius v. Oregon,* 412 U.S. 470 (1973), where discovery rules place a particular burden on the defense, due process requires that the defense must have reciprocal discovery rights against the prosecution. Federal Rule of Criminal Procedure 16 provides defendants with a number of discovery and inspection rights, essentially providing the prosecution with reciprocal rights where the defense has chosen to exercise its rights first. The Federal Rules do not require either party to provide a pretrial list of all witnesses, but federal judges have discretion to order the government to provide a witness list.

■═■

Quicknotes

DISCOVERY Pretrial procedure during which one party makes certain information available to the other.

PERJURY The unlawful communication of a false statement knowingly and under oath.

■═■

Griffin v. California

First-degree murder court (D) v. State (P)

380 U.S. 609 (1965).

NATURE OF CASE: Certiorari from a murder conviction.

FACT SUMMARY: Griffin (D), during his trial for first-degree murder, did not testify on the issue of his guilt, and both the prosecutor and judge subsequently commented on this failure to the jury, before it convicted him.

🏛 RULE OF LAW

The Fifth Amendment Self-Incrimination Clause implicitly forbids comment by the prosecution on an accused's failure to testify, or instructions by the court that such failure is evidence of guilt.

FACTS: Griffin (D) refused to testify at his trial for first-degree murder, invoking the Fifth Amendment privilege against self-incrimination. Before the jury deliberated on the issue of guilt, the prosecutor commented on this failure to testify and suggested that guilt should be inferred therefrom. During instructions to the jury, the court stated that if Griffin (D) failed to explain facts within his knowledge that tended to indicate his guilt, then the jury could take that failure as "tending to indicate the truth of such evidence," but that such failure alone does not by itself "warrant an inference of guilt." Upon conviction, and affirmance of that conviction by the California Supreme Court, Griffin (D) brought a petition for certiorari to the U.S. Supreme Court.

ISSUE: Does comment by a judge or prosecutor on an accused's failure to testify violate his Fifth Amendment privilege against self-incrimination?

HOLDING AND DECISION: (Douglas, J.) Yes. Comment by a judge or prosecutor on an accused's failure to testify violates his Fifth Amendment privilege against self-incrimination. The Fifth Amendment Self-Incrimination Clause forbids comment by the prosecution on an accused's failure to testify, or instructions by the court that such failure is evidence of guilt. Such comment by the prosecution or court is a "remnant of the inquisitorial system of criminal justice which the Fifth Amendment protects against." Such comment penalizes the exercise of a constitutional privilege to refrain from self-incrimination and, as such, cannot be allowed. It may be true that there is a natural inference of guilt from a failure to testify as to facts within the knowledge of an accused, but the jury must make this inference on its own without comment from the court. Here, therefore, Griffin's (D) conviction must be reversed.

CONCURRENCE: (Harlan, J.) Since within the federal system the Fifth Amendment bars adverse comment by federal prosecutors and judges on a defendant's failure to take the stand in a criminal trial, there is no legitimate escape from

today's decision. Unfortunately, the decision exemplifies the creeping paralysis with which the Supreme Court "incorporation" doctrine is infecting the operation of the federal system.

DISSENT: (Stewart, J.) In examining whether an accused's privilege against self-incrimination has been violated, "compulsion" is the focus of inquiry (i.e., such privilege has only been violated if the accused was "compelled to be a witness against himself"). The Court, however, fails to identify any such compulsion in the comments of the court and prosecutor. First, such comment does not compel an accused's testimony by creating awareness in the jury of his failure to testify, since that failure is obvious by itself. Second, no compulsion may be assumed on the ground that the inferences drawn by the jury that has heard such comments will be detrimental to an accused, especially where the Court has carefully controlled its comments. The trial court here carefully instructed the jury that Griffin's (D) failure to testify "does not by itself warrant an inference of guilt." It is doubtful that a jury without such instructions would have observed such a limitation. The comment in this case was a means of articulating and rationally discussing a fact that is necessarily impressed on the jury's consciousness (i.e., the failure to testify). The state has an important interest in such discussion, which should not arbitrarily be cut off.

▶ ANALYSIS

This case illustrates the rule applicable to "direct comment" on an accused's failure to "testify." Note, however, that it does not prevent a prosecutor from commenting on an accused's "failure to offer evidence" on critical aspects of the case. It has been held that a court's comment, that an accused's "failure to explain" possession of recently stolen property should be considered in determining whether he knew the goods were stolen, does not violate *Griffin* (*Barnes v. United States*, 412 U.S. 837 (1973)). Of course, what is considered permissible depends upon the wording of the prosecutor's comments. If he emphasizes an accused's failure to present other evidence instead of the fact that he "personally" offered no explanation, there is probably no violation of *Griffin*. Note further that *Griffin* does not prevent a prosecutor from commenting to a jury upon an accused's "refusal to submit to reasonable tests or examinations," the results of which would have been admissible on the issue of guilt or innocence. Note, finally, that *Griffin* does prevent counsel for one of several co-defendants from commenting on the failure of other co-defendants to testify.

■=■

Continued on next page.

Quicknotes

CERTIORARI A discretionary writ issued by a superior court to an inferior court in order to review the lower court's decisions; the Supreme Court's writ ordering such review.

FIRST DEGREE MURDER The willful killing of another person with deliberation and premeditation; first-degree murder also encompasses those situations in which a person is killed within the perpetration of, or attempt to perpetrate, specified felonies.

PRIVILEGE AGAINST SELF-INCRIMINATION A privilege guaranteed by the Fifth Amendment to the federal Constitution in a criminal proceeding for communications made by an accused and protecting an accused or witness from having to give testimony that may incriminate himself.

United States v. Thomas

Federal government (P) v. Convicted drug dealer (D)

116 F.3d 606 (2d Cir. 1997).

NATURE OF CASE: Appeal from conviction under federal narcotics laws.

FACT SUMMARY: After retiring to deliberate, numerous jurors complained about the conduct of one of their number; that juror was dismissed and a verdict returned.

🏛 RULE OF LAW

If there is any indication that the request to discharge a juror is based on that juror's view of the sufficiency of the evidence, the request must be denied.

FACTS: In a trial where all the defendants were black, a jury was selected with one black member, identified as Juror No. 5. The prosecution attempted to remove Juror No. 5 by means of a peremptory challenge, but the challenge was denied. During the defense summation, several jurors complained that Juror No. 5 was showing agreement with defense counsel. However, in interviews with each juror, including Juror No. 5, the jurors indicated they would be able to apply the law to the facts as sworn. After the jurors retired to deliberate, several jurors complained again about Juror No. 5, informing the court that he was unyieldingly in favor of acquittal. Several jurors cited various reasons for Juror No. 5's apparent behavior, such as his statements that the defendants were "his people" or were "good people." Other jurors recalled him discussing his opposition to conviction in terms of the evidence, and challenging the sufficiency or reliability of the prosecution's witnesses. Juror No. 5 himself, in an interview with the court, said nothing to indicate that he was not making a good-faith effort to apply the law to the facts of the case. Finally, the court dismissed Juror No. 5, and the remaining eleven jurors returned a verdict.

ISSUE: If there is any indication that the request to discharge a juror is based on that juror's view of the sufficiency of the evidence, must the request be denied?

HOLDING AND DECISION: (Cabranes, J.) Yes. If there is any indication that the request to discharge a juror is based on that juror's view of the sufficiency of the evidence, the request must be denied. If a juror is ignoring the law, the court has the authority to remove that juror. Jurors do not have a right to engage in the practice described as nullification. However, that power must be exercised with great caution. A court may not delve deeply into a juror's motivations because it may not intrude on the secrecy of deliberations. Because there was some evidence here—his own statements, as well as the statements of other jurors—that Juror No. 5 was weighing the evidence and was unconvinced by the government's case, it was inappropriate to dismiss him. Reversed.

▶ ANALYSIS

Judge Cabranes discusses at some length the double-edged sword of jury nullification. On the one hand, he recalls the case of John Peter Zenger, acquitted of criminal libel in 1735; and the acquittals in prosecutions under the fugitive slave laws in the nineteenth century. However, he also notes cases—more numerous and more recent—such as the two hung juries in the prosecution of Byron De La Beckwith for the murder of NAACP secretary Medgar Evers.

■=■

Quicknotes

JURY NULLIFICATION The inherent power of a jury to ignore the strength of evidence and override the decision-making authority of the forum, to render a binding verdict acquitting the defendant according to its own impulses.

■=■

CHAPTER 17

Sentencing

Quick Reference Rules of Law

Mistretta v. United States

Criminal defendant (P) v. Federal government (D)

488 U.S. 361 (1989).

NATURE OF CASE: Challenge to the constitutionality of the Sentencing Commission [implied from casebook excerpt].

FACT SUMMARY: [Facts not stated in casebook excerpt.]

🏛 RULE OF LAW
[Implied from casebook excerpt.] The Sentencing Commission is constitutional.

FACTS: [Facts not stated in casebook excerpt.]

ISSUE: [Implied from casebook excerpt.] Is the Sentencing Commission constitutional?

HOLDING AND DECISION: (Blackmun, J.) [Implied from casebook excerpt.] Yes. The Sentencing Commission is constitutional. .

Congress enacted specific guidelines that were meant to establish a range of determinate sentences for categories of offenses and defendants according to various specified factors, "among others." The maximum of the range ordinarily may not exceed the minimum by more than the greater of 25 percent or six months, and each sentence is to be within the limit provided by existing law. The Sentencing Commission was established "as an independent commission in the judicial branch of the United States." In addition to the duty the Commission has to promulgate determinative-sentence guidelines, it is under an obligation periodically to "review and revise" the guidelines. It is to "consult with authorities on, and individual and institutional representatives of, various aspects of the Federal criminal justice system." It must report to Congress "any amendments of the guidelines." It is to make recommendations to Congress whether the grades or maximum penalties should be modified. It must submit to Congress at least annually an analysis of the operation of the guidelines. It is to issue "general policy statements" regarding their application. And it has the power to "establish general policies . . . as are necessary to carry out the purposes" of the legislation; to "monitor the performance of probation officers" with respect to the guidelines; to "devise and conduct periodic training programs of instruction in sentencing techniques for judicial and probation personnel and others; and to perform such other functions as are required to permit federal courts to meet their responsibilities" as to sentencing. [Constitutionality of the Sentencing Commission is implied from the casebook excerpt.]

proposals for sentencing reform. It rejected strict determinate sentencing because it concluded that a guideline system would be successful in reducing sentence disparities while retaining the flexibility needed to adjust for unanticipated factors arising in a particular case. The Judiciary Committee rejected a proposal that would have made the sentencing guidelines only advisory.

■■■

▶ ANALYSIS

The *Mistretta* Court noted that before settling on a mandatory-guideline system, Congress considered other competing

Williams v. New York

Death row convict (P) v. State (D)

337 U.S. 241 (1949).

NATURE OF CASE: Appeal from a conviction for murder.

FACT SUMMARY: Following a conviction for murder, the trial judge sentenced Williams (P) to death using out-of-court records and reports to reach his decision.

🏛 RULE OF LAW
The use of additional out-of-court records and reports by a trial judge in sentencing does not violate the Due Process Clause.

FACTS: Williams (P) was tried for first-degree murder. The evidence proved a wholly indefensible murder committed by a person engaged in a burglary. The jury returned a verdict of guilty with a recommendation for life sentence. The judge imposed the death penalty, stating that the presentence investigation of Williams's (P) past criminal record and psychiatric reports revealed that he was a menace to society. Consideration of this additional information was pursuant to the New York Criminal Code. The court of appeals affirmed the conviction and sentence over Williams's (P) contention that the statute as construed violated the Due Process Clause of the Fourteenth Amendment in that the information was supplied by witnesses with whom Williams (P) had not been confronted and had no opportunity to cross-examine. Williams (P) appealed.

ISSUE: Does the use of additional out-of-court information by a trial judge in sentencing violate the Due Process Clause?

HOLDING AND DECISION: (Black, J.) No. The procedural policy grounded in the Due Process Clause of the Fourteenth Amendment provides in part that no person shall be tried and convicted of an offense unless he is given reasonable notice of the charges against him and is afforded an opportunity to confront and examine adverse witnesses. That the Due Process Clause does provide these protections where the question is the guilt of a defendant is clear. However, a sentencing judge is not confined to the narrow issue of guilt. Essential to his selection of an appropriate sentence is the possession of the fullest information possible concerning a defendant's life and characteristics. Thus, the use of additional information by a trial judge in sentencing does not violate the Fourteenth Amendment. Williams (P) was found guilty after a fairly conducted trial. His sentence followed a hearing conducted by the judge in which Williams (P) testified as to his sentence. The case went to the highest state court, which affirmed the sentence. Williams (P) was not denied due process of law. Affirmed.

DISSENT: (Murphy, J.) Here, the judge exercised his discretion to deprive a man of his life in reliance on material made available to him in a probation report, consisting almost entirely of evidence that would have been inadmissible at the trial. In a capital case, against the unanimous recommendation of a jury, when the report would concededly not have been admissible at the trial, and was not subject to examination by the defendant, the high commands of due process were not obeyed. Due process of law includes at least the idea that a person accused of crime shall be accorded a fair hearing through all the stages of the proceedings against him.

▶ ANALYSIS

In *Gardner v. Florida,* 430 U.S. 349 (1977), the Court held that a sentence of death imposed at least in part on the basis of information in a presentence report that the defendant had no opportunity to contest was unconstitutional. Distinguishing its holding in *Williams,* the Court said that the death penalty had now been recognized by a majority of the Court as "a different kind of punishment than any other that may be imposed in this country."

■=■

Quicknotes

DUE PROCESS CLAUSE Clause found in the Fifth and Fourteenth Amendments to the United States Constitution providing that no person shall be deprived of "life, liberty, or property, without due process of law."

■=■

McMillan v. Pennsylvania

Felony convict (D) v. State (P)

477 U.S. 79 (1986).

NATURE OF CASE: Appeal of sentence imposed upon conviction.

FACT SUMMARY: McMillan (D) was sentenced under a Pennsylvania law that required a minimum sentence of five years for certain felonies if the sentencing judge finds by a preponderance of the evidence that the offender was in "visible possession of a firearm" during commission of the crime.

RULE OF LAW
Due process does not require a sentencing court to find any facts used in sentencing to be proven beyond a reasonable doubt, by clear and convincing evidence, by a preponderance of the evidence, or by any other burden of proof.

FACTS: McMillan (D) was sentenced under a Pennsylvania law that required a minimum sentence of five years for certain felonies if the sentencing judge finds by a preponderance of the evidence that the offender was in "visible possession of a firearm" during commission of the crime. McMillan (D) appealed his sentence, arguing that due process requires "visible possession of a firearm" to be proven by at least clear and convincing evidence.

ISSUE: Does due process require a sentencing court to find any facts used in sentencing to be proven by clear and convincing evidence?

HOLDING AND DECISION: (Rehnquist, J.) No. Due process does not require a sentencing court to find any facts used in sentencing to be proven beyond a reasonable doubt, by clear and convincing evidence, by a preponderance of the evidence, or by any other burden of proof. Sentencing courts traditionally have heard evidence and found facts without any burden of proof at all. So long as the fact to be proven is not an element of the offense, as here, no burden of proof need be imposed simply because the fact concerns the crime, as opposed to the background or character of the offender. Thus, McMillan (D) was properly sentenced. Affirmed.

DISSENT: (Stevens, J.) There must be some constitutional limits on the power of a state to define the elements of criminal offenses. The high standard of proof is required because of the immense importance of the individual interest in avoiding both the loss of liberty and the stigma that results from a criminal conviction. It follows that if a state provides that a specific component of a prohibited transaction shall give rise to both a special stigma and to a special punishment, that component must be treated as a fact necessary to constitute the crime. Here, the constitutional significance of the special sanction cannot be avoided by the cavalier observation that it merely "ups the ante" for the defendant.

▶ ANALYSIS

The defense in *McMillan* pointed to prior Supreme Court decisions holding that due process required proof by at least clear and convincing evidence in involuntary commitment procedures and procedures to terminate parental rights. However, the Court distinguished sentencing procedures from those types of cases, because where an offender is being sentenced he has already been proven guilty of a crime beyond a reasonable doubt. The Court also held that the aggravating factor of visible possession of a firearm can constitutionally be treated as a sentencing consideration as opposed to an element of the charged offense.

■=■

Quicknotes

BURDEN OF PROOF The duty of a party to introduce evidence to support a fact that is in dispute in an action.

DUE PROCESS The constitutional mandate requiring the courts to protect and enforce individuals' rights and liberties consistent with prevailing principles of fairness and justice and prohibiting the federal and state governments from such activities that deprive its citizens of life, liberty, or property interest.

FELONY A criminal offense of greater seriousness than a misdemeanor; felonies are generally defined pursuant to statute as any crime that is punishable by death or by a term of imprisonment exceeding one year.

■=■

Apprendi v. New Jersey

Hate crime convict (D) v. State (P)

530 U.S. 466 (2000).

NATURE OF CASE: Appeal from conviction under state hate crime statute.

FACT SUMMARY: Apprendi (D) fired shots into the home of an African-American family because he allegedly did not want the occupants of the home in the neighborhood because of their race.

🏛 **RULE OF LAW**
Any fact that increases the penalty for a crime beyond the statutory minimum, other than the fact of a prior conviction, must be submitted to a jury and proven beyond a reasonable doubt.

FACTS: Apprendi (D) fired shots into the home of an African-American family. When he was arrested he stated that he did not want the family in the neighborhood because of their race. He was indicted on 23 counts, none of which referred to the New Jersey hate crime statute or alleged that Apprendi (D) acted with a racially motivated purpose. After an evidentiary hearing on the issue of Apprendi's (D) motive for the shooting, the judge concluded that the crime was motivated by racial bias and he was sentenced to 12 years to run consecutively with his other sentences. Apprendi (D) appealed.

ISSUE: Must any fact that increases the penalty for a crime beyond the statutory minimum, other than the fact of a prior conviction, be submitted to a jury and proven beyond a reasonable doubt?

HOLDING AND DECISION: (Stevens, J.) Yes. Any fact that increases the penalty for a crime beyond the statutory minimum, other than the fact of a prior conviction, must be submitted to a jury and proven beyond a reasonable doubt. Here the issue is whether the Due Process Clause of the Fourteenth Amendment requires a factual determination authorizing an increase in the maximum prison sentence for an offense from 10 to 20 years be made by a jury on the basis of proof beyond a reasonable doubt. In *Jones v. United States,* under the Due Process Clause of the Fifth Amendment and the notice and jury trial guarantees of the Sixth Amendment, any fact increasing the maximum penalty for a crime must be charged in an indictment, submitted to a jury, and proven beyond a reasonable doubt. The Fourteenth Amendment requires the same conclusion in this case. [Here, the constitutional proscription against deprivation of liberty without due process of law and the guarantee that in all criminal prosecutions the accused enjoy the right to a speedy and public trial by an impartial jury.] While traditionally judges were bound to the sentence proscribed by statute, judges have been accorded wide latitude in sentencing so long as such discretion is limited to the

range of sentencing options prescribed by the legislature. While trial practice procedures may change, they must at least adhere to the basic principles of trying to a jury all facts necessary to constitute the offense and proving such facts beyond a reasonable doubt. Prosecution subjects a criminal defendant both to the risk that he will lose his liberty and stigmatization. Thus the standard of reasonable doubt is imposed to ensure that he will not be subject to such deprivation erroneously. Constitutional limits exist to states' authority to eliminate facts necessary to constitute a criminal offense. State statutory schemes that keep from the jury facts that may expose defendants to greater or additional punishment raise serious constitutional issues. Here the statutory scheme in issue allows a jury to convict a defendant of a second-degree offense based on a finding beyond a reasonable doubt that he unlawfully possessed a weapon, and then allows a judge to impose punishment following a second and subsequent hearing equal to crimes of the first degree based on a finding by the preponderance of the evidence that defendant's purpose was intimidation of the victim based on a particular characteristic the victim possessed. This practice cannot stand. Reversed and remanded.

CONCURRENCE: (Scalia, J.) The founders of the republic were not prepared to leave criminal justice to the States, which is why the jury-trial guarantee was one of the least controversial provisions of the Bill of Rights. Furthermore, as a guarantee of fairness, an individual's guilt will be determined beyond a reasonable doubt by the unanimous vote of twelve fellow citizens, and a criminal will never get more punishment than he bargained for when he did the crime. To allow a single employee of the State to determine the length of a sentence is not the system envisioned by a Constitution that guarantees trial by jury. In addition, the guarantee that "[i]n all criminal prosecutions, the accused shall enjoy the right to . . . trial, by an impartial jury" has no intelligible content unless it means that all the facts that must exist in order to subject the defendant to a legally prescribed punishment must be found by the jury.

CONCURRENCE: (Thomas, J.) The Constitution requires a broader rule than adopted by the Court here. A "crime" includes every fact that is by law a basis for imposing or increasing punishment. If the legislature defines some core crime and then provides for increasing punishment of that crime upon a finding of some aggravating fact, then the two constitute an aggravated crime and the aggravated fact is an element of the aggravated crime.

DISSENT: (O'Connor, J.) The Court has long recognized that not every fact that bears on a defendant's

Continued on next page.

punishment need be charged in an indictment, submitted to a jury and proven beyond a reasonable doubt. Instead this Court has held that the legislature's definition of the elements is usually dispositive and courts proceed with caution before deciding that a certain fact must be treated as an offense element despite the legislature's decision not to characterize it as such. The Court's rule is unsupported by history and case law.

DISSENT: (Breyer, J.) The majority's rule promotes an ideal that juries determine the existence of those facts upon which punishment turns. There are practically speaking too many sentencing factors for all of them to be submitted to a jury. The solution lies not in prohibiting the legislature from enacting sentencing factors, but in sentencing rules that determine punishment on the basis of properly defined relevant conduct, with procedural and Due Process safeguards.

▶ *ANALYSIS*

Here the Court annunciates a broad rule with the effect of precluding the state and federal government from invoking sentence enhancements in order to increase a maximum sentence.

■══■

Quicknotes

BILL OF RIGHTS Refers to the first ten Amendments to the U.S. Constitution, setting forth individual rights and liberties.

DUE PROCESS CLAUSE Clause found in the Fifth and Fourteenth Amendments to the United States Constitution providing that no person shall be deprived of "life, liberty, or property, without due process of law."

■══■

Blakely v. Washington

Convicted kidnapper (D) v. State (P)

542 U.S. 296 (2004).

NATURE OF CASE: Appeal from a conviction for kidnapping.

FACT SUMMARY: When Blakely (D) was sentenced by a judge to more than three years beyond the statutory maximum for the crime to which he had pleaded guilty (because of a statutory enhancement based on a fact not included within the guilty plea), he argued that a sentencing procedure which deprives a defendant of the right to a jury determination of all facts essential to the sentence violates the Sixth Amendment.

RULE OF LAW

A sentencing procedure which deprives the defendant of the right to a jury determination of all facts essential to the sentence violates the Sixth Amendment.

FACTS: The State (P) charged Blakely (D) with first-degree kidnapping. Upon reaching a plea agreement, however, the State (P) reduced the charge to second-degree kidnapping involving domestic violence and use of a firearm. Blakely (D) entered a guilty plea admitting the elements of the second-degree kidnapping and the domestic violence and firearm allegations, but no other relevant facts. The case proceeded to sentencing. The facts of his plea, standing alone, supported a maximum sentence of 53 months. Pursuant to state law, however, the judge imposed an "exceptional" sentence of 90 months after making a judicial determination that Blakely (D) had acted with "deliberate cruelty." Faced with an unexpected increase of more than three years in his sentence, Blakely (D) argued that since the State's (P) sentencing procedure deprived him of the right to a jury determination of all facts essential to the sentence, his Sixth Amendment rights were violated. The state court of appeals affirmed the conviction, and the Washington Supreme Court denied discretionary review. Blakely (D) appealed to the U.S. Supreme Court.

ISSUE: Does a sentencing procedure which deprives the defendant of the right to a jury determination of all facts essential to the sentence violate the Sixth Amendment?

HOLDING AND DECISION: (Scalia, J.) Yes. A sentencing procedure which deprives the defendant of the right to a jury determination of all facts essential to the sentence violates the Sixth Amendment. Blakely (D) was sentenced to prison for more than three years beyond what the law allowed for the crime to which he confessed, on the basis of a disputed finding that he had acted with "deliberate cruelty." The Framers would not have thought it too much to demand that, before depriving a person of three more years of liberty, the state should suffer the "modest inconvenience" of submitting its accusation to the unanimous suffrage of twelve of the accused's equals and neighbors,

rather than a lone employee of the State. Here, the facts supporting the finding of "deliberate cruelty" were neither admitted by Blakely (D) nor found by a jury. The statutory maximum a judge may constitutionally impose must be based solely on the basis of the facts reflected in the jury verdict or admitted by the defendant. In other words, the relevant statutory maximum is not the maximum sentence a judge may impose after finding additional facts, but the maximum he or she may impose "without any additional findings." Finally, whether the judge's authority to impose an enhanced sentence depends on finding a specified fact, one of several specified facts, or an aggravating fact, it remains the case that the jury's verdict alone does not authorize the sentence. Reversed.

DISSENT: (O'Connor, J.) The effect of today's decision will be greater judicial discretion and less uniformity in sentencing. It is implausible that the Framers would have considered such a result to be required by the Due Process Clause or the Sixth Amendment. Prior to Washington's sentencing reform legislation, the state's unguided discretion inevitably resulted in severe disparities in sentencing received and served by defendants committing the same offense and having similar criminal histories. Because of today's decision, over 20 years of sentencing reform are all but lost, and tens of thousands of criminal judgments are in jeopardy.

DISSENT: (Breyer, J.) As a result of the majority's ruling, sentencing must now take one of three forms, each of which risks impracticality, unfairness, or harm to the jury trial right the majority purports the strengthen. This circumstance reveals that the majority's Sixth Amendment interpretation cannot be correct. First, creating a "determinate" sentencing system, although assuring uniformity, would do so at an intolerable cost by imposing identical punishments on people who committed their crimes in very different ways. Second, "indeterminate" sentencing systems in which the sentence is entirely discretionary with the judge, may produce unfair disparities in the punishments of similarity situated defendants, the so-called "what the judge ate for breakfast" on the day of sentencing test. Third, the "structured" sentencing system contains so many complexities and difficult choices for the defendant as to make it unworkable and provides an unreasonable extent to which a prosecutor can control the outcome through what charges might be brought for the same offense. Hence, the majority today ignores the adverse consequences inherent in its conclusion. While there are many faults to the guidelines systems, they will be better cured through legislation with reasoned input from the criminal

Continued on next page.

justice community than by an unchangeable decision of the Court.

▶ *ANALYSIS*

As the Supreme Court stresses in *Blakely*, the need to provide intelligible content to the right of jury trial is no mere procedural formality, but a fundamental reservation of power in our constitutional structure. The *Blakely* case was not about whether determinate sentencing is constitutional, only about how it can be implemented in a way that respects the Sixth Amendment.

■━■

Quicknotes

SIXTH AMENDMENT Provides the right to a speedy and public trial by impartial jury, the right to be informed of the accusation, the right to confront witnesses, and the right to have the assistance of counsel in all criminal prosecutions.

■━■

North Carolina v. Pearce

State (P) v. Retried rapist (D)

395 U.S. 711 (1969).

NATURE OF CASE: Petitions for writs of habeas corpus.

FACT SUMMARY: Pearce (D) obtained a reversal of his conviction. Upon retrial, he was sentenced to eight years in prison which, when added to the time he had already served, amounted to a longer total sentence than that originally imposed. Rice (D) also obtained a reversal of his conviction. Upon retrial, he was sentenced to a harsher sentence than his original sentence, and no credit was given for the time he'd already served.

RULE OF LAW
The Double Jeopardy Clause does not prohibit, upon a reconviction, imposition of a harsher sentence than imposed after the first conviction so long as the court's reasons affirmatively appear.

FACTS: Pearce (D) was sentenced to 12 to 15 years in prison for assault with intent to rape. He obtained a reversal of his conviction. Upon retrial, he was convicted and sentenced to eight years, which, when added to the time he had already served, amounted to a longer sentence than that originally imposed. Rice (D) was sentenced to ten years in prison after pleading guilty to burglary. He obtained a reversal of his conviction. Upon his retrial, he was convicted upon three of the original four counts and sentenced to a term totaling 25 years. No credit was given for the time he had already served. Pearce (D) was granted habeas corpus on the ground that the longer sentence was unconstitutional. Rice (D) was also granted habeas corpus as it was found that the state was punishing him for his having exercised his post-conviction right of review.

ISSUE: Does the Double Jeopardy Clause prohibit, upon a reconviction, imposition of a harsher sentence than imposed after the first conviction so long as the court's reasons affirmatively appear?

HOLDING AND DECISION: (Stewart, J.) No. The Double Jeopardy Clause does not prohibit, upon a reconviction, imposition of a harsher sentence than imposed after the first conviction so long as the court's reasons affirmatively appear. The guarantee against double jeopardy does not include restrictions upon length of a sentence imposed upon reconviction since the original conviction has, at the defendant's request, been nullified. Nevertheless, an accused may not be punished for exercising the constitutional right to appeal and have a tainted sentence set aside. Accordingly, to ensure absence of a retaliatory motivation on the part of the judge who performs the second sentencing, the reasons for a harsher second conviction must affirmatively be set forth. Furthermore, the Double Jeopardy Clause protects

against multiple punishments as well as multiple prosecutions, hence any punishment already exacted must be fully credited in imposing sentence upon a new conviction for the same offense. In both the *Pearce* and *Rice* cases the State did not justify the harsher sentences imposed, which violates the Due Process Clause. Reversed.

CONCURRENCE: (White, J.) The Court should authorize an increased sentence on retrial based on any objective, identifiable factual data not known to the trial judge at the time of the original sentencing proceeding.

ANALYSIS

In *Green v. U.S.,* 355 U.S. 184 (1957), mentioned in one of the concurring opinions, the defendant had originally been charged with first-degree murder, but was convicted of second-degree murder. His appeal resulted in the reversal of his conviction, and he was retried on the original charge. The second jury convicted him of first-degree murder. The Supreme Court held that double jeopardy barred conviction on that charge, since Green had already been in peril of being convicted and punished for first-degree murder at his first trial. In *Tucker v. Peyton,* 357 F.2d 115 (4th Cir. 1956), it was held that where a prisoner serving consecutive sentences succeeded in having one of the sentences invalidated after it had been fully or partially served, the state must give credit on the sentence remaining for the time served. In *Miller v. Cox,* 443 F.2d 1019 (4th Cir. 1971), it was held that a defendant who had served 21 years on a void conviction was not entitled to credit against subsequently committed felonies.

Quicknotes

DOUBLE JEOPARDY A prohibition against a second prosecution for the same offense after an acquittal or conviction for that offense in a prior proceeding or against multiple punishments for the same offense.

REVERSAL The annulment of a trial court decision by a reviewing court.

WRIT OF HABEAS CORPUS A proceeding in which a defendant brings a writ to compel a judicial determination of whether he is lawfully being held in custody.

Double Jeopardy

Quick Reference Rules of Law

Blockburger v. United States

Drug convict (D) v. Federal government (P)

284 U.S. 299 (1932).

NATURE OF CASE: Appeal from a conviction for violation of the Harrison Narcotic Act.

FACT SUMMARY: Blockburger (D) was charged with several different crimes arising from the same essential transaction.

RULE OF LAW
(1) Each of several successive sales under the Harrison Narcotic Act constitutes a distinct offense, however closely they follow each other.
(2) The sale of morphine hydrochloride not in or from the original stamped package, and without a written order, constitutes two separate offenses, although the transaction was the same.

FACTS: Blockburger (D) was charged in a five count indictment with violating provisions of the Harrison Narcotic Act. He was found guilty on three of the counts that charged him with a sale of morphine hydrochloride to the same purchaser on consecutive days. The judgment was affirmed on appeal, and Blockburger (D) appealed to the U.S. Supreme Court.

ISSUE:
(1) Do each of several successive sales under the Harrison Narcotic Act constitute a distinct offense, however closely they follow each other?
(2) Does the sale of morphine hydrochloride not in or from the original stamped package, and without a written order, constitute two separate offenses, although the transaction was the same?

HOLDING AND DECISION: (Sutherland, J.)
(1) Yes. Each of several successive sales of narcotics without compliance with the Harrison Narcotic Act constitutes a distinct offense, however closely the sales may follow each other. Here, the sales, although made to the same person, were distinct and separate sales made at different times. The test is whether the individual acts are prohibited, or the course of action that they constitute. If the former, then each act is punishable separately. If the latter, there can be but one penalty. Here, the first transaction, resulting in a sale, had come to an end. The next sale was not the result of the original impulse, but of a fresh one, namely, of a new bargain.
(2) Yes. The sale of morphine hydrochloride not in or from the original stamped package, and without a written order, constitutes two separate offenses, although the transaction was the same. The face of the statute creates two distinct offenses. Here, each of the offenses created required proof of a different element. When the same act or transaction constitutes a violation of two distinct statutory provisions, the test to be applied to determine whether there are two offenses or only one is whether each provision requires proof of an additional fact that the other does not. Affirmed.

ANALYSIS

In *Blockburger,* the Court noted that the Narcotic Act was not aimed at sales of the forbidden drugs qua sales, a matter entirely beyond the authority of Congress, but at sales of such drugs in violation of the requirements set forth in sections 1 and 2, enacted as aids to the enforcement of the stamp tax imposed by the act.

Brown v. Ohio

Convicted car thief (D) v. State (P)

432 U.S. 161 (1977).

NATURE OF CASE: On certiorari from appellate court judgment upholding Brown's (D) auto theft conviction.

FACT SUMMARY: After serving his sentence for a joyriding conviction, Brown (D) was tried and convicted of auto theft.

🏛 RULE OF LAW
Successive prosecutions for the same offense and course of conduct may not be brought merely by dividing the conduct into different segments of time.

FACTS: Brown (D) was convicted of "joyriding"—taking or operating a vehicle without the owner's consent. The date charged in the complaint was December 8, 1973, the date he was apprehended. After serving a jail term, Brown (D) was indicted for auto theft arising out of the same taking; the indictment specified that the vehicle had been stolen on or about November 29, 1973.

ISSUE: May successive prosecutions for the same offense and course of conduct be brought merely by dividing the conduct into different segments of time?

HOLDING AND DECISION: (Powell, J.) No. Successive prosecutions for the same offense and course of conduct may not be brought merely by dividing the conduct into different segments of time. For purposes of the Double Jeopardy Clause, the two crimes charged constitute the same offense, as joyriding is a lesser included offense of auto theft. Joyriding requires proof of the unauthorized taking of a vehicle, but not proof of intent to permanently deprive the owner of his property. The prosecutor who proves auto theft has established all the elements of joyriding. However, we disagree with the court of appeals that Brown (D) may be prosecuted twice merely by focusing on different aspects of his nine-day joyride. Under Ohio law, the theft and operation of a single car is a single offense. The judgment of the court of appeals is reversed.

CONCURRENCE: (Brennan, J.) The Double Jeopardy Clause, except in extremely limited circumstances not present here, requires the prosecution of all charges in a single proceeding that grow out of a single criminal act. The "single-transaction" test applies, even if the offenses may be viewed as discrete for charging purposes.

DISSENT: (Blackmun, J.) Nine days elapsed between the two incidents that are the basis of Brown's (D) convictions. A time must have come when he stopped driving the car. When he operated it again in a different community, the Ohio courts could find that the acts were sufficiently distinct to justify a second prosecution.

▶ ANALYSIS

The "same offense" test used by the Court to bar the successive prosecution of a statutory offense as well as a lesser included offense was enunciated in *Blockberger v. United States,* 284 U.S. 299 (1932). Some commentators have criticized *Blockberger* for being too generous, saying that "the same offense" means exactly that. Others have said the *Blockberger* rule is not generous enough, allowing multiple prosecution under statutes that overlap substantially, where neither is wholly included in the other.

Quicknotes

DOUBLE JEOPARDY A prohibition against a second prosecution for the same offense after an acquittal or conviction for that offense in a prior proceeding or against multiple punishments for the same offense.

LESSER INCLUDED OFFENSE One that is necessarily established by proof of the greater offense; the greater offense requires proof of all the elements of the lesser offense in order to sustain a conviction.

Missouri v. Hunter

State (P) v. Convicted robber (D)

459 U.S. 359 (1983).

NATURE OF CASE: On certiorari from state supreme court judgment setting aside conviction for armed criminal action.

FACT SUMMARY: Hunter (D) was convicted, in the same trial, for first-degree robbery and for the crime of armed criminal action, and sentenced for each.

🏛 RULE OF LAW
Where a legislature specifically authorizes punishment under two statutes, regardless of whether one is a lesser included offense of the other, the court may impose cumulative punishment.

FACTS: Hunter (D) was convicted under a Missouri (P) statute of first-degree robbery. He was also convicted in the same trial for the crime of armed criminal action. The latter crime requires proof of a felony committed with the use of a dangerous or deadly weapon. The statute proscribing armed criminal action specifies that punishment under the statute shall be administered in addition to the punishment for the underlying offense.

ISSUE: Where a legislature specifically authorizes punishment under two statutes, regardless of whether one is a lesser included offense of the other, may the court impose cumulative punishment?

HOLDING AND DECISION: (Burger, C.J.) Yes. Legislatures, not courts, proscribe the scope of punishment. With respect to cumulative sentences imposed in a single trial, the Double Jeopardy Clause does no more than prevent the sentencing court from imposing greater punishment than the legislature intended. The Missouri Supreme Court recognized that the Missouri (P) legislature intended that punishment for these statutes be cumulative. The judgment of the Missouri Supreme Court is reversed and Hunter's (D) sentence is upheld.

DISSENT: (Marshall, J.) A scheme that permits the prosecution to obtain two convictions and two sentences for the same is not equivalent to a single conviction, even if the one conviction carries a sentence of equal severity to the two separate convictions. Each of the two convictions imposes an additional stigma and does additional damage to the defendant's reputation. Such multiple convictions are thus not permitted by the Double Jeopardy Clause.

▶ *ANALYSIS*

The dissent stated that in the context of multiple prosecutions, prosecutions for an offense and a lesser included offense arising out of the same conduct violated the Double

Jeopardy Clause, regardless of legislative intent. Justice Marshall was prepared to apply the same rationale to the single prosecution context; however, the majority deferred to the legislature where the case involved multiple punishments arising out of a single criminal act.

◼━◼

Quicknotes

CUMULATIVE PUNISHMENT Consecutive penalties that are imposed on the same person.

DOUBLE JEOPARDY A prohibition against a second prosecution for the same offense after an acquittal or conviction for that offense in a prior proceeding or against multiple punishments for the same offense.

LESSER INCLUDED OFFENSE One that is necessarily established by proof of the greater offense; the greater offense requires proof of all the elements of the lesser offense in order to sustain a conviction.

◼━◼

Fong Foo v. United States

Corporation and its employees (D) v. Federal government (P)

369 U.S. 141 (1962).

NATURE OF CASE: On certiorari from writ of mandamus vacating an acquittal in federal district court.

FACT SUMMARY: A corporation and two of its employees (D) were tried before a jury on an indictment charging conspiracy and concealment of material facts. After seven days of testimony, the district judge ordered a directed verdict of acquittal as to all the defendants. The record shows that the judge's action was based on supposed improper action by the prosecutor, an assistant United States attorney, and upon a supposed lack of credibility in the testimony of one of the Government's (P) witnesses.

> ## RULE OF LAW
> A verdict of acquittal may not be reviewed without putting the defendant twice in jeopardy.

FACTS: A corporation and two of its employees (D) were indicted on charges of conspiracy and concealment of material facts. They were tried before a jury in federal district court. After several witnesses for the prosecution testified, the judge directed a verdict of acquittal as to all defendants. The order was based on the supposed improper conduct of the prosecutor and the supposed lack of credibility in the testimony of one of the witnesses who had testified for the Government (P). On appeal, the court of appeals reversed the acquittal and ordered a new trial.

ISSUE: May an appellate court review a judgment of acquittal?

HOLDING AND DECISION: (Per curiam) No. A verdict of acquittal may not be reviewed without putting the defendant twice in jeopardy. Although the court of appeals thought, not without reason, that the acquittal was based on an egregiously erroneous foundation, the acquittal was final and could not be reviewed without violating the Double Jeopardy Clause of the Constitution. The judgment of the court of appeals is reversed.

CONCURRENCE: (Harlan, J.) Retrial of petitioners should be permitted if the acquittal was clearly based solely on the exercise of a power the trial judge unquestionably did not have. However, the record fails to indicate that the district court judge based his order solely on the exercise of a nonexistent judicial power.

DISSENT: (Clark, J.) The trial judge clearly had no power to direct a verdict of acquittal. The word "acquittal" is no magic "open sesame"; in this case, the judgment of acquittal was null and void.

▶ *ANALYSIS*

Federal law prohibits an appeal from an acquittal, even to clarify a point of law, because of the "case and controversy" requirement of Article III. In some states, the Government (P) may appeal an acquittal to seek clarification of the law; however, the acquittal will stand even if the state prevails on the point of law.

■■■

Quicknotes

CONSPIRACY Concerted action by two or more persons to accomplish some unlawful purpose.

DIRECTED VERDICT A verdict ordered by the court in a jury trial.

PER CURIAM Denotes a decision that represents the opinion of the entire court.

WRIT OF MANDAMUS A court order issued commanding a public or private entity, or an official thereof, to perform a duty required by law.

■■■

Ashe v. Swenson

Poker game robber (D) v. Court (P)

397 U.S. 436 (1970).

NATURE OF CASE: Petition for writ of habeas corpus after conviction of robbery.

FACT SUMMARY: Three or four men robbed six men and stole one of the victims' cars. Each alleged robber was charged with seven separate offenses. Ashe (D) was acquitted on the robbery charge as to one of the victims. At that trial, the State's proof that the robbery had occurred and that the alleged victim was one of the victims was unassailable. The evidence that Ashe (D) was one of the robbers was weak. At a second trial for the robbery of a second victim, Ashe (D) was convicted.

RULE OF LAW

The doctrine of collateral estoppel is embodied in the Fifth Amendment guarantee against double jeopardy, and, accordingly, an acquittal based on a factual issue that is also presented as an essential element of a second charge bars trial on that charge.

FACTS: Three or four men robbed six men who were playing poker and stole one of the victims' cars. (It was never clear whether there were three or four robbers.) Three men were arrested near the abandoned stolen car. Ashe (D) was arrested separately some distance away. Each of the four was charged with six robbery counts and the theft of the car. At Ashe's (D) trial for the robbery of Knight, the proof that the armed robbery had occurred and that Knight had been a victim was unassailable. The State's evidence that Ashe (D) had been one of the robbers was weak. The jury found Ashe (D) not guilty. Six weeks later, Ashe (D) was brought to trial for the robbery of Roberts. The witnesses were the same but their testimony on Ashe's (D) identification was much stronger. One of the victims whose identification testimony had been negative at the first trial was not called at the second. The jury found Ashe (D) guilty, and he was sentenced to 35 years.

ISSUE: Is collateral estoppel a part of the Fifth Amendment's guarantee against double jeopardy?

HOLDING AND DECISION: (Stewart, J.) Yes. Collateral estoppel is a part of the Fifth Amendment's guarantee against double jeopardy. Collateral estoppel means that when an issue of ultimate facts has once been determined by a valid and final judgment, that issue cannot be litigated again between the same parties in any future lawsuit. Although first developed in civil litigation, the doctrine has long been held applicable in criminal cases. Where a previous judgment of acquittal was based upon a general verdict, as is usually the case, the court must examine the records of the prior proceedings to determine whether a rational jury could have grounded its verdict upon any issue other than the one that the defendant seeks to foreclose from consideration. Looking to the record here, there is no indication that the first jury could have rationally based its verdict on a finding that the robbery did not occur or that Knight had not been a victim. The only rationally conceivable issue in dispute before the jury was whether Ashe (D) had been one of the robbers. The jury, by its verdict, found that he had not. We hold that the doctrine of collateral estoppel is embodied in the Fifth Amendment guarantee against double jeopardy; a state could not constitutionally bring Ashe (D) before a second jury to decide whether he was one of the robbers after a first jury had already held that he was not. Reversed and remanded.

DISSENT: (Burger, C.J.) Nothing in the language or any of the gloss previously placed on the Double Jeopardy Clause remotely justifies the majority's treatment of the collateral estoppel doctrine. The essence of the concurring opinion is that all that occurred in this case was one transaction or episode. "For me it demeans the dignity of the human personality and individuality to talk of a 'single transaction' in the context of six separate assaults on six individuals."

▶ ANALYSIS

Ashe deprives the prosecution of a major tactical advantage in trying separately, closely related offenses arising from a single transaction. The effect of the collateral estoppel doctrine is to prevent the prosecutor from "treating the first trial as no more than a dry run for a second prosecution" on a second charge. With this tactic eliminated, the prosecutor may find less advantage in separate prosecutions in such situations. In *Harris v. Washington,* 404 U.S. 55 (1971), the Court held that the constitutional guarantee applies, irrespective of whether the jury considered all relevant evidence, and irrespective of the State's good faith in bringing successive prosecutions. There a bomb sent through the mail killed Burdick and the defendant's son. After his acquittal on a charge of murdering Burdick, the defendant was charged with murdering his son. It was contended that the issue of identity had not been fully litigated because the trial judge had wrongly excluded a threatening letter written by the defendant.

Quicknotes

COLLATERAL ESTOPPEL A doctrine whereby issues litigated and determined in a prior proceeding are binding upon all

Continued on next page.

subsequent litigation between the parties regarding that issue.

DOUBLE JEOPARDY A prohibition against a second prosecution for the same offense after an acquittal or conviction for that offense in a prior proceeding or against multiple punishments for the same offense.

FIFTH AMENDMENT Provides that no person shall be compelled to serve as a witness against himself, or be subject to trial for the same offense twice, or be deprived of life, liberty, or property without due process of law.

■≡■

Downum v. United States

Defendant (D) v. Federal government (P)

372 U.S. 734 (1963).

NATURE OF CASE: On certiorari from conviction in state court.

FACT SUMMARY: Two days after discharge of the jury, a second jury was impaneled and Downum (D) was tried and convicted.

🏛 RULE OF LAW
Where the prosecution allows a jury to be selected despite the absence of a key prosecution witness, jeopardy may attach as soon as the jury is sworn.

FACTS: A jury was selected and sworn to try Downum (D) on seven counts. The prosecution then asked that the jury be discharged because a key witness on two counts was absent. Over Downum's (D) motion to dismiss those two counts and proceed on the rest of the charges, the judge discharged the jury. A second jury was impaneled two days later; over Downum's (D) plea of double jeopardy, he was tried and convicted.

ISSUE: Where the prosecution allows a jury to be selected despite the absence of a key prosecution witness, may jeopardy attach as soon as the jury is sworn?

HOLDING AND DECISION: (Douglas, J.) Yes. Where the prosecution allows a jury to be selected despite the absence of a key prosecution witness, jeopardy may attach as soon as the jury is sworn. The Double Jeopardy Clause must be broadly construed; its prohibition is not against being twice punished, but against twice being put in jeopardy. We resolve any doubt in favor of the liberty of the citizen. Each case must be judged on its facts—here, the prosecution opposed Downum's (D) motion to proceed with the trial on the counts unaffected by the absence of the witness. The conviction is reversed.

DISSENT: (Clark, J.) The circumstances in which the prosecutor found himself resulted from excusable oversight, rather than any deliberate action. Downum (D) was never formally arraigned by the first jury, it heard no evidence, and he was not prejudiced in any way. The "ends of public justice" require that the government have an opportunity to present its case.

▶ ANALYSIS

There are some situations in which a second trial may be had after a jury is discharged without reaching a verdict. The most common of these is the hung jury, where the jurors are discharged because they are unable to agree.

Quicknotes

DOUBLE JEOPARDY A prohibition against a second prosecution for the same offense after an acquittal or conviction for that offense in a prior proceeding or against multiple punishments for the same offense.

HUNG JURY The failure of a jury to reach agreement on a verdict resulting in a mistrial.

IMPANELED The selection of a jury.

MOTION TO DISMISS Motion to terminate a trial based on the adequacy of the pleadings.

■━■

Bartkus v. Illinois

Accused robber (D) v. State (P)

359 U.S. 121 (1959).

NATURE OF CASE: On certiorari from state court conviction for robbery.

FACT SUMMARY: Bartkus (D) was tried and acquitted in federal district court; he was then tried and convicted in state court for the same conduct.

🏛 RULE OF LAW
Prosecution in a state court following acquittal for the same conduct in a federal court does not place a defendant twice in jeopardy, nor is it necessarily a violation of due process.

FACTS: Bartkus (D) was tried and acquitted by a jury in a federal district court for the robbery of a federally insured savings and loan. He was then tried on robbery charges in a state court, and was sentenced to life imprisonment. The prosecutions were conducted independently although there were some connections; for example, the federal investigator turned all the evidence he had gathered over to state prosecutors.

ISSUE: Does prosecution in a state court following acquittal for the same conduct in a federal court place a defendant twice in jeopardy?

HOLDING AND DECISION: (Frankfurter, J.) No. Prosecution in a state court following acquittal for the same conduct in a federal court does not place a defendant twice in jeopardy. We have repeatedly held in this Court that a defendant may be punished for the same conduct in successive state and federal prosecutions. A citizen of the United States is also a citizen of a state, and may be held accountable by both sovereigns. As to the question of due process, several states have enacted laws barring or limiting such successive prosecutions. We believe that the individual state legislatures are more competent to deal with this issue and thus develop a rational, integrated body of criminal law. The conviction is upheld.

DISSENT: (Black, J.) The Court takes the position that a second trial is less offensive if one is conducted by the federal government and the other by the state. This distinction is too subtle for me to grasp. Whether by two "sovereigns" or one, in either case a man is forced to face danger twice for the same conduct.

DISSENT: (Brennan, J.) The record shows that the extent of participation of the federal authorities here constituted this state prosecution actually a "second federal prosecution" of Bartkus (D). This conviction should be set aside because it is the product of unconstitutional federal action.

▶ ANALYSIS

Justice Brennan, joined by two other justices, voted to set aside the conviction on factual grounds alone, criticizing the conduct of the federal prosecutors. In his view, the participation by federal prosecutors in the state trial was so great that the state prosecution was "actually a second federal prosecution of Bartkus" and thus impermissible.

■=■

Quicknotes

ACQUITTAL The discharge of an accused individual from suspicion of guilt for a particular crime and from further prosecution for that offense.

CERTIORARI A discretionary writ issued by a superior court to an inferior court in order to review the lower court's decisions; the Supreme Court's writ ordering such review.

■=■

Post-Trial Process

Quick Reference Rules of Law

Jackson v. Virginia

Convicted murderer (D) v. State (P)

443 U.S. 307 (1979).

NATURE OF CASE: On habeas corpus from court of appeals decision upholding murder conviction.

FACT SUMMARY: Jackson (D) was convicted of first-degree murder.

🏛 RULE OF LAW
In reviewing a habeas corpus challenge to the sufficiency of the evidence, an appellate court must do more than determine whether any quantum of the slightest record evidence supported the charges.

FACTS: Jackson (D) appealed his first-degree murder conviction in federal court, then petitioned the court of appeals for review in a habeas corpus proceeding. The court of appeals, considering Jackson's (D) argument that the evidence was insufficient to permit a rational factfinder to conclude that the killing was premeditated, noted that there was some evidence in the record to support that conclusion, and upheld the conviction.

ISSUE: In reviewing a habeas corpus challenge to the sufficiency of the evidence, must an appellate court do more than determine whether any quantum of the slightest record evidence supported the charges?

HOLDING AND DECISION: (Stewart, J.) Yes. In reviewing a habeas corpus challenge to the sufficiency of the evidence, an appellate court must do more than determine whether any quantum of the slightest record evidence supported the charges. In *Thompson v. Louisville*, 362 U.S. 199 (1960), this Court stated that we could "find no evidence whatever in the record to support these charges." This statement has been wrongly interpreted by the courts of appeals in habeas corpus proceedings to stand for the proposition that the presence of the merest modicum of evidence in the record supporting each element of the crime is all that is needed to deny a challenge to the sufficiency of the evidence. The correct test is for the reviewing court to consider all the evidence from the record in the light most favorable to the prosecution; and to inquire whether any rational factfinder, aware of the requirement of proof beyond a reasonable doubt, could have reached a verdict of guilty on the basis of the evidence so viewed. The judgment of the court of appeals is reversed.

CONCURRENCE: (Stevens, J.) The Supreme Court, in its majority opinion, does not require the reviewing court to view just the evidence most favorable to the prosecution and then to decide whether that evidence convinced it beyond a reasonable doubt, nor whether, based on the entire record, rational triers of fact could be convinced of guilt beyond a reasonable doubt. Instead, and without explanation, it

chooses a still narrower standard that merely asks whether, "after viewing the evidence in the light most favorable to the prosecution, any rational trier of fact could have found the essential elements of the crime beyond a reasonable doubt." It seems to me that if logic allows this choice after *Winship*, it should also allow the presumption that the Court has rejected—that trial judges and juries will act rationally and honestly in applying the reasonable-doubt standard, at least so long as the trial is free of procedural error and the record contains evidence tending to prove each of the elements of the offense. Time may prove that the rule the Court has adopted today is the wisest compromise between one extreme that maximizes the protection against the risk that innocent persons will be erroneously convicted and the other extreme that places the greatest faith in the ability of fair procedures to produce just verdicts. But the Court's opinion should not obscure the fact that its new rule is not logically compelled by the analysis or the holding in *Winship* or in any other precedent, or that the rule reflects a new policy choice rather than the application of a pre-existing rule of law.

▶ ANALYSIS

Justice Stevens described the majority holding as an unnecessary encroachment upon the guarantee of substantive fairness heretofore left almost entirely to the trial courts. Stevens criticized the decision as inappropriately diminishing the power of the trial courts to determine the sufficiency of the evidence.

■=■

Quicknotes

HABEUS CORPUS COLLATERAL REVIEW An independent review of whether a prisoner is being lawfully imprisoned.

PROOF BEYOND A REASONABLE DOUBT Standard of proof necessary to convict a defendant, requiring the absence of evidence that would cause a reasonable person to hesitate in making an important decision in his personal affairs.

QUANTUM An essential amount; a modicum of the required degree.

■=■

Arizona v. Fulminante

State (P) v. Confessing first-degree murderer (D)

499 U.S. 279 (1991).

NATURE OF CASE: Appeal from grant of motion to suppress confessions.

FACT SUMMARY: In Arizona's (P) criminal action against Fulminante (D) for first-degree murder, the Arizona Supreme Court, reversing the trial court's ruling, granted Fulminante's (D) motion to suppress two confessions he allegedly made in respect to the murder.

🏛 RULE OF LAW
Admission of a coerced confession may be harmless if it appears beyond a reasonable doubt that its admission did not contribute to the verdict obtained.

FACTS: After his incarceration for federal charges relating to possession of a firearm, Fulminante (D) allegedly confessed to one Sarivola, an undercover FBI agent, that he sexually assaulted and murdered his daughter prior to his incarceration. Nearly one year after this alleged confession and after his release from prison on the firearms charge, Fulminante (D) allegedly made another confession to Sarivola's fiancee regarding the same incident. As a result of these confessions, Fulminante (D) was charged with the first-degree murder of his daughter, leading to his eventual conviction and a death sentence despite his pretrial motion to suppress the alleged confessions, which the trial court denied. On appeal, however, the Arizona Supreme Court granted Fulminante's (D) motion, holding that Fulminante's (D) alleged confessions were coerced and, thus, inadmissible, and ruling that the harmless error analysis was not applicable to coerced confessions. Arizona (P) appealed.

ISSUE: May admission of a coerced confession be harmless if it appears beyond a reasonable doubt that its admission did not contribute to the verdict obtained?

HOLDING AND DECISION: (White, J.) Yes. Admission of a coerced confession may be harmless if it appears beyond a reasonable doubt that its admission did not contribute to the verdict obtained. This rule merely applies the rule as laid down in *Chapman v. California*, 386 U.S. 18 (1967), which made clear that federal constitutional error may be held harmless if it is declared harmless beyond a reasonable doubt. In applying *Chapman*'s rule to confessions, it is especially noteworthy that confessions are probably the most probative and damaging evidence that can be admitted against a defendant. Indeed, a full confession in which the defendant discloses the motive for and means of the crime may tempt the jury to rely upon that evidence alone in reaching its verdict. Accordingly, a reviewing court must exercise extreme caution before determining that the admission of a confession at trial was harmless. In the instant case, since the transcript discloses that a successful prosecution depended on

the jury believing the two confessions, that both confessions were impeachable standing alone, and that the admission of the first confession led to the admission of other evidence prejudicial to Fulminante (D), Arizona (P) has failed to prove beyond a reasonable doubt that the admission of the coerced confessions was harmless. Fulminante's (D) motion to suppress the confessions was properly granted. Affirmed.

CONCURRENCE: (Kennedy, J.) Although having reservations about the involuntariness of Fulminante's (D) confessions, the majority's holding that the confessions were coerced, inadmissible and, therefore, its admission did not constitute harmless error, is acceptable.

DISSENT: (Rehnquist, C.J.) When reviewing the erroneous admission of an involuntary confession, an appellate court must simply review the remainder of the evidence against the defendant to determine whether its admission was harmless beyond a reasonable doubt. In such event, a harmless error analysis is appropriate, and the instant case constitutes a classic example of harmless error. Here, a second confession providing even more details of the crime was in fact properly admitted into evidence.

▶ *ANALYSIS*

By opening the door to harmless error analysis, the above case creates the risk of erroneous harmless error determinations; and erroneous determinations are most likely to take place in cases in which there is strong independent evidence of a defendant's guilt. Thus, the above case may lead in practice, if not in rhetoric, to a harmless error standard for involuntary confessions that is similar to the lax standard rejected in *Payne v. Arkansas,* 356 U.S. 560 (1958).

■■■■

Quicknotes

COERCED CONFESSION A statement made by a person charged with the commission of a criminal offense acknowledging his guilt in respect to the charged offense, made when the confessor's free will was overcome as a result of threats, promises, or undue influence, and that is inadmissible at trial.

HARMLESS ERROR An error taking place during trial that does not require the reviewing court to overturn or modify the trial court's judgment in that it did not affect the appellant's substantial rights or the disposition of the action.

■■■■

Teague v. Lane

Robbery convict (P) v. Prosecution (D)

489 U.S. 288 (1989).

NATURE OF CASE: Review of denial of habeas corpus.

FACT SUMMARY: Teague (P) argued in a habeas proceeding that a post-conviction judicial decision had rendered his conviction invalid.

🏛 RULE OF LAW
Except in special circumstances, case law will not be retroactively applied in collateral review.

FACTS: Teague (P) was charged with various felonies. An all-white jury convicted Teague (P), a black man, of attempted murder, robbery, and battery. The prosecution had used all its peremptory challenges to exclude blacks from the jury. Teague (P) appealed, contending that this denied him due process. On appeal the conviction was upheld. Teague (P) subsequently petitioned for habeas corpus, contending that he had been entitled to a jury consisting of a cross section of the community. The district court denied his petition on the merits, as did the court of appeals. The U.S. Supreme Court granted review.

ISSUE: Except in special circumstances, will case law be retroactively applied in collateral review?

HOLDING AND DECISION: (O'Connor, J.) No. Except in special circumstances, case law will not be retroactively applied in collateral review. Habeas corpus provides an avenue for upsetting judgments that otherwise would be final. It is not intended to be a substitute for direct review. Both the state and criminal defendants have an interest in leaving concluded litigation in a state of repose. If new rules of constitutional law were to be applied retroactively, any litigation might be reopened if the new rule were to be applicable. Further, the purpose of habeas is that its presence creates an incentive for trial and appellate judges to conduct their proceedings in a manner consistent with established constitutional principles. To apply new principles retroactively would actually subvert this purpose. Therefore, the Court concludes that, unless the post-conviction rule announced is so fundamental to the concept of ordered liberty that it would be unconscionable not to retroactively apply it, retroactive application will not be given. A necessary corollary to this rule is that no new rule of constitutional criminal procedure should be announced in a habeas proceeding. Here, to rule as Teague (P) urges would amount to that. Therefore, without ruling on the merits of the claim, the denial of habeas must be affirmed.

DISSENT: (Brennan, J.) When collateral review challenges have merit, the plurality's decision would prevent vindication of constitutional rights, hence denying a check against further violations until the same claim is presented on direct review. The plurality's adherence to treating like cases alike amounts to "letting the tail wag the dog" when it stymies the resolution of substantial constitutional questions. Uniform treatment of habeas petitioners is not worth the price the plurality is willing to pay.

▶ ANALYSIS

The opinion in fact announces two rules, the first being that stated above and the second being that new constitutional issues cannot be announced in a habeas proceeding. The latter rule is potentially much more significant than the first. It is important to note, however, that only four justices joined the section announcing that rule, which limits its precedential value.

■═■

Quicknotes

PEREMPTORY CHALLENGE The exclusion by a party to a lawsuit of a prospective juror without the need to specify a particular reason.

WRIT OF HABEAS CORPUS A proceeding in which a defendant brings a writ to compel a judicial determination of whether he is lawfully being held in custody.

■═■

Wainwright v. Sykes

Court (P) v. Intoxicated homicide suspect (D)

433 U.S. 72 (1977).

NATURE OF CASE: Habeas corpus challenge to a murder conviction.

FACT SUMMARY: Sykes (D) sought a review of his murder conviction via a habeas corpus proceeding, but he had failed to comply with state procedural rules in not raising the underlying claim at trial.

> ## RULE OF LAW
> One who did not comply with state procedural rules by not raising his federal claim at trial cannot obtain federal habeas corpus review of his state criminal conviction unless he shows "cause" for noncompliance and shows "prejudice" as a result of the claimed error in the original proceeding.

FACTS: Sykes (D) violated a state procedural rule by not raising, at trial, his claim that the incriminating statements admitted against him were involuntary because he did not understand the *Miranda* warnings that he had been given. When he was convicted in state court for murder, Sykes (D) then presented a federal habeas corpus challenge to that conviction based on the aforementioned contention. Opposing such action, Wainwright (P) argued that the rule in *Francis v. Henderson* should be extended to cover this case. That rule was that federal habeas corpus review was barred absent a showing of "cause" and "prejudice" where the challenge was to the makeup of a grand jury. Sykes (D) argued that *Fay v. Noia* had laid down an all-inclusive rule rendering state timely-objection rules ineffective to bar review of underlying federal claims in federal habeas corpus proceedings absent a showing of "knowing waiver" or a "deliberate bypass" of the right to so object.

ISSUE: In order to obtain federal habeas corpus review of his state criminal conviction, must one who did not comply with state procedural rules in raising his federal claim at trial show "cause" for noncompliance and show "prejudice" resulting from the claimed error in the original proceeding?

HOLDING AND DECISION: (Rehnquist, J.) Yes. If one who suffered a state criminal conviction did not comply with state procedural law by bringing up his federal claim at trial, he cannot obtain federal habeas corpus review of the conviction unless he shows "cause" for noncompliance and shows "prejudice" as a result of the claimed error in the original proceeding. A state's contemporaneous objection rule is designed to insure that constitutional claims are heard when they are fresh, not years later in a federal habeas corpus proceeding. Furthermore, to apply the "knowing waiver" or "deliberate bypass" standard, the more lenient of

those suggested, would encourage "sandbagging" by lawyers who would take their chances on a not guilty verdict at trial with the intent to raise their constitutional claims in a federal habeas corpus court if their initial gamble does not pay off. The "cause" and "prejudice" rule herein adopted attempts to make the state trial on the merits the "main event" rather than a "tryout on the road." In this case, the required showing of cause was not made. Remanded with instructions to dismiss the petition for a writ of habeas corpus.

DISSENT: (Brennan, J.) The Court is not justified in imposing a stricter standard than the deliberate bypass test. It is the harshest test possible that still distinguishes between intentional and inadvertent noncompliance by counsel with procedural rules. Most procedural defaults are born of the inadvertence, negligence, inexperience, or incompetence of trial counsel, and it is unfair to make the criminal defendant accountable for the naked errors of his attorney. The mistakes of a trial attorney should be visited on the head of a federal habeas corpus applicant only when this Court is convinced that the lawyer actually exercised his expertise and judgment in his client's service, and with his client's knowing and intelligent participation, where possible.

ANALYSIS

One possible result of this case may be that defendants are pushed into making more claims based on ineffectiveness of counsel to fulfill the requirement that they show "cause." That is, a particular procedural default will simply be cited as an example of general incompetence of counsel. The effect would be merely to transform the old claims alleging deprivation of constitutional rights to new claims alleging ineffectiveness of counsel, with all the attendant problems which that will engender.

Quicknotes

WRIT OF HABEAS CORPUS A proceeding in which a defendant brings a writ to compel a judicial determination of whether he is lawfully being held in custody.

Smith v. Murray

Convicted murderer-rapist (D) v. Government official (P)

477 U.S. 527 (1986).

NATURE OF CASE: On certiorari from denial of habeas corpus petition.

FACT SUMMARY: Smith (D) was convicted of rape and murder; a psychiatrist testified under cross-examination by the prosecutor to the content of statements made by Smith (D) during the course of his examination.

🏛 RULE OF LAW
A tactical decision by defense counsel not to pursue an objection on appeal does not provide a basis for reviving the issue under the rubric of an ineffective assistance of counsel claim.

FACTS: Smith (D) raped a woman at knifepoint near his home. He then murdered her by means of choking, drowning and stabbing. At his trial on rape and murder charges, Smith's (D) appointed counsel requested that a psychiatrist be appointed to examine Smith (D). On cross-examination, the prosecutor elicited damaging information from the psychiatrist, including the fact that Smith (D) told the psychiatrist during the examination that he had come close to raping a schoolgirl on a bus, and had torn off the girl's clothes before abandoning the attack. On appeal, Smith (D) did not raise the issue of the inadmissibility of the psychiatrist's testimony under the Fifth and Fourteenth Amendments' prohibition against self-incrimination. He later petitioned for writ of habeas corpus which was denied on the grounds that Smith (D) had forfeited the claim by failing to press it in earlier proceedings. Smith (D) argued that the issue was preserved because his attorney's failure to raise the claim constituted ineffective assistance of counsel and thus provided cause for not pursuing the claim on appeal.

ISSUE: Will a tactical decision by defense counsel not to pursue an objection on appeal provide a basis for reviving the issue under the rubric of an ineffective assistance of counsel claim?

HOLDING AND DECISION: (O'Connor, J.) No. A tactical decision by defense counsel not to pursue an objection on appeal does not provide a basis for reviving the issue under the rubric of an ineffective assistance of counsel claim. The process of winnowing out weaker arguments on appeal and focusing on those more likely to prevail, far from being evidence of incompetence, is the hallmark of effective appellate advocacy. The decision not to pursue an objection to the admission of the psychiatrist's testimony fell well within the wide range of professionally competent assistance. The decision of the district court to deny the writ of habeas corpus is upheld.

DISSENT: (Stevens, J.) To the extent there has been a procedural "default," it is exceedingly minor. The Court has lost its way in a procedural maze of its own creation and grossly misevaluated the federal court's statutory mission under the federal habeas corpus statute.

▶ ANALYSIS

The dissent raises an issue of sharp concern; that because of failure to adhere to the finer points of procedure, whether or not "excusable" under the standards of post-conviction review, a legally innocent defendant might be put to death. The issue becomes even more significant when a claim of factual innocence is maintained. There is an "actual innocence" exception to the rule barring revival of defaulted claims. However, a defendant seeking to show that the defaulted claim deprived the factfinder of exculpatory evidence must show that it is more likely than not that no reasonable juror would have convicted him in light of the new evidence.

Quicknotes

EXCULPATORY EVIDENCE A statement or other evidence that tends to excuse, justify, or absolve the defendant from alleged fault or guilt.

HABEAS CORPUS A proceeding in which a defendant brings a writ to compel a judicial determination of whether he is lawfully being held in custody.

PRIVILEGE AGAINST SELF-INCRIMINATION A privilege guaranteed by the Fifth Amendment to the federal Constitution in a criminal proceeding for communications made by an accused and protecting an accused or witness from having to give testimony that may incriminate himself.

Glossary

Common Latin Words and Phrases Encountered in the Law

A FORTIORI: Because one fact exists or has been proven, therefore a second fact that is related to the first fact must also exist.

A PRIORI: From the cause to the effect. A term of logic used to denote that when one generally accepted truth is shown to be a cause, another particular effect must necessarily follow.

AB INITIO: From the beginning; a condition which has existed throughout, as in a marriage which was void ab initio.

ACTUS REUS: The wrongful act; in criminal law, such action sufficient to trigger criminal liability.

AD VALOREM: According to value; an ad valorem tax is imposed upon an item located within the taxing jurisdiction calculated by the value of such item.

AMICUS CURIAE: Friend of the court. Its most common usage takes the form of an amicus curiae brief, filed by a person who is not a party to an action but is nonetheless allowed to offer an argument supporting his legal interests.

ARGUENDO: In arguing. A statement, possibly hypothetical, made for the purpose of argument, is one made arguendo.

BILL QUIA TIMET: A bill to quiet title (establish ownership) to real property.

BONA FIDE: True, honest, or genuine. May refer to a person's legal position based on good faith or lacking notice of fraud (such as a bona fide purchaser for value) or to the authenticity of a particular document (such as a bona fide last will and testament).

CAUSA MORTIS: With approaching death in mind. A gift causa mortis is a gift given by a party who feels certain that death is imminent.

CAVEAT EMPTOR: Let the buyer beware. This maxim is reflected in the rule of law that a buyer purchases at his own risk because it is his responsibility to examine, judge, test, and otherwise inspect what he is buying.

CERTIORARI: A writ of review. Petitions for review of a case by the United States Supreme Court are most often done by means of a writ of certiorari.

CONTRA: On the other hand. Opposite. Contrary to.

CORAM NOBIS: Before us; writs of error directed to the court that originally rendered the judgment.

CORAM VOBIS: Before you; writs of error directed by an appellate court to a lower court to correct a factual error.

CORPUS DELICTI: The body of the crime; the requisite elements of a crime amounting to objective proof that a crime has been committed.

CUM TESTAMENTO ANNEXO, ADMINISTRATOR (ADMINISTRATOR C.T.A.): With will annexed; an administrator c.t.a. settles an estate pursuant to a will in which he is not appointed.

DE BONIS NON, ADMINISTRATOR (ADMINISTRATOR D.B.N.): Of goods not administered; an administrator d.b.n. settles a partially settled estate.

DE FACTO: In fact; in reality; actually. Existing in fact but not officially approved or engendered.

DE JURE: By right; lawful. Describes a condition that is legitimate "as a matter of law," in contrast to the term "de facto," which connotes something existing in fact but not legally sanctioned or authorized. For example, de facto segregation refers to segregation brought about by housing patterns, etc., whereas de jure segregation refers to segregation created by law.

DE MINIMIS: Of minimal importance; insignificant; a trifle; not worth bothering about.

DE NOVO: Anew; a second time; afresh. A trial de novo is a new trial held at the appellate level as if the case originated there and the trial at a lower level had not taken place.

DICTA: Generally used as an abbreviated form of obiter dicta, a term describing those portions of a judicial opinion incidental or not necessary to resolution of the specific question before the court. Such nonessential statements and remarks are not considered to be binding precedent.

DUCES TECUM: Refers to a particular type of writ or subpoena requesting a party or organization to produce certain documents in their possession.

EN BANC: Full bench. Where a court sits with all justices present rather than the usual quorum.

EX PARTE: For one side or one party only. An ex parte proceeding is one undertaken for the benefit of only one party, without notice to, or an appearance by, an adverse party.

EX POST FACTO: After the fact. An ex post facto law is a law that retroactively changes the consequences of a prior act.

EX REL.: Abbreviated form of the term "ex relatione," meaning upon relation or information. When the state brings an action in which it has no interest against an individual at the instigation of one who has a private interest in the matter.

FORUM NON CONVENIENS: Inconvenient forum. Although a court may have jurisdiction over the case, the action should be tried in a more conveniently located court, one to which parties and witnesses may more easily travel, for example.

GUARDIAN AD LITEM: A guardian of an infant as to litigation, appointed to represent the infant and pursue his/her rights.

HABEAS CORPUS: You have the body. The modern writ of habeas corpus is a writ directing that a person (body) being detained (such as a prisoner) be brought before the court so that the legality of his detention can be judicially ascertained.

IN CAMERA: In private, in chambers. When a hearing is held before a judge in his chambers or when all spectators are excluded from the courtroom.

IN FORMA PAUPERIS: In the manner of a pauper. A party who proceeds in forma pauperis because of his poverty is one who is allowed to bring suit without liability for costs.

INFRA: Below, under. A word referring the reader to a later part of a book. (The opposite of supra.)

IN LOCO PARENTIS: In the place of a parent.

IN PARI DELICTO: Equally wrong; a court of equity will not grant requested relief to an applicant who is in pari delicto, or as much at fault in the transactions giving rise to the controversy as is the opponent of the applicant.

IN PARI MATERIA: On like subject matter or upon the same matter. Statutes relating to the same person or things are said to be in pari materia. It is a general rule of statutory construction that such statutes should be construed together, i.e., looked at as if they together constituted one law.

IN PERSONAM: Against the person. Jurisdiction over the person of an individual.

IN RE: In the matter of. Used to designate a proceeding involving an estate or other property.

IN REM: A term that signifies an action against the res, or thing. An action in rem is basically one that is taken directly against property, as distinguished from an action in personam, i.e., against the person.

INTER ALIA: Among other things. Used to show that the whole of a statement, pleading, list, statute, etc., has not been set forth in its entirety.

INTER PARTES: Between the parties. May refer to contracts, conveyances or other transactions having legal significance.

INTER VIVOS: Between the living. An inter vivos gift is a gift made by a living grantor, as distinguished from bequests contained in a will, which pass upon the death of the testator.

IPSO FACTO: By the mere fact itself.

JUS: Law or the entire body of law.

LEX LOCI: The law of the place; the notion that the rights of parties to a legal proceeding are governed by the law of the place where those rights arose.

MALUM IN SE: Evil or wrong in and of itself; inherently wrong. This term describes an act that is wrong by its very nature, as opposed to one which would not be wrong but for the fact that there is a specific legal prohibition against it (malum prohibitum).

MALUM PROHIBITUM: Wrong because prohibited, but not inherently evil. Used to describe something that is wrong because it is expressly forbidden by law but that is not in and of itself evil, e.g., speeding.

MANDAMUS: We command. A writ directing an official to take a certain action.

MENS REA: A guilty mind; a criminal intent. A term used to signify the mental state that accompanies a crime or other prohibited act. Some crimes require only a general mens rea (general intent to do the prohibited act), but others, like assault with intent to murder, require the existence of a specific mens rea.

MODUS OPERANDI: Method of operating; generally refers to the manner or style of a criminal in committing crimes, admissible in appropriate cases as evidence of the identity of a defendant.

NEXUS: A connection to.

NISI PRIUS: A court of first impression. A nisi prius court is one where issues of fact are tried before a judge or jury.

N.O.V. (NON OBSTANTE VEREDICTO): Notwithstanding the verdict. A judgment n.o.v. is a judgment given in favor of one party despite the fact that a verdict was returned in favor of the other party, the justification being that the verdict either had no reasonable support in fact or was contrary to law.

NUNC PRO TUNC: Now for then. This phrase refers to actions that may be taken and will then have full retroactive effect.

PENDENTE LITE: Pending the suit; pending litigation under way.

PER CAPITA: By head; beneficiaries of an estate, if they take in equal shares, take per capita.

PER CURIAM: By the court; signifies an opinion ostensibly written "by the whole court" and with no identified author.

PER SE: By itself, in itself; inherently.

PER STIRPES: By representation. Used primarily in the law of wills to describe the method of distribution where a person, generally because of death, is unable to take that which is left to him by the will of another, and therefore his heirs divide such property between them rather than take under the will individually.

PRIMA FACIE: On its face, at first sight. A prima facie case is one that is sufficient on its face, meaning that the evidence supporting it is adequate to establish the case until contradicted or overcome by other evidence.

PRO TANTO: For so much; as far as it goes. Often used in eminent domain cases when a property owner receives partial payment for his land without prejudice to his right to bring suit for the full amount he claims his land to be worth.

QUANTUM MERUIT: As much as he deserves. Refers to recovery based on the doctrine of unjust enrichment in those cases in which a party has rendered valuable services or furnished materials that were accepted and enjoyed by another under circumstances that would reasonably notify the recipient that the rendering party expected to be paid. In essence, the law implies a contract to pay the reasonable value of the services or materials furnished.

QUASI: Almost like; as if; nearly. This term is essentially used to signify that one subject or thing is almost analogous to another but that material differences between them do exist. For example, a quasi-criminal proceeding is one that is not strictly criminal but shares enough of the same characteristics to require some of the same safeguards (e.g., procedural due process must be followed in a parole hearing).

QUID PRO QUO: Something for something. In contract law, the consideration, something of value, passed between the parties to render the contract binding.

RES GESTAE: Things done; in evidence law, this principle justifies the admission of a statement that would otherwise be hearsay when it is made so closely to the event in question as to be said to be a part of it, or with such spontaneity as not to have the possibility of falsehood.

RES IPSA LOQUITUR: The thing speaks for itself. This doctrine gives rise to a rebuttable presumption of negligence when the instrumentality causing the injury was within the exclusive control of the defendant, and the injury was one that does not normally occur unless a person has been negligent.

RES JUDICATA: A matter adjudged. Doctrine which provides that once a court of competent jurisdiction has rendered a final judgment or decree on the merits, that judgment or decree is conclusive upon the parties to the case and prevents them from engaging in any other litigation on the points and issues determined therein.

RESPONDEAT SUPERIOR: Let the master reply. This doctrine holds the master liable for the wrongful acts of his servant (or the principal for his agent) in those cases in which the servant (or agent) was acting within the scope of his authority at the time of the injury.

STARE DECISIS: To stand by or adhere to that which has been decided. The common law doctrine of stare decisis attempts to give security and certainty to the law by following the policy that once a principle of law as applicable to a certain set of facts has been set forth in a decision, it forms a precedent which will subsequently be followed, even though a different decision might be made were it the first time the question had arisen. Of course, stare decisis is not an inviolable principle and is departed from in instances where there is good cause (e.g., considerations of public policy led the Supreme Court to disregard prior decisions sanctioning segregation).

SUPRA: Above. A word referring a reader to an earlier part of a book.

ULTRA VIRES: Beyond the power. This phrase is most commonly used to refer to actions taken by a corporation that are beyond the power or legal authority of the corporation.

Addendum of French Derivatives

IN PAIS: Not pursuant to legal proceedings.

CHATTEL: Tangible personal property.

CY PRES: Doctrine permitting courts to apply trust funds to purposes not expressed in the trust but necessary to carry out the settlor's intent.

PER AUTRE VIE: For another's life; during another's life. In property law, an estate may be granted that will terminate upon the death of someone other than the grantee.

PROFIT A PRENDRE: A license to remove minerals or other produce from land.

VOIR DIRE: Process of questioning jurors as to their predispositions about the case or parties to a proceeding in order to identify those jurors displaying bias or prejudice.

Casenote Legal Briefs